Catherine
Houghton

Honesty,

Humility,

Enthusiasm

Nature
relieves
architecture.

Architecture
relieves
nature.

Gardens never end . . .

. . . and buildings never begin.

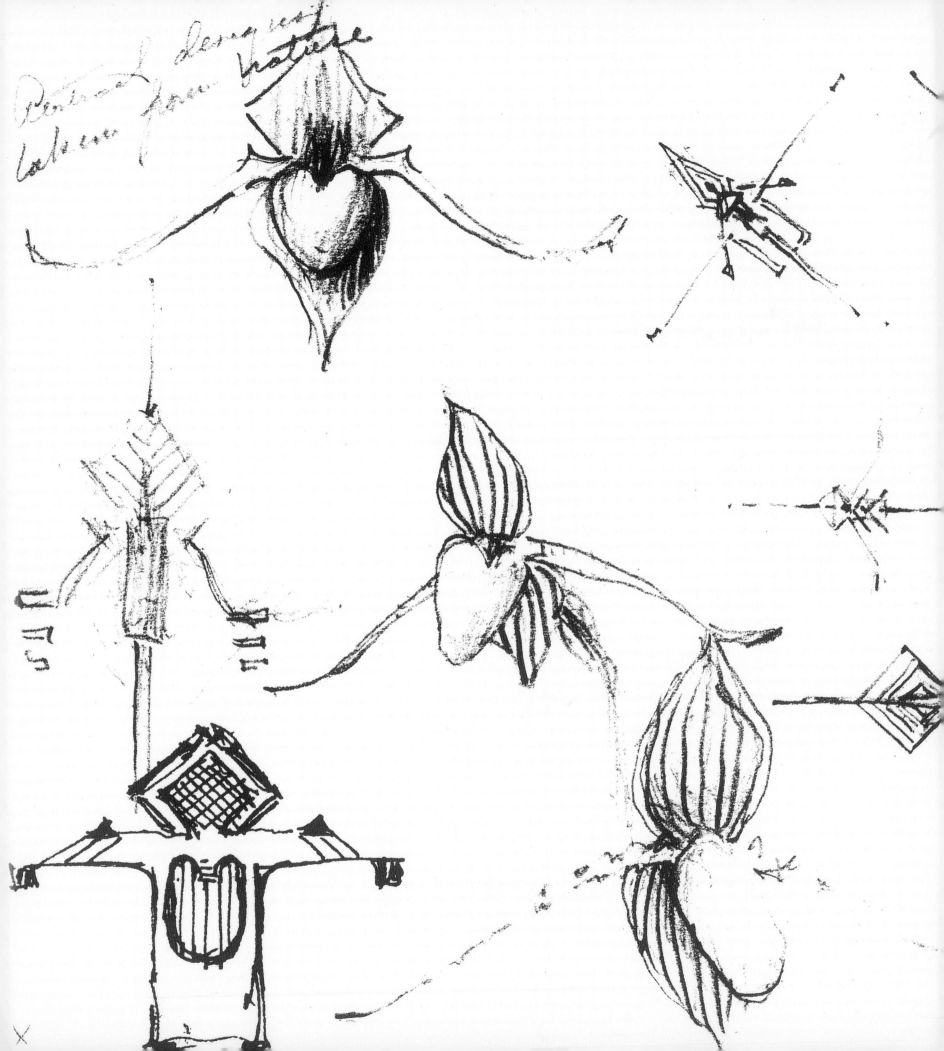

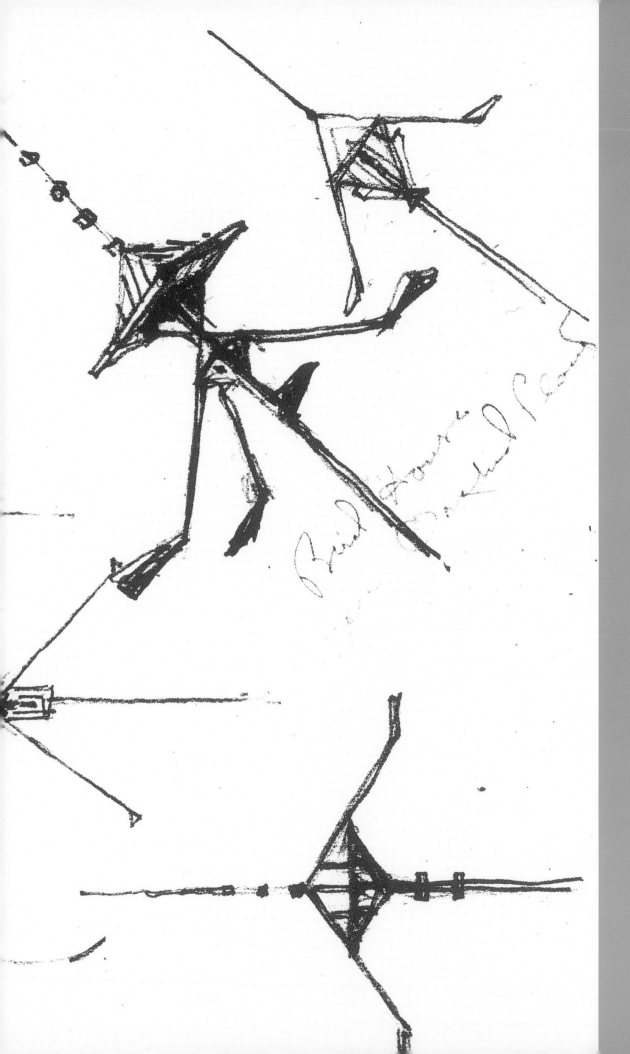

Buildings must relate, first one part to another, then all parts to the whole.

This composed order is much like the arrangement of flowers.

Where there
is an art, there
is a science.

Where there
is a science,
there is an art.

Art is feeling …
science is fact.

Feelings must be
combined with
facts before
anything new,
of value, can be
created.

Fun can be found almost everywhere.

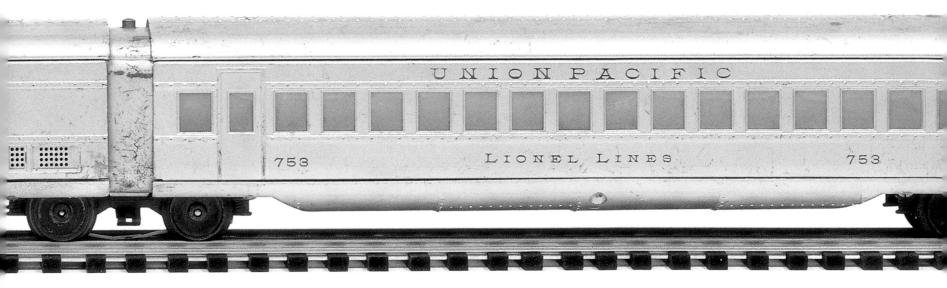

If one works to find it, only then is it elusive.

ALDEN B. DOW

DIANE MADDEX

MIDWESTERN MODERN

ALDEN B. DOW HOME AND STUDIO

MIDLAND, MICHIGAN

CONTENTS

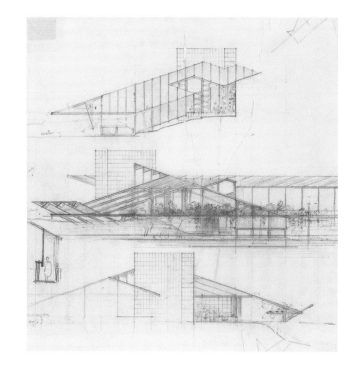

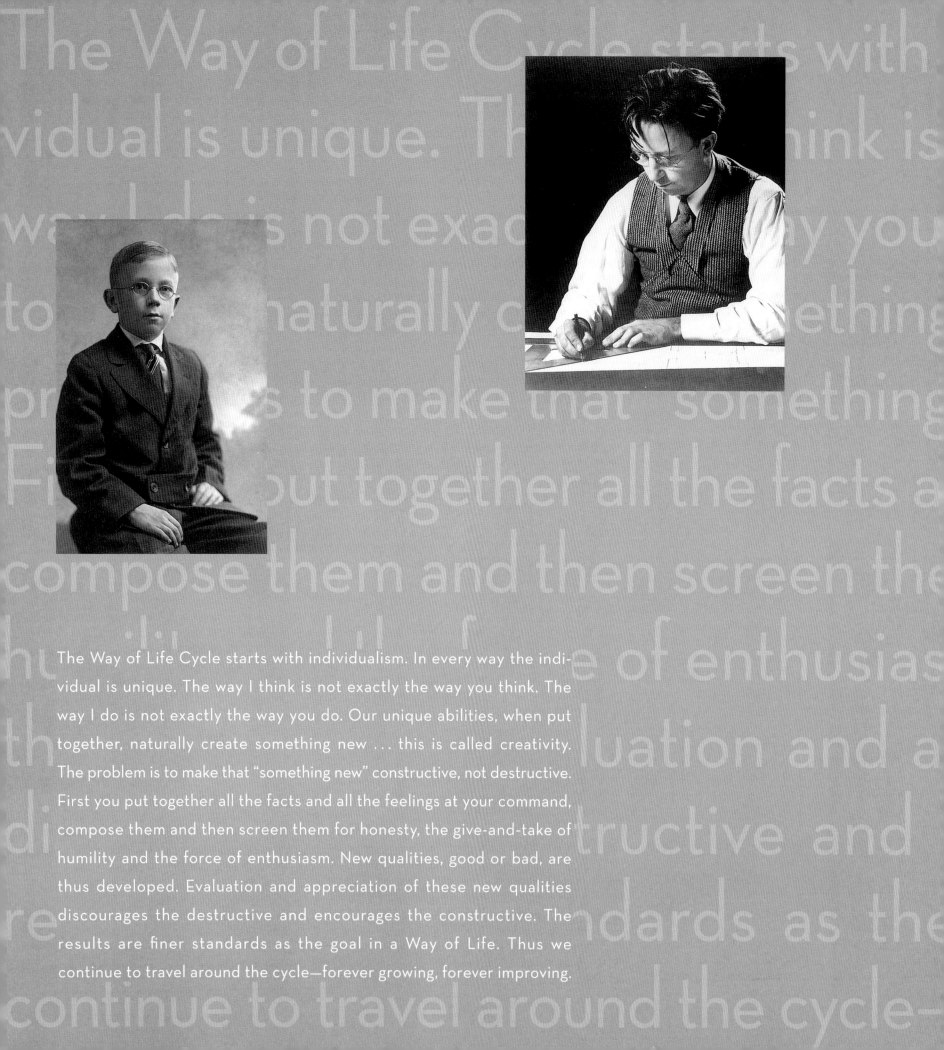

The Way of Life Cycle starts with individualism. In every way the individual is unique. The way I think is not exactly the way you think. The way I do is not exactly the way you do. Our unique abilities, when put together, naturally create something new ... this is called creativity. The problem is to make that "something new" constructive, not destructive. First you put together all the facts and all the feelings at your command, compose them and then screen them for honesty, the give-and-take of humility and the force of enthusiasm. New qualities, good or bad, are thus developed. Evaluation and appreciation of these new qualities discourages the destructive and encourages the constructive. The results are finer standards as the goal in a Way of Life. Thus we continue to travel around the cycle—forever growing, forever improving.

MIDWESTERN MODERN

■ Alden Ball Dow (1904–83) began life in an oven, for want of a proper incubator. This start slowed him down hardly at all over the next eight decades, as he took a path through life different from that of his father, Herbert H. Dow, founder of The Dow Chemical Company in Midland, Michigan. Before the son was forty, he was being heralded as "one of the country's most famous architects"—winner of a prestigious international competition, designer of an extraordinary studio and home, and an articulate voice for a more rational, humane way of building. Over a long career he created design chemistry worthy of the Dow name. ■ As an architect his work mediated between European modernism (the new International Style) and the organic architecture of Frank Lloyd Wright. But as a young man in the 1930s, Dow forcefully stated: "I dislike the word 'modernistic.' It implies a fad or a style—something here today and gone tomorrow."

ALDEN B. DOW

Instead he urged, optimistically, "Do not burden it now with a name. Because architecture in the past has been a matter of style, do not think for a minute that it is building its future on such a weak basis." Dow's design sources were multifaceted: nature (always), reason and practicality, the arts of Japan, the color wheel, the joy of play. He excelled at creating houses and churches, buildings whose scale was intrinsically humane. ■ Dow judged his work and his own life using a three-letter shorthand, HH&E, signifying honesty, humility, and enthusiasm. The first and last are fairly self-explanatory, but he often felt the need to define *humility*. "By this I mean the ability to give and take gracefully," he explained. "It seems to be a combination of justice, respect, and love. A building that has humility must contribute something to the land it sits on and the land in turn must contribute something to the building." Dow was equally humble, disliking the Wrightian kind of showmanship. The fame of this architect, a Midlander practically his entire life, may have been more regional than national. However, as a writer pointed out in 1961, "Although Dow's roots are deep into the Midwest … there is nothing provincial about either the man or his work." ■ In 1942 the noted architecture critic Talbot Hamlin perfectly caught Dow's spirit. "Alden Dow … has not been content to accept the accepted, merely to ring new changes on current tunes," he wrote. "He has sought to create out of building materials a poetry of plane and line, of outside and in, of color and form…. Yet his work is never a matter of equations or fixed relationships; it is rather the production of a mind seeking to create out of building materials objects that somehow plumb the more unusual depths of human experience…. Here is a man not content with building mere comfortable and efficient shelters but a man who conceives that architecture, in order to realize its potential contribution to human living, must also create buildings which enlarge the imagination and enrich the emotional life of those who dwell in them." ■ In 1983, the last year of his life, one of Dow's final honors was to be named architect laureate of Michigan, a class of respect usually bestowed on poets. But how fitting that his lifelong reach for poetry in architecture would be so recognized by his home state, whose motto is *"Si quaeris peninsulam amoenam, circumspice"* ("If you would seek a pleasant peninsula, look around you"). This advice recalls the famous epitaph for the architect Christopher Wren in St. Paul's Cathedral, London: *"Si monumentum requiris circumspice"* ("If you would see his monument, look around"). To find Alden Dow's legacy, start in Midland, the center of Dow's world—and look around. ■

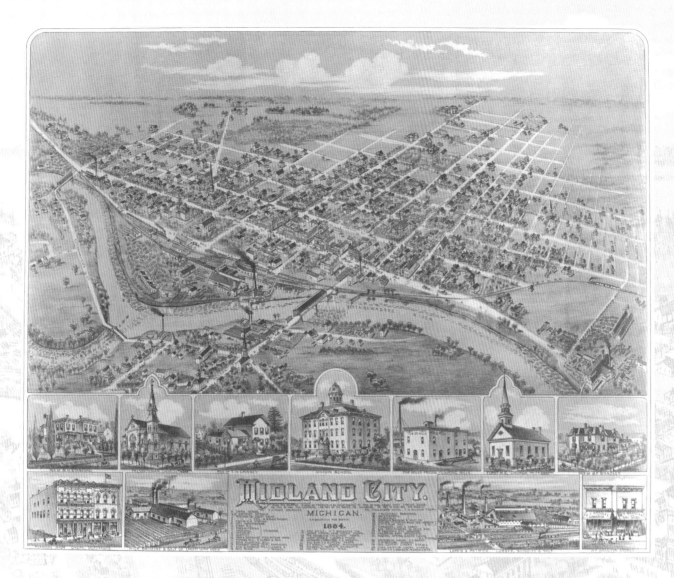

Little more than a half century after it was first surveyed, Midland—located near the thumb in the Michigan "mitt"—was on its way by 1884 to becoming a "City of Beautiful Churches" that would soon build an opera house. Both the "cork pine" and the wealth it brought traveled the town's rivers mainly to enrich Bay City and Saginaw.

Preceding page: Like an arrow skimming across a pond, the conference room of Alden Dow's studio marks the spot where the built and the natural worlds meet. It sits below the water level; behind it, stepping stones seem to have escaped from the building—each one serving to bridge the two elements of land and water.

TOMORROW'S CITY TODAY

Chapters in the story of Midland, Michigan, are inscribed on the walls of its Tudor-style courthouse. Colorful murals by Paul Honoré depicting Indians, trappers, traders, early settlers, towering Norway pines, and the woodsmen who harvested them trace the tale of this special place in the middle of America. From its first residents to the scientists drawn here beginning at the dawn of the twentieth century, Midland has been a pioneering town—a laboratory in many ways.

"Midland County slumbered for centuries under a deep-pile green carpet of *Pinus strobus*, 150-feet-tall white pine trees," noted the historian Dorothy Langdon Yates. The Chippewas arrived first, attracted to this Eden's "magic white sand," a great salt basin. Where the Tittabawassee and Chippewa Rivers met became known to traders in beaver skins as the Forks; their last trading post closed in 1840. A decade later came a "green rush" of Paul Bunyans ready to extract Michigan's own white gold—its tall pines—and then float immense logs down to the Saginaw River. The total board feet of Michigan white pine cut from 1850 to 1897 was enough to build ten million six-room houses.

Not far behind the lumberjacks were the millers. Two years after Midland County was founded in 1850, John Larkin arrived from the East and soon set up a lumber mill that later became the town's main industry. He built Midland's

■ THE RIVER WINDING THROUGH IS BEAUTIFUL. WE OUGHT TO USE IT AS MUCH AS WE CAN. ■

first hotel as well as a steamboat, the *City of Midland,* but he did not neglect the resources below ground; several wells reaching down to the briny depths were among those that helped Michigan at the time produce half the nation's salt. With its saloons and hotels that attracted lumbermen as well as its settlers who farmed just steps away from wilderness, Midland remained a bawdy town until at least the Civil War. By the end of the century the woods were lumbered out, and fires and floods further threatened Midland's security.

From a township population of 2,389 in 1908, the number of residents rose to 27,188 (driving 4,650 automobiles) by 1927. What was the secret of this turnaround? In a word: Dow. The arrival and success of The Dow Chemical Company beginning in 1897 helped shape this county seat into a cosmopolitan oasis—a middle-class, family-oriented place to live with the benefits of a city but the feeling of a small town. Called a "City of Modern Merlins," Midland attracted some of the nation's best scientific minds. Their families wanted and got good schools, parks, recreational facilities, libraries, cultural centers, and a country club. As Dow Chemical prospered, so did its hometown. The Great Depression of the 1930s passed it by.

If it can be said that one Dow—Herbert—put Midland on the map, then it was one of his sons—Alden—who redrew that template. While the father made the town into an industrial giant, the son built it into an architectural mecca. As early as 1939, reporters called it a model city, one of the most modern in the United States. An architectural island created in the middle of Michigan's sea of salt, Midland remains comparable to only one other small American town: Columbus, Indiana, which, thanks to the vision of J. Irwin Miller, an industrialist like Herbert Dow, is a display case of the country's notable architects.

What sets Midland apart, however, is that one architect was chiefly responsible for shaping "Tomorrow's City Today." Beginning with that up-to-the-minute country club in 1931, Alden Dow left Midland sixty-three houses, two residential complexes, ten religious buildings, eleven education buildings, eight civic buildings, and fifteen commercial and industrial structures, not to mention bridges and other refinements to his father's gardens. He served on the planning commission and spurred such a burst of tree planting on Main Street that Midland eventually gained designation as a Tree City, USA. Today most local children learn in Dow-designed schools, their parents work in Dow offices, and families go to the library, arts center, churches, and band shell designed by Alden Dow. He had the opportunity to design an entire town—Lake Jackson, Texas—but Midland is his monument. No U.S. city has been so profoundly affected by the vision of a single architect or enjoyed such a familial relationship with one. Alden Dow, boasted a writer in 1943, was Midland's "unofficial architect-in-chief" and gave his hometown "a greater harmony of design than even London in the days of Christopher Wren."

▶

Herbert Dow, who showed architectural inclinations of his own, urged Midland to build its Tudoresque 1926 courthouse—promoting a 1919 bond issue, underwriting some costs, and bringing Bloodgood Tuttle from Cleveland to design it. Fieldstone for the walls came from farms across the county. A shovel and a trowel used for the groundbreaking and cornerstone were made of lightweight Dowmetal, "Midland's wonder metal." Murals outside and in, picturing the county's history, similarly benefited from Dow Chemical expertise: made of magnesite stucco, a brine product, the frescoes are colored with pigment and ground glass developed over several months by Dow scientists and the artist.

THE WORKS

When Herbert Henry Dow stepped off the train in Midland one hot August day in 1890, what he saw before him might as well have been a town in the Old West. Wooden sidewalks on Main Street marking the infamous Saloon Row were still scarred from lumberjack boots, and the street itself flowed from mud to dust. It would have been considered a backwoods town if there had been many woods left in Michigan. Yet it wasn't tall pines that this young scientist from Cleveland craved—it was the prehistoric sea of brine just below the earth's crust.

Dow had briefly visited Midland two years earlier, when as a graduate of Case School of Applied Science in Cleveland he had come in search of good brine close to the surface. Some Michigan entrepreneurs were evaporating salt from this underground resource, using waste wood for heat, but the young college chemistry instructor had the idea that greater treasures—notably bromine, used in patent medicines and photographic supplies—could be mined from the salty brine. Even though electricity had not yet arrived in Midland, he planned to avail himself of this new invention by using his own generator.

Herbert Dow, born in Belleville, Ontario, in 1866, was already well on his way to a life of invention, following the example of his father, Joseph H. Dow, a master mechanic and inveterate tinkerer from an old New England family (descended from Henry Dow, a native of Norfolk, England, who settled in Massachusetts in 1637). The Industrial Revolution had spawned an age of discovery in the late 1800s. Herbert Dow followed his own dreams by forming the Canton Chemical Company in 1889 to harvest bromine from brine through a "blowing out" process. The path to the world-renowned Dow Chemical Company was not straight, however, as Dow struggled over the next decade to find economical ways to process chemicals while placating financial backers. On the road to establishing an American chemical industry independent of

Herbert Dow grew a handlebar mustache and later added a beard to lend gravity to his young man's persona, making him a distinguished-looking thirty-one in 1897. But spurred by World War I, he suddenly came to work in 1919 clean shaven. "It looked too Prussian," said the leader of America's chemical industry.

Even while struggling to get his company up and running, Dow found time to court Grace Anna Ball, the school-teacher daughter of Midland pioneers Amelia and G. Willard Ball, who owned a hardware store. The Dows were married on November 16, 1892, and soon Grace began to help her husband watch over his bromine boilers on late winter nights, sleeping on a cot.

Herbert Dow wasted no time in 1890 in leasing space for his new chemical works. The Evens Flour Mill at the west end of Main Street became the first home of Dow's industrial empire. The tower housed a brine well that Dow used to prove that bromine could be extracted electrolytically from the buried ancient sea. He and a three-man crew worked around the clock.

A decade after Dow started experimenting in the old gristmill, his burgeoning chemical complex had taken over the Larkin farm on the banks of the Tittabawassee River at Midland's opposite end. The underground brine lasted until 1987.

foreign producers, he formed three companies before the one bearing his own name, temporarily relocating from Midland to Ohio. His indomitable optimism helped him persevere against those who nicknamed him "Crazy Dow."

A year after The Dow Chemical Company was formed in 1897, it released its first product: bleach, created from chlorine captured from Midland's copious hidden sea. "Our success," Dow later explained, "is based on making use of what the other fellow throws away." In addition to potassium bromide crystals and chlorine, he pioneered the manufacture of chemicals such as chloroform, indigo dye, antiknock additives for gasoline, synthetic phenol explosives, lightweight magnesium metal (called Dowmetal), ethylene, iodine, Epsom salts, and aspirin, among many others. ("If all the headaches in the world were laid end to end," the *Detroit News* suggested in 1939, "Midland, Mich., could furnish enough aspirin to cure them.")

Like Henry Ford working to the south in Detroit, Dow was a true American innovator. He used mechanization techniques like those pioneered by the Model T maker (and bought himself a Ford touring car in 1912). The "man with a million ideas" took out 107 patents for chemical and mechanical devices, of which Dow was the sole inventor of ninety-one. He broke the German and British monopolies on bromine and bleach. He diversified Dow products, helping the company and its hometown weather World War I and depressions. He spent little time in his office, preferring to walk among his workers offering advice. Beginning in 1901 he allowed his employees to share in the profits of the business he worked so hard to nourish. In 1930 Henry Ford himself observed of Dow, "As technician, and as business man, his policy is founded upon a rare conception of chemistry's place in our national economics." Dow, who was recognized with two honorary doctorates and elected posthumously to the National Inventors Hall of Fame, was chosen in 1929 as "the American chemist who has most distinguished himself by his service to applied chemistry" and the next year

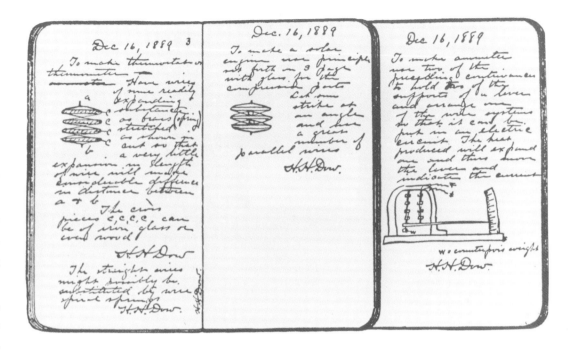

was awarded the prestigious Perkin Medal in industrial chemistry. Years earlier, one of his stockholders had complained that his "ideas come too rapidly for one man to reduce to practice."

Despite his success, the modest Dow for many years pedaled a bicycle along Main Street to and from the plant, which his family called the Works. As far as the town was concerned, the determined alchemist of The Dow Chemical Company was its own "first citizen." In addition to making state and national contributions, he found time to serve as a member of the town council and board of education, and Dow began a family legacy of philanthropy by supporting community interests such as the park system and individual gardens, the airport, churches, swimming pools, and the new courthouse (he appears in a lobby mural). With the aid of this ardent temperance advocate, Midland's saloons succumbed to a 1908 vote in favor of prohibition. "Crazy Dow" had been transformed into "Dr. Dow." Along the way he groomed two sons to carry on his leadership—one in expanding the reach of The Dow Chemical Company and the other in continuing to shape the town that Herbert Dow had made his own in 1890.

▲ In 1887 Herbert Dow began to record the large and small events of daily living in a series of notebooks that grew to number forty-eight by 1928. Many document his early scientific theories, such as his first drawing of an electrolytic cell for "blowing out" bromine from brine, dated December 16, 1889 (and patented in 1891). He detailed everything from inventions and expenses to his home, gardens, and travels.

A "TIGHT SHIP"

Before Herbert Dow and Grace Ball were married in 1892, they liked to stroll through a wooded area off Main Street called the Pines. Within seven years they would come to own that pine grove. It was one piece of a ten-acre home site assembled over two years for their expanding family, which in 1899 included Helen, Ruth, Willard, and by year's end Osborn (named after one of Dow's business partners). For a man with his meticulous attention to detail, the chance to build his own home proved an enticing challenge—and a welcome diversion from business—for Herbert Dow.

The Bay City architects Clark and Munger were the designers of record, but the fastidious head of The Dow Chemical Company shadowed them at every corner and cornice. For a model, he and Grace suggested a house they had seen near Chicago. "While we admire the Colonial style for other people," Dow admonished his architects, "we do not care for any of it on our house." Changes were made to follow Dow's persistent written and oral communications, but because of time and cost constraints a few Colonial Revival moldings slipped through. The Dow Homestead's prominent gable and asymmetrical form link it to the era's Shingle Style—itself based on colonial designs—yet features such as the house's broad sloping roof and rustic cobblestone porch at least acknowledge the progressive Arts and Crafts movement then capturing public attention. It was above all a comfortable home—a "nest in the Pines," as brother-in-law Thomas Griswold dubbed it, adding his own verse:

> This is that mansion fine, Sir,
> that Dow, the halogen man,
> Has built for his loving wife, Sir,–
> Just show me the likes, if you can!
> Its founded on Amperes and Volts, Sir,–
> It[']s built out of Natural Brine;
> And Midland's the town where it stands, Sir,
> At the close of '99.

Herbert Dow's backers had worried that he was devoting too much attention to building his home. But aside from his family, it was his main diversion from the struggles of turning The Dow Chemical Company into a viable enterprise. He brought to architectural challenges the same rigor and thoroughness that he employed at work. Money was in short supply both places, so counting his dollars and cents for building materials came naturally. The total cost came to $4,812.

Inside, "Mother ran a 'tight ship,'" her son Alden recalled long afterward. "Her house and her work days were models of efficiency." She took as her credo godliness and cleanliness. "Every spring and every fall our house was completely cleaned, top to bottom," he added. "Everything, and I mean everything, was taken out of every room in the house, thoroughly cleaned, and put back in its place, in almost sterile condition. All the children had to help in this task, and I can remember thinking it wasn't exactly fun but Mother had a knack of making it exciting. It was kind of a game."

The children all fell in line. "She was a stickler for order and punctuality. I remember how we all gathered in the living room before meals and sat down to eat as a group," said Alden. "Mother did

Grace Dow's fourth child, Osborn Curtiss, was born a week after the family moved into its new home in November 1899. He was preceded by, from left, Willard Henry in 1897, Helen in 1894, and Ruth Alden in 1895. Osborn died of spinal meningitis shortly after this photograph was taken.

The Main Street lot was still wooded in 1899 when the Dows and their first three children came to visit their new house, which from then on would be Herbert and Grace Dow's only home in Midland.

Showing a broad porch terminating in a porte-cochère, this revised sketch of the Dow Homestead, now known as The Pines, was made by their architect, Averton Munger, on April 27, 1899. Final inspiration came from an architectural plan book. "It is not the kind of home most people would suppose sheltered Herbert H. Dow ... unless they knew him well," observes Tawny Ryan Nelb in *The Pines*.

not condone stragglers." A church bell got everyone's attention. Herbert Dow forbade talk of "scandal" at the dinner table, he never drank, and he even disapproved of sugar, although Sunday breakfast more than once included toast with cream as thick as cheese from their own cow. Dow seldom talked at meals—Alden could recall times when his father would come home for lunch, eat, and return to the plant without saying a word. Grace Dow, known to her grandchildren as Nena, was reported to have tossed a piece of bread at her husband, asking, "Why don't you say something?"

Guests added divertissements for the family. "Much of our entertainment took place in our home," reminisced Alden Dow. "We constantly were visited by fascinating people known to my father. In the course of some evenings we might be entertained by some music. Well, my father, who did not have a voice, dearly loved to sing. On some occasions, my father's dissonance was matched only by my mother's chagrin." An annual picnic for local businesses, club meetings, and other gatherings kept the family in touch with their fellow townspeople. Feeling at home in his house and in Midland, Dow ensured that his company would remain headquartered in the place where it was born.

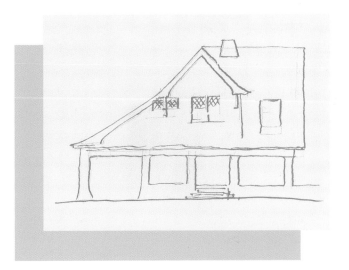

The Dows upgraded floors and furnishings in 1904, inspired by a visit to the St. Louis World's Fair. A decade later their three-bedroom home was expanded upstairs and downstairs with the addition of a sun parlor off the dining room, a sleeping porch off the master bedroom suite above, and a "Pullman Car" offering more sleeping accommodations toward the back of the house for family upstairs and servants downstairs. Later in life, pointing to the irregular floor plan and the way the rooms at The Pines open into one another, Alden Dow gave the assessment of an accomplished architect: "You know, my father had a modern idea when he built that house."

The three-story house in which Alden Dow grew up is dominated on the front by a swooping gable and a dramatic cutaway roof with a cross-gable to the left. Colonial-style pediments crown window pairs front and back. The clapboard siding was painted white until 1904.

Following a 1914 addition that expanded the house on the first and second stories, Alden had a room of his own in the new back wing. Before that he and Willard had shared a former guest room.

Special care was lavished on the entrance hall, including stained-pine woodwork and a fireplace (later removed). As finances improved, the Dows added oak parquet flooring, the large art-glass window above the landing, oriental carpets, and carefully chosen landscape paintings. To the left is a reception and music room and to the right is the living room.

▲ In 1904 Herbert Dow ordered upgrades for his home. In the living room, Persian rugs were laid down on oak floors that replaced the less expensive pine installed originally. Here the family spent evenings reading, studying, or sewing.

▲ Serving the original girls' bedroom on the house's front side, this bathroom was renovated in 1931 by Alden as one of his first design projects. Dorothy probably chose the blue tile and lavender fixtures for this chic Art Deco retreat.

SANCTUARY

Grace Dow told her husband that taking care of their home was her job. His was the garden.

Come just about every Sunday, Herbert Dow's family knew to find him outside, weather permitting. He got up early and disappeared into his "back lot" with a shovel and a pail of water. "About dinner time Father would be missed by the family, and we would go out looking for him," Alden Dow later recalled. "After much looking about we would stumble on his coat . . . , next we might find the pail, and finally the hole, and down inside would be Father digging." Herbert Dow's garden was also a place for retreat when he was faced with problems down at the Works. He would sometimes leave the plant and come home to dig sandy soil from around the base of his trees. Topsoil and fertilizer would arrive soon afterward to nourish needy plantings trying to thrive in Midland's sandy soil and frosty climate. Said his grandson Herbert Dow Doan: "I like to think that for him, his house and gardens were his personal haven, and allowed him to build things that he could see and feel in a very personal way. He was a great builder."

While the house was still in blueprints in the spring of 1899, Dow had a vision in mind for turning his land into a farm and sowing an orchard on it. From his mother came his love of gardening, and from experience as a boy raising vegetables came practical know-how, coupled with his considerable knowledge of chemistry. In May 1899 he wrote his father: "I planted an orchard yesterday," meticulously itemizing his ninety-two fruit trees (apple, pear, cherry, plum), ten grape varieties, one mulberry tree, and four lilac bushes.

Herbert Dow continued to acquire more specimens and more land, amassing a hundred apple varieties and sixty each of plum and pear within a decade. Eventually five thousand trees, including spectacular crab apples, stretched across some 125 acres. His first sale of apples was made

▶

Holding a photograph of his home, Herbert Dow in 1913 inspects a tree in his orchard. He declared in 1927: "I know more or less the history of every tree in my orchard." Although he grew and sold apples, including a "Dow apple" with banana-like flesh, he did not eat them himself.

The rock-lined swimming pool built in 1925 behind the Dow Homestead replaced a natural pond that had served as a gathering place for neighborhood children in summer and winter. "My idea of a beautiful garden," said Herbert Dow, "is one in which there is a small pool, some stones on one edge, a fine mist from an invisible source dropping on the stones and dripping off into the water, and all of it surrounded by shrubbery or plants."

▼

in 1907. To Dow, the orchard was another of his experiments—a place to discover if he could produce good fruit on "pine stump lands." It was his hobby, one that also put food on his family's table, provided an abundance to be donated, gave him displays for the Michigan State Fair, and served as a demonstration site for visiting horticulturalists documenting the possibilities of using chemicals for agriculture. The orchard never became as strong a commercial venture as he would have liked, but his work there ultimately led to establishment of The Dow Chemical Company's agricultural chemical department.

Within a year of starting the orchard, Dow had turned his attention to the remainder of his estate. In 1900 he persuaded company employee Elzie Cote to help set in motion the creation of another landscape palette: the Dow Gardens. First came annual and perennial flower beds to quickly add natural color to the site. Then followed more intense reshaping of the land according to Dow's personal philosophy. To add surprise and extend the sense of space, irregular swaths, paths, and waterways were created with horse-drawn scrapers. To broaden the appearance of lawns, convex forms were changed to concave. To punctuate long vistas, special features and bridges were built. Native trees and shrubs were planted along with vegetables. The Dow "farm"—complete with chickens, cows, and horses—became a sylvan retreat for family and, in 1931, for public visitors as well.

"The Dow Gardens were strictly an outlet for my father's creative interest in gardening," observed Alden Dow. "He was more interested in developing ideas rather than using those of the experts." Herbert Dow himself explained his affinity for nature in a March 1912 talk to Midland's Monday Club: "A man who has money enough can go out and within one year build a very magnificent house, but he cannot build beautiful trees. A house grows old and out-of-date every year. A tree becomes more beautiful and valuable with age."

▲ In 1920 Herbert Dow hired the British artist Arthur Henry Knighton-Hammond to paint the Dow Chemical works, and his eye must have been turned by the family orchards. Knighton-Hammond captured this tractor cultivating a pathway in *The Works* and also painted another view showing a horse-drawn wagon used for spraying the trees.

▶
Herbert Dow pauses in his gardens to view the swans near this rustic bridge, built around 1904 with cinder clinkers salvaged from Dow Chemical furnaces. It was replaced in 1979 by the Sun Bridge, a concrete span designed by Alden Dow.

BORN TO BUILD

"I was born into a family of chemists—a profession that was making earthshaking discoveries every day," Alden Dow recalled at age seventy. Some may have expected any son of Herbert Dow to follow the family passion for science, but Alden instead melded both his father's scientific bent of mind and his mother's artistic sensibilities. As he liked to say,

> Where there is an art, there is a science.
> Where there is a science there is an art.
> Art is feeling … science is fact.
> Feelings must be combined with facts
> before anything new, of value, can be created.

Alden and his two younger sisters, Margaret and Dorothy, benefited from being the Dow household's second generation of children. Under the watchful eyes of their personal protectors—Alden, the first child to arrive after the death of Osborn in 1902, was Ruth's "baby"—the youngest children had almost unlimited freedom in and around the large house on Main Street. By age five, Alden was raking rows of leaves on the lawn to outline rooms in imaginary castles; little Margaret annoyed him by running through the "walls." For Dorothy he built a multiroom playhouse, but before she could make it hers he moved it (at Herbert Dow's request) to a hill behind the house and converted it in turn into a chemistry laboratory, a boys' club, and a rabbit hutch; soon a basement dug beneath became a secret meeting place.

Up in his parents' bedroom, Alden tackled the early engineering toy Meccano, wielding a wrench and screws to coax the pieces into exotic shapes. "He was always building," remembered Dorothy. Not far behind among his interests was drawing, an activity his mother encouraged. In 1911, when he was seven, a neighbor girl asked him what he wanted to be when he grew up. "An architect," he replied. "Why?" she knowingly retorted. "They don't make any money!"

Reading was difficult for Alden until he was eight. "Nobody could figure out why he had trouble

Alden Ball Dow was born prematurely at home on April 10, 1904, weighing only about four pounds. While the doctor was tending to Grace Dow, Herbert Dow wrapped the baby in blankets and placed him in the best incubator the scientist could find quickly—the family oven. (Dow had invented and sold hen incubators as a boy.) Alden was named after the Puritan John Alden, a distant ancestor.

learning to read until they suddenly discovered he couldn't see a single letter," said Margaret. As far as Meccano was concerned, "I suppose he felt and screwed things together in the way he wanted them to go. He built things in spite of his eyes."

From 1911 to 1918 Alden was schooled at home along with Margaret and Dorothy and occasional classmates. The older Dow children had been taught by a German woman at a small private school. Grace Dow, who was never heard to raise her voice, had taught for a year at Midland's Post Street School before marrying Herbert Dow but was happy to turn over her young children's education to other teachers. Desks were set up for morning classes in the new sleeping porch off the master bedroom. At noon the teacher left, and then the students of the Dow school did their homework, played in the master bedroom–library, or put on amateur theatricals in the attic. By 4:30 on weekdays, all toys had to be put away so the family could gather downstairs with Father. The founder of The Dow Chemical Company did not play with his children—indeed, he had "very little sense of play," said Alden, who added: "I felt I never knew him." Dr. Dow preferred solitaire, chess, checkers, and timing his own speed in completing jigsaw puzzles. No one played games on Sunday.

Dorothy remembers the World War I era as a sober time, as she would. She fell ill during the Spanish influenza epidemic of 1918, and her sister Helen Hale, her aunt Helen Griswold, and the family's private teacher died. That fall Alden and Margaret entered Midland High School at the same time despite their two years' age difference. As Dows they had to set a good example once they were in public school.

For a child who began life in an oven and who could barely see until age eight, Alden wasted little time in diving into vigorous and innovative activities outdoors and in. Along with the Dows themselves, the young of Midland gravitated to the ponds in the Dow gardens in winter to skate and ski downhill in back of the family's barn. For street skating Alden had special skates with two wheels—a forerunner of today's inline skates. In high school

Alden liked to ride, whether on four wheels or four legs. Atop Sorry, the family horse, he helped with work on the gardens of the Dow Homestead.

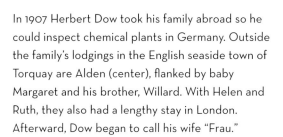

In 1907 Herbert Dow took his family abroad so he could inspect chemical plants in Germany. Outside the family's lodgings in the English seaside town of Torquay are Alden (center), flanked by baby Margaret and his brother, Willard. With Helen and Ruth, they also had a lengthy stay in London. Afterward, Dow began to call his wife "Frau."

Herbert Dow was a strict but loving father to his children, including his sons, Willard and Alden. When the family went to church on Sunday, the patriarch typically preferred to stay home and tend to his orchard and gardens.

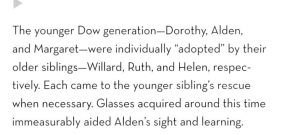

The younger Dow generation—Dorothy, Alden, and Margaret—were individually "adopted" by their older siblings—Willard, Ruth, and Helen, respectively. Each came to the younger sibling's rescue when necessary. Glasses acquired around this time immeasurably aided Alden's sight and learning.

he played football; without his glasses, remembered his brother-in-law Harry Towsley, he could not see down the field and just hoped that the ball would reach its target. He was the first boy in Midland to have a set of golf clubs, his friend Ormond Barstow recalled. Model trains were constant companions, a hobby that accompanied the boy into adulthood.

Alden (class of 1922) was teased in the yearbook's tongue-in-cheek sophomore class history for being a Dow: "November 16—Dow spent five cents." The next year, as a junior, he was voted "Greatest Talker (male)," but this award may likewise have been bestowed in jest given his measured cadence. He invariably chaired his high school decorating committees. "The resulting combinations of lights and crêpe paper" said Barstow, "were beautiful and romantic beyond words." Informal summer dances on the Dows' front porch offered other opportunities for Alden to innovate with Japanese lanterns, lights, and flowers. Like his mother and his sister Helen, Alden was also musical. His violin teacher reported that he played with "marvelous feeling," although he could not read the notes.

Few things fascinated Alden as much as taking pictures—a love of film that he pursued the rest of his life. He graduated to a movie camera as soon as the "Movette," with its miniature 17½ mm film, was offered about 1917. From this great invention came comic productions in high school, featuring fast-forward and reverse scenes to amuse his friends. In the 1920s going to the picture shows became a family affair for the Dows, topped off by Saturday matinees with friends. On August 11, 1923, Alden rushed with his still camera to document Midland's first train wreck after an engine jumped the track near the Dow home, killing the engineer and the fireman; his photograph illustrated the newspaper story the next day. When Eastman Kodak introduced its 16 mm film in 1923, Alden found a perfect medium for capturing the world around him—and creating new worlds of his own making. He was a young man in motion, as if he were speeding to make up for any time lost because of his small size and less-than-perfect eyesight.

▲ At eight years of age, Alden took hammer to hand to create his very first building about 1912. Before long Herbert Dow decided that the view from the Homestead would be improved if the three-room playhouse were moved behind the house, where a basement was excavated for it.

◄

Alden was "always sketching" as a boy, his sisters remembered. This childhood drawing may have been the start of his fascination with birch trees, which he later planted around his own Home and Studio.

■ THE PROBLEM IS NOT FINDING AN IDEA BUT KNOWING WHEN YOU HAVE A GOOD ONE. ■

Then about fourteen years old, Alden Dow (standing) joined his family in their gardens in 1918. From left are Herbert Dow's Connecticut cousin Lucy Curtiss, Grace Dow, Uncle Frank Curtiss, Herbert Dow, and Alden's sister Margaret (seated).

Alden's high school classmates were surprised when the 136-pounder decided to try out for the football team in 1921. After a friend called him puny, a showdown ensued. With some quick dance steps, victory was his. "In all modesty, while I probably was never a candidate for the Great White Hope, I was an apt student," remembered "Doc Dow," as he was nicknamed.

SETTING SAIL

Herbert Dow's far-flung business interests almost guaranteed that no family member would be confined to Midland. He and Grace simply gathered up their younger, home-schooled children and took them along on trips to New York City and farther afield. Each visit to New York called for a tour of the Metropolitan Museum of Art, followed by Broadway musicals or light operas.

The Dows had traveled abroad before, but the trip they treated Alden to at the age of eighteen left a life-altering impression. This voyage to Japan via Hawaii in late 1922 and early 1923 delayed Alden's enrollment in college but proved an education in itself. Herbert Dow, who went to immerse himself in the aesthetics of Japanese gardens, booked his family into new accommodations in Tokyo just nearing completion: Frank Lloyd Wright's exotic Imperial Hotel. Alden liked its scale and ornament ("a pure composition of abstract forms"), although he came to conclude that there was too much ornament. "We all found that a most fascinating place, the kind of building you could think about," he said, "and from then on my mind ran in that direction." An architectural mentor was confirmed and an aesthetic philosophy revealed. "Seeing Japan with my own eyes was a revelation," Dow later recalled. "I saw composed order in landscaping, buildings, floral arrangements … in fact, it seemed to be the backbone of the Japanese culture."

By the fall of 1923 Alden put aside his desire from the age of seven to be an architect and began his formal education in chemical and mechanical engineering, as his brother, Willard, had before him. As in Wright's case, engineering was a career path that Alden was destined to leave behind. Although he wrote his parents from the University of Michigan in Ann Arbor that he "enjoyed force diagrams and physics," he knew more about what was going on in the architecture school. He looked for diversions: pledging Willard's fraternity, going to the movies, taking a plane ride with his brother, giving in to "automobile fever," looking

into a new Kodak motion picture camera, and buying some land. On a Grand Tour of Europe and Algiers in the summer of 1925, Alden was the only family member who dared to fly from Paris to London on a Fokker passenger plane, taking just over two hours. From the crow's nest of the RMS *Mauretania* to the peak of the Eiffel Tower, he captured the trip on four reels of motion picture film, stopping only when the *Homeric* brought him to "the familiar sky-line of little old New York," as the Midland newspaper reported.

That year Alden finally confessed to his parents that his marks looked "partly discouraging but I know I can do better next semester." He had to disclose that he had been placed on probation but begged his mother: "Please Mama for my sake try not to worry." By the next year Alden was sure that he did not want to return to Ann Arbor, and the engineering school agreed. "I know you and Dad are awful discouraged with me but I don't think that you always will be," he asserted.

Herbert Dow was more understanding than might be expected. "I think it is a mistake for any young man to stay in College too long," he had written to his younger son in 1924. After working at his father's company in the summer, as he had done for several years, Alden decided that he was not destined to be a chemist. One morning he came to breakfast and announced that he was going that very day with his father on a business trip to New York. "I want to enter Columbia University's School of Architecture," he explained. Herbert Dow was speechless at first. He had tried to persuade Alden that architecture was not a real profession—too dependent on "personal feeling," unlike science, and thus impractical.

Years later Alden began to repeat one of his father's guiding principles: "Never copy. If you cannot figure out a way to do a thing better than it has been done before, don't do it, for otherwise you are just inviting cut-throat competition." For Alden, "It was this point of view that put me into architecture. I was sure I could build a better house than was being built."

Herbert and Grace Dow were fortunate to have their own photographer along on their travels—their son. During the family's 1923 sojourn in Japan, Alden captured his father absorbing some garden ideas to guide him back in Midland. Herbert Dow hoped to build his own unique garden, "one that is not Japanese, nor Italian, nor anything else except artistic."

Frank Lloyd Wright's Imperial Hotel (1915) made an indelible impression on Alden Dow during his 1923 visit to Tokyo. Both the repeated geometric motifs and the molded stone used inside and out made appearances in Dow's own work. The hotel survived an earthquake later in 1923 but was demolished in 1968.

Perhaps to deflect attention from having to admit to his mother that he was on probation, Alden included a meticulously crafted plan of his college room in one of his 1925 letters home. It came complete with an explanatory legend.

"I guess I wasn't made to go to school," Alden wrote in 1925 to his parents from the University of Michigan. He preferred courses in landscape design, surveying, and physics to the math-oriented engineering curriculum.

SCHOOLED IN THE JAZZ AGE

When Alden Dow arrived in New York City in late September 1926, it was the best of times. Wall Street was up, and the Jazz Age was in full swing. Architects such as Raymond Hood were building a city of towers—inventing a new American modernism. A 1926 poster said it all: "The Wonder City of the World."

The young man from Midland, residing first at 340 West 55th Street for $10 a week, slowly launched his new career by taking a class in architectural planning at Columbia University. "It surprises me how easy it is for me," he wrote his parents. "I never dreamed that I could really draw and I think that I am better than most of them." He got around by subway. "Can you imagine me sitting in the center of a big room in the Metropolitan Museum sketching some old vase or the design on some old piece of furniture?" he asked, noting that he was also trying his hand at watercolors. "I am sure glad that the family is satisfied with me coming down here because I sure am and I am going to stick to this sort of work," he promised.

Manhattan's delights beckoned. One night Alden attended a dance recital that may have helped shape his own musical inventions decades later. "It was interesting to see how well they could express their thoughts just by movements," he told the Dows in Michigan. But he was left mystified by an exhibit of modern art in Brooklyn— likely the startling 1926 Société Anonyme show featuring three hundred works of a hundred artists from Miró to Mondrian. "I never saw such 'stuff' in my life," he reported. "It all looked like the kind of work that the kids do in kindergarten." He went to the opera and of course to see the latest advancement in photography: "It is what they call a vitaphone picture or a talking motion picture," the amateur photographer wrote home. "It is rather a new thing but it seems to be getting away very good here in New York."

The Paramount Theatre—the marble and crystal picture palace in Times Square designed by the

The excitement of building a new architecture for a new age flowed from the pen of the architectural draftsman Hugh Ferriss in the 1920s. New York's groundbreaking skyscraper style found its way into Alden Dow's work while he was still at Columbia.

▲ To connect his brother Willard's house to the family gardens in Midland, Alden in 1927 designed a concrete footbridge inspired by the new pared-down style emanating from European ateliers. It was constructed that summer, along with another concrete bridge he designed for the sixth green of Midland's golf course.

preeminent theater designers Rapp and Rapp—opened in 1926, and Alden joined the throngs as soon as he could. "I have absolutely never been so thrilled over such a thing before in my life," he exclaimed. "It is absolutely the biggest and most gorgeous theatre that I have ever seen and it must be the most wonderful one in the world." Instead of describing it all, he wanted Herbert and Grace Dow to be surprised when they saw it for themselves. Alden was thrilled in turn by the first talkies such as *The Jazz Singer* of 1927 and the first color motion pictures.

Early 1927 saw Alden taking courses at Columbia to earn credits needed to enter architecture school as a full-time student. When he came upon the 1925 compilation of Frank Lloyd Wright's work originally published in the Dutch journal *Wendingen,* it proved a revelation to him; the book was filled with "knockout" photographs, Alden suggested, as well as drawings and critical assessments that inspired admirers around the world. That summer the innovations were all his when two bridges that he designed—both abstractions in concrete—came to life in Midland.

What architecture should look like and accomplish was much on his mind. "My idea is to do something entirely different from the type of buildings around home but more on the modern French style," he wrote his parents, adding that European designers' "best work has been on interiors but the idea is suggested in the two bridges we built this summer, which although … crude suggest many possibilities." He was also getting ideas from department store windows and furniture offerings. "At Christmas time I am going to use this same type of decoration at the Michigan party and I think that you will like it," he announced to the Dows.

By September 1927 Alden was primed to officially begin his four-year program at Columbia. The architecture school, hardly a proponent of the new European moderne style that he found so appealing, still hewed to a rigorous Beaux-Arts training. Its emphasis was on formalism, classical style, symmetry, and drawing. One of Alden's first classes was assigned a war memorial project. While his fellow students dutifully drew classical columns with Doric, Ionic, or Corinthian capitals, Alden figured out a better way to solve the problem: with a large shell-shaped sculpture ringed with the ruins of war. "This passes on its originality," responded the professor when he dispensed the grades, "but don't ever do it again." Alden spent the rest of his time at Columbia "following orders and waiting to get out."

Immersing himself in the history of architecture, architectural rendering, perspective, charcoal drawing, and similar courses, Alden grew increasingly confident in his intended life's work. Yet in 1928 he turned down an offer to design a garage for his father, thinking it "too early," and he resisted Herbert Dow's pleas to design needed housing for workers in Midland. Around this time Alden announced that he was working on a small-house design that was "out of the ordinary" and creating attention. Hardly two weeks after the stock market crashed on October 24, 1929, he had a country club on his mind. "I heard the other day they are getting serious about building a golf club house at home," he told his mother, "so I have been trying to get something ready for them.... I had better take the job while I can get it." His plan was to do the work under the official tutelage of an architecture firm in Saginaw.

Black Tuesday was followed by an economic depression that seeped into every corner of American life. Then came Herbert Dow's sudden death on October 15, 1930, from liver failure. In Manhattan the skyscraper spree created by the likes of the Chrysler Building, Empire State Building, and Rockefeller Center—"cloud-cathedrals of the religion of Success," as the writer Lloyd Morris put it—was coming to a halt. From flappers to the Four Hundred, from the denizens of the Cotton Club in Harlem to the margin speculators on Wall Street, the Jazz Age was playing its last set. It was no longer the best of times, but in 1931 Alden Dow received his bachelor's degree in architecture and prepared to return home to a safer world.

▲ Alden Dow (seated behind the fourth student from the right in the first row) told his sister Dorothy that while he was at Columbia, "there was something new every day coming out to get excited about." One noted Columbia graduate, Morris Ketchum, called Dow the "most talented designer and draftsman in the school."

◄ In 1929 the twenty-five-year-old Alden Dow stood five feet, seven inches tall and weighed 143 pounds. He had gained weight, which must mean that New York's cuisine agreed with him.

▲   ▶

With several friends, Alden embarked on another tour of Europe in the summer of 1929 by sea, air, and auto, but he announced that he wanted to see only new buildings—no relics. Taking the wheel himself for about 2,500 miles, he nonetheless savored historic sites and Gothic cathedrals from London and France to Italy, Germany, Austria, and Amsterdam. Paris, he concluded, got its ideas from Vienna and improved them, "just as New York gets its ideas from Paris." He took these and other photographs to use in his studies.

▶

Alden kept no paintings or drawings in his studio office except this sketch of his wife, Vada, drawn by an artist named Haley to accompany their 1931 engagement announcement in the *Midland Republican*.

VADA

Alden Dow first met Vada Lomyra Bennett, so the family story goes, when he saw her riding her tricycle to kindergarten about 1911. She was five and he was seven, and it was love at first sight: Alden, who had a lifelong affinity for fast wheels, fell in love with her tricycle. Over the next decade, while Alden was home schooled, they had little contact except for skating on the Dow pond. By the time he was fourteen, wearing corduroy knickers with long black stockings, he had his chance to turn Vada's head with his own driving machine, known variously as "the bus" and "the buckboard." As she later remembered: "It had four wheels and a steering gear and a little gasoline motor. The floor was open." It carried two or three riders, required no license, and could easily go off road. One of Alden's friends dubbed it "the greatest invention ever made."

Vada (1906–91) was the first of eight children born to Eva and Earl Willard Bennett of Midland. The family lived on Main Street two blocks from the Dow Homestead. Earl Bennett was a legend at The Dow Chemical Company. Armed with a business-school degree to round off the edges of his youthful experience as a lumber-camp cook, Bennett arrived in Midland in 1900 to visit his grandmother and quickly acquired a job with Herbert Dow. The pay was $25 a month, for which the new bookkeeper also got to sweep out the office. Over the next half century, he rose to be a vital financial adviser, member of the board of directors, treasurer, and finally chairman of the board in 1949.

When the Dow children entered public school, Alden's sisters Margaret and Dorothy began to pick up Vada along the way. And she began to notice Alden. Their first date was a Campfire Girls party. "We could each ask a boy, and so I asked Alden," Vada recalled. "He loooooved to waltz!" Alden drove the Dow family car, which broke down on the way home. The two walked the rest of the way, but Alden was so upset, she said, that "he didn't even take me to the door." Their romance nonetheless grew quietly but assuredly over the years, once he showed Vada that he did indeed have a sense of humor. As a close friend, Peters "Pat" Oppermann, later observed, "I don't think that Alden or Vada had another interest to any degree at any time in their life."

After graduation from Midland High School in 1923, Vada earned a bachelor of arts degree at Kalamazoo College and went on to receive her master's degree in education from Teacher's College at Columbia University in New York. At first she hesitated to go to New York, fearful that people would say that she was following Alden there. "It will look awful," she thought. But Vada wanted to pursue early-childhood education and moved east anyway. She later did practice teaching at nursery schools at Vassar's Euthenics Institute

■ I CAN'T IMAGINE A GIRL MORE IDEAL FOR ME. SHE HAS EVERYTHING THAT I LACK AND THEN SOME. ■

As a student at Kalamazoo College in the early 1920s, Vada Bennett was inspired by a professor to embark on a career in sociology. When she learned more about the new nursery-school movement, she made that her main area of study. Later she founded her own innovative program, the Parents' and Children's School, in Midland.

A Theta Delta Chi fraternity photograph from 1924 at the University of Michigan shows Vada Bennett and Alden Dow (front row, left), then a steady couple. His sister Margaret is second from the right in the back row.

Alden Dow and Vada Bennett were married at the First Presbyterian Church in Midland on September 16, 1931. Two hundred guests joined the couple for the reception and dinner at the Midland Country Club. It was the social event of the season.

and in Mamaroneck, New York, and East Orange, New Jersey.

Alden delighted in having Vada visit while he was studying at Columbia. "I want to show you something beautiful," he would say on their Sunday walks, taking her to architectural treasures such as St. Bartholomew's Church on Park Avenue. On December 9, 1929, Alden wrote his mother to say that he couldn't wait to give her the news: "Vada and I are *eventually* going to get married." It was to be such a long way off, he suggested, that the two did not want to call themselves engaged. "I feel like a million dollars," he exclaimed. "She is really head and shoulders above any other girl I have ever met in every way. I can't imagine a girl more ideal for me. She has everything that I lack and then some."

Two years later, following their graduations, they returned to Midland and were married on September 16, 1931. Few young bridegrooms could offer a site to match the one in which the new couple toasted their new married life: the Midland Country Club, designed by the groom himself even before he obtained his architecture license and just barely finished in time for the reception. Alden, an inveterate traveler by now, had planned a three-month western Grand Tour of a honeymoon with a gift of $5,000 from his mother—enough to buy a house in those depression years. They took a rough flight from Detroit to Chicago and then set a slower course by rail west on the Empire Builder to see places such as Los Angeles, San Francisco, and Yosemite National Park. In October the newlyweds sailed to Hawaii, where they spent a luxurious five weeks, stopping at the Royal Hawaiian Hotel, a landmark even in 1931. On the return trip they detoured to Phoenix to see the Arizona Biltmore Hotel, which bears the imprint of Frank Lloyd Wright, to compare with several Wright houses they had inspected en route. "Vada was as crazy about them as I was," Alden wrote home, excited to find "new ideas for building." After a bout of homesickness on Vada's part, both were "glad to get back to dear old Midland."

AVANT GARDE

Launching a career in architecture in the depression year of 1931 was daunting for most young graduates, with the possible exception of Alden Dow. Even Frank Lloyd Wright was having a hard time finding commissions. One of Dow's fellow newcomers, looking back ten years later for an exhibition entitled Forty Architects Under Forty at the Architectural League in New York City, noted poignantly:

We were just getting out of school or into practice when the stockbrokers were jumping out of windows. This was also the time of the big switch from Beaux Arts to Bauhaus.... We weren't sure what kind of architecture we wanted to do, but we were agreed on one thing: Roman baths were no place for railroad trains, nor medieval nunneries for undergraduates.

The skyscrapers were all built. So were the state capitols.... [In] comparison with the twenties, the sum total was neither impressive nor very profitable. Nevertheless, we started something.

Alden Dow had started something even before leaving Columbia: Midland's first country club, a building embodying tenets of the "new architecture" that had captured his attention in New York and abroad. In this first major work he strongly resolved any artistic tension he may have felt in school—between the classical and modern approaches to architecture—in favor of the new. Echoing the current architectural mantras in Europe, he told Midlanders in 1931 that a building was "a machine" that should "be dressed to suit its function."

After Gilbert A. Currie, a lawyer and ardent golfer, concluded in 1926 that Midland needed a golf course, Herbert Dow suggested that his son design its permanent clubhouse. Alden, although several years away from being licensed, produced a sketch in 1930 for a building that was almost immediately executed in association with Frantz and Spence architects of Saginaw. Dow's design, for one of Midland's most important public structures after the 1926 courthouse sponsored by his father, was a clear break with that mural-embellished, Tudoresque predecessor. Where the earlier structure was a romantic evocation of the past, the son's work was an emphatic vote for the future. Its streamlined, cubistic forms created their own ornament. Its taut stucco skin in a neutral, monochromatic tone signaled functionalism. Its strong

Dow sited the three-story Midland Country Club in a ravine so that the locker rooms could be entered from the ground floor at the rear. Generous windows as well as a covered terrace in the 32,000-square-foot, cinder-block structure give panoramic views onto the golf course. Herbert Dow's gardener, Elzie Cote, supervised the landscaping, and Dow products were used in construction. Today the clubhouse has been significantly altered.

▼

geometric planes turned the clubhouse into three-dimensional sculpture.

The country club, which opened on May 1, 1931, was a tour de force for a twenty-seven-year-old who could not attend the celebration because he had to prepare for graduation. The *Midland Republican* produced a special edition lauding the young man's accomplishments in everything from the colorful furnishings (the lounge and dining room carpets were purple; walls were salmon and green; some furniture was aluminum) to the modern heating and plumbing equipment to the gifts and time contributed by Dow family members. Most striking of all, glowing ceiling and floor lighting bathed club members in an unexpected rainbow of colors.

How did a student from the American Midwest come to share some of the most progressive ideas in architecture? Living in New York and traveling abroad certainly broadened his perspective. Lessons from the 1925 Exposition Internationale des Arts Décoratifs et Industrials Moderne in Paris,

which gave rise to the Art Deco movement, can be seen in the crisp setbacks and vertical articulation of the clubhouse facade. Familiarity with the nascent International Style from visits to the Netherlands, Germany, Vienna, and Paris (in 1929–31 Le Corbusier's Villa Savoie was on the drawing boards) shows itself in the clubhouse's horizontality, ribbon windows at the back, and conception as a machine for play. Stylized fireplace murals inside evoke Wright's work at Midway Gardens (1913) and the Imperial Hotel (1915), and doors and windows inset with geometric art glass recall his Prairie years; even the square logo Dow developed to sign his drawings paid homage to this eminence grise. In his first building Dow brought the world to Midland. "If we will continue to develop this character," he prophesied, "Midland will become one of the most interesting towns in the country."

After a decade of work, the writer of the Forty Architects Under Forty catalogue concluded in 1941: "Our big job has been to break down the prejudices of an outworn eclecticism and to replace them with something more positive and vital." Among the exhibition's select group who had set out on this path were Eero Saarinen, Edward Durell Stone, Harwell Hamilton Harris, George Nelson—and Alden Dow.

TALIESIN, WISCONSIN
Photographed in 1946
By Alden B. Dow

FELLOWSHIP

"I first became interested in Frank Lloyd Wright in about 1920 listening to my father tell of the houses Wright was building in Chicago and Wright's fascination for Bechstein pianos," Alden Dow remembered a half century later. The family's 1923 visit to the Imperial Hotel in Tokyo had cemented Alden's fascination with the architect. Beginning in 1929 as a Columbia student, he resolved to ask Wright if he could work with him for a summer. "I might take you if I liked you," Wright icily responded in 1930, but even after Dow went to hear him lecture at Princeton University, it did not happen. Dow held out the hope of getting in "after I finish school." Following graduation from Columbia in 1931, however, Dow commuted from Midland to Saginaw to work with Frantz and Spence, where he sketched out a number of speculative projects.

In 1932, in part to keep the wolves at bay during the Great Depression, Wright established the Taliesin Fellowship at the urging of his wife, Olgivanna. Now a formal system was in place for accepting students to work at the feet of the master, and Dow signed himself up in spring 1933, barely a half year after the first apprentices had arrived at Wright's home and studio in Spring Green, Wisconsin.

Alden and Vada left Midland in late April that year for what he thought would be sessions of deep conversation with Wright about architecture. Instead he was put on the dishwashing team. As Alden, who was about a decade older than the other apprentices, recalled: "Most of the time there was spent in running the farm, taking care of the existing buildings, and building a little theatre and a large drafting room all at Hillside. ... I spent weeks on this, as well as cutting stone and putting it in place for the chimney in the drafting room. ... In the field we did everything from planting to harvesting."

It was the same life lived by the other student architects, and Vada joined in after three lonely weeks in Madison, an hour away. She had thought

◄

Vada Dow, who grew close to Olgivanna Wright, became a painting fellow at Taliesin and joined in the afternoon gatherings with Wright in Taliesin's tea circle. "It will be long before we ever get people in the Fellowship like you and Alden," Olgivanna Wright wrote several months after their departure.

◄

Dow's motion pictures of life in Spring Green—from the apprentices in the field to the master at work—remain one of the most complete records of the Fellowship experience. He returned in 1946 to supplement views taken in 1933. Picnics in the field, captured by Pedro E. Guerrero, another Taliesin apprentice, were a regular opportunity for the Wrights to mingle with the apprentices.

The two architects maintained a warm friendship over the next fifteen years, with Dow contributing gifts as varied as apples from the family orchards to recipes for oxidizing copper copings to financial aid for the always-needy Wright. In 1937 the sage of Taliesin even came to Midland—calling it "an outpost of civilization"—to give a talk in which he graciously commended Dow for embracing the Wrightian principles of organic architecture. But all that came to an end in 1949, when Dow was awarded the commission to design the Phoenix Civic Center—practically in Wright's own back yard. The city had found Wright too expensive. Hurtful letters were exchanged, with Wright crying, "I feel as though I had lost a son to find a cheap competitor." Dow replied with gardening analogies, wishing for "a rose without thorns." Amends were finally made after a chance meeting at the Plaza Hotel in New York in the early 1950s, and when the first Frank Lloyd Wright Creativity Award was presented by Olgivanna Wright in 1982, it went to Alden Dow. She called him "my late husband's spiritual son."

"I consider Frank Lloyd Wright the greatest architect that ever lived," Dow had divulged to a correspondent in 1970. "I can't think of a form or an idea that has been used in building since his time that he did not experiment with years ago.... His buildings truly represent this country and I am sure we eventually will awaken to the contributions he made to our way of living through architecture." Both were inspired by nature, used geometric modules as the basis of their designs, dreamed that architecture might cure social ills, relished challenging sites, excelled at designing homes, and built flexibility into their buildings. As Tobias S. Guggenheimer observes in *A Taliesin Legacy: The Architecture of Frank Lloyd Wright's Apprentices*: "Dow seems to have had little interest in subordinating his own ambitions or in helping Wright construct his perfect world. Rather, it appears that Dow's brief tenure at Taliesin, like that of others yet to come, was meant to affirm through personal contact the truths he had perceived in Wright's work long before he actually met the man."

that she might study at the University of Wisconsin, but Wright persuaded her to come to Taliesin and pay tuition as part of the Fellowship. "We have both decided that this is the ideal way to live ...," Alden wrote his mother during the first of six months spent there. One of the inveterate filmmaker's lasting contributions was to document the Taliesin Fellowship's first year in motion pictures.

Dow went to Taliesin to immerse himself in Wright's revolutionary ideas about architecture, to confirm and sharpen his own theories. He also took with him plans for a house he had been working on at Frantz and Spence, for Earl Stein, a Dow Chemical employee. Wright, providing suggestions that improved the concept, urged that the house be the Fellowship's first official project. Soon after construction of the Stein House got under way in the fall of 1933—and not wishing to linger too long under Wright's large shadow—Dow returned to Midland, where architectural opportunity awaited. He had admitted to his mother that he saw in Wright qualities of his father: "He just keeps moving on no matter what is in his way."

NOT YOUR FATHER'S HOUSE

When Alden Dow left the Taliesin Fellowship in the fall of 1933, America's deepening depression had hardly surfaced in Midland. Employment at The Dow Chemical Company reached a peak in 1934. The only problem the town had in common with the rest of the country was a housing shortage. What Midland needed was its own architect, one whose innovative ideas would appeal to Midland's scientific and professional community. What Dow found were eager clients in his family's circle and among the members of the country club who were enjoying his strikingly modern clubhouse.

Even before joining the Taliesin Fellowship, Dow had received his first residential commission in 1932. His clients, as for a number of later works, came from family: his sister Margaret and her husband, Dr. Harry Towsley, who were just setting up their household in Ann Arbor. Not yet

registered to practice architecture—his license was awarded in June 1933, when he was at Taliesin—Dow drew the plans in association with the Saginaw architects Frantz and Spence, as he had for the country club.

With its broad hipped roof and pronounced horizontality, the small Towsley House recalled in some respects elements from Wright's Prairie Style; the open plan would also have met with Wright's approval. But its standing-seam copper roof was a feature that Dow would make his own, and the bright whites used for exterior and interior walls pointed in the direction of the International Style. Dow's selection of textured Acoustex panels for interior walls showed his proclivity for new and experimental materials—as one would expect of Herbert Dow's son. Trying to maintain a low profile for the three-bedroom house, the young architect ended up doing battle with code officials over 7½-foot-high ceilings that the city insisted be 8 feet. Dow lost the fight

The complex massing found at the rear of the Towsley House in Ann Arbor contrasts with the residence's simple facade, notable for diamond-pane windows similar to those of the home in which Alden Dow grew up. At the back, under sloping copper roofs, the house and its garage enclose a welcoming terrace. Dow's sister Margaret and her husband, Harry Towsley, lived here for six decades.

A cozy inglenook in the Towsley House contrasts with the general openness of the layout—a melding of old and new ways of designing a home. Frosted-glass panels concealed both lighting above the fireplace and a built-in cabinet opposite the kitchen. The door at right leads to the house's two bedrooms.

this time (although he documented his battle in a humorous strip of plaques by Paul Honoré placed near the door), but he returned over the years to enlarge the house without altering its compact appearance from the street.

More houses followed, as it became prestigious in Midland to own a house designed by the son of Dow Chemical's founder. The first built in his hometown was for the family of Earl Stein, soon to be the city's mayor. Low-slung, brick, with an oversized chimney anchoring a sheltering copper roof, the design was tweaked by Wright and reworked by Dow during his Taliesin stay. "Everyone here likes the house," he wrote his client, "including the very critical Mr. Wright." Once his new teacher urged Dow to take advantage of the house's parklike setting, he projected terraces and garden walls into the landscape and created a sunken garden in the back to open up the ground-level bedrooms. Inside, views snake around corners to expand the sense of space

and add surprise—a key design principle of Wright's that Dow learned firsthand in his father's gardens. The architect told Stein that he hoped the house would be regarded as "one of the best examples of modern architecture."

Dow soon began to turn out the scores of houses that would build his international reputation. His 1933 design for Joseph Cavanagh, a previous Midland mayor, was also sketched out at Taliesin and continued the general L-shaped form, materials, and open plans of the Towsley and Stein Houses. As word spread about Dow's progressive residences, more commissions followed in the same vein—among them the accomplished Diehl and MacCallum Houses of 1935. However, plans drawn for two houses in 1933, one built and one not, set Dow on a different course. In them he put to the full test one of his favorite maxims from his father: "Never copy." He went in search of a better way to build than the competition.

▲

Inside the Stein House, the living room ceiling is cut away to add height and interest as well as a skylight. For a beginning architect not yet thirty, Dow skillfully played up design and textural contrasts throughout— rough against smooth, dark against light, low against high.

▲

Generous roof overhangs on the three-story Stein House, in addition to the overall massing, harken back to Wright's Prairie houses. Changes have been made since it was completed in 1934, but the house remains a landmark of Dow's early career. It was one of the first buildings constructed by a Taliesin apprentice.

"GEOMETRIC POETRY"

While designing homes for mayors and other prominent citizens of Midland, Alden Dow was beginning a long quest to produce attractive houses for people whose budgets were much more modest. One such low-cost home, the Lewis House (designed in 1933 and completed the next year for $2,500), was built around a welcoming hearth assembled from a type of concrete block new to Midland. A decade earlier Frank Lloyd Wright had experimented with what he called textile blocks for four houses in the Los Angeles area. Dow liked the idea of using blocks because they would be inexpensive to manufacture, provide their own structural support, and offer aesthetic variety. Like Wright, he was taken with the potential of harnessing the machine to improve architecture.

Dow had already been using a unit-based design system similar to Wright's, laying out his plans on a four-foot module. "I think Mr. Wright's great contribution to architecture was his modular design approach," Dow wrote to his great-niece Martha Whiting in 1969. "I have used this on all houses I've done." Geometric modules, he explained, allowed for building components that could be duplicated

Dow patented his series of Unit Blocks in 1938, noting that the continuous lines they produced were "less disturbing to the eye" than the zigzagging joints of concrete blocks and bricks. Sixteen variants were designed to meet special needs such as corners, wall caps, and window and door openings.

▼

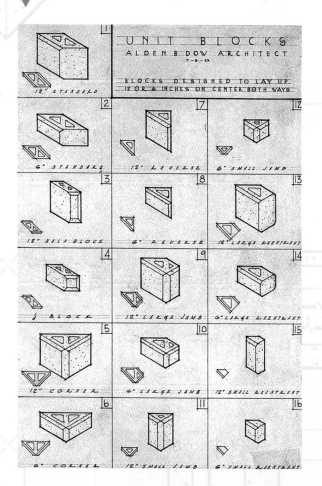

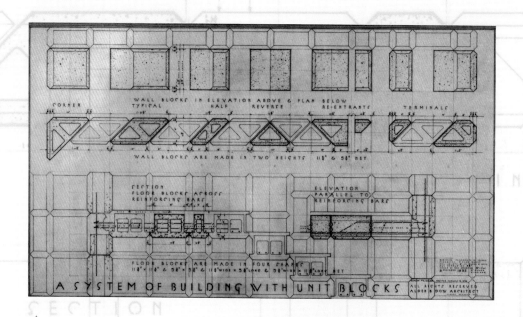

▲

With their rhomboid shapes, Dow's Unit Blocks made a strong bond because one course was angled to the right, the next to the left. Structural steel, wire conduits, and piping could be threaded through the hollow interiors. Air in the center space created natural insulation.

▶

In the Lewis House (1933) in Midland, Dow's first low-cost residence to be built, family life centered around the Unit Block hearth. Rooms in the square house fanned out in a pinwheel from this physical and visual focal point.

easily by a machine. At this time, standard cinder blocks were plain eight-by-sixteen-inch rectangles. Dow reasoned that cinder ash residue from the coal furnaces at The Dow Chemical Company might be recycled into what he began to call Unit Blocks. He had experimented, unsatisfactorily, with plain cubic blocks before going to Taliesin. When he returned he created a new beveled block one foot square on its face but angled forty-five degrees behind; this offered greater structural integrity because the joints would be offset from course to course. The blocks, lighter in weight than concrete blocks but structurally as strong, became a way to organize architectural space both horizontally and vertically.

The first house Dow designed entirely using his Unit Blocks, dated 1933, was for the Lynn Heatleys in Midland. With its rhythmic walls of concrete blocks, flat roof, dominant horizontality, three levels, glassy expanses, and raised clerestory, the house was apparently too unusual for the Heatleys. It was never built. Other clients welcomed the chance to be part of Dow's experiment. The first Unit Block design actually built was the four-bedroom Heath House of 1934, which cut an even more strikingly horizontal line. A dozen more would follow.

▶

The Unit Blocks, flat roof, and streamlined appearance that Dow introduced in the Heath House of 1934 became his signature for the remainder of the decade. The architect showed his love of color by choosing blue trim.

As the Heath House shows, Dow's kitchens were thoroughly modern for the 1930s. Unit Blocks in two sizes add texture, while the clerestory fills the room with light.

▼

After the Heath House came another Unit Block house in 1934 for Vada Dow's brother-in-law Alden Hanson; built just two houses away on a three-foot, rather than a four-foot, module, it was designed to grow with the family, as it did in 1938. A third house designed in 1934, for John Whitman, another former Midland mayor, garnered honors well beyond Midland. Blocks for his own and other Unit Block houses were made by Whitman's cinder-block company. (He also aided Dow in refining the basic composition of the blocks.) An assured composition of five living levels arising from a five-foot unit system helped

the house gain the grand prize for residential design at the 1937 Paris Exposition of Arts and Technology. It was a rare acknowledgment by Europeans that American design of the period was worth their notice.

The Ball House of 1935, suggested the architecture critic Talbot Hamlin, offered "a new sense of the interrelation of rectangular forms—a kind of geometric poetry." This was followed by more homes constructed of Dow's blocks: in 1935 for his chief draftsman Robert Goodall, a former Wright employee who helped Dow with the block design; one in 1936 for Charles W. Bachman in East Lansing and

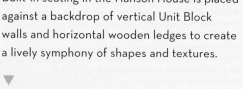

Built-in seating in the Hanson House is placed against a backdrop of vertical Unit Block walls and horizontal wooden ledges to create a lively symphony of shapes and textures.

From its windowed street facade, the Hanson House of 1934 appears smaller than its actual size. The full extent of Dow's ability to sculpt three-dimensional forms and meld textures becomes obvious on the entrance side. The oversized chimney with a scattering of quarter-size blocks anchors the composition.

In the Whitman House of 1934, five levels are compacted into what was made to appear an over-ridingly horizontal design, emphasized by the broad stucco wall. To the left the living room windows push out from the wall, while windows on the top level are set back to add to the architectural dynamism.

Receiving the Grand Prix from the Paris Exposition in 1937 for the Whitman House and his studio, Dow's new international recognition put him in league with the designers of the Empire State Building and Rockefeller Center, fellow winners.

Inserted into its own level above the dining room, the Whitman living room seems to float in space. Built-in seating snuggles around the fireplace inglenook. The National Register of Historic Places commended the house for "Alden Dow's remarkable ability to manipulate space and materials."

another for the architect's aunt Mary Dow in Saginaw. That same year he also designed a summer home in Midland for Elsa and James Pardee, a college classmate of Herbert Dow's, in time for Pardee's election as Dow Chemical's board chairman. Taking advantage of its sloping site on Main Street, the architect tucked three levels into the ninety-foot-long T-shaped Pardee residence. Interior spaces flow effortlessly from living room down to dining room and up to the bedrooms. Elegant finishings made it a home fit for a captain of industry.

This success was followed by still more Unit Block houses (Dow was designing other house types at the same time). His hundred-foot-long design of 1938 for Alden Hodgkiss in Petoskey was simplified to one level to focus on the view of Lake Michigan. The next year Dow produced one of his largest and most expensive residences yet for his sister Dorothy and her husband, Anderson Arbury, outside Midland. This was followed by 1940 designs for homes with more squared-up plans near Detroit for Robbie Robinson, a window salesman with whom Dow had worked, and in Algonac for LeRoy Smith. Pairs of masterful proposals for Margaret Mitts (1935) in Saginaw and K. T. Keller (1938), head of the Chrysler Corporation, on Lake

St. Clair went unbuilt along with the earlier Heatley House.

Dow's first twelve Unit Block houses managed to be surprisingly varied—testimony to the seemingly infinite variations possible with this material. Yet they form a cohesive group bound by common features. They were designed on a unit system, tend to present a strongly horizontal appearance, and offer a sculptural dynamism in their plans. Painted white to mask the gray cinder material, the Unit Blocks offered almost solid planes of color. Flat roofs make the residences seem to hug the ground, while massive chimneys add a vertical counterpoint. The front door is often hidden to add mystery, windows are prominent, and clerestories bring light into otherwise dark places. Public and private spaces are clearly delineated, with living and sleeping areas set into separate zones; transitions may be marked by just a few steps. The resulting multiple levels enliven the interiors in a thoroughly modern way. Large expanses of glass and use of the same building blocks outside and in help erase distinctions between outdoors and indoors. A trellis may carry the line of the house out to nature. Garages are thoughtfully integrated into the plan, often connected to the house with a sheltering walkway or carport. Altogether the houses exhibit an assured mix of forms, materials, planes, and colors. Each one has its own personality, and, as one historian concluded about the Ball House, "Nothing is predictable."

It did not take the architectural press long to home in on Dow's accomplishments. In December 1936 *Architectural Forum* pronounced the Heath House "an ingenious plan" with "interesting interior vistas" and a "great deal of originality." The following April the magazine cited the Hanson House for being "a three-dimensional object, in contrast to the average small house which is designed as a series of elevations." In 1942 Talbot Hamlin weighed in with an overview in the magazine *Pencil Points*. The critic expressed some personal reservations about the "insistent rhythms"

▲ Visitors to the Pardee House of 1936 are sheltered under a broad roof overhang as they approach the secluded entrance. The exterior unfolds in intersecting planes and contrasting materials—glass framed in wood, cinder blocks meshed with glass blocks, a crown of copper awnings.

▲ In the Pardee living area and hall, space is brilliantly manipulated into an interlocking skein of levels. Stairs lead down to the dining area and up to bedrooms and a sunroom. Mrs. Pardee tried to persuade Dow to change both the Unit Blocks and the large expanses of windows, but he prevailed.

of the blocks, but he was generally enthusiastic about Dow's houses. A half century later it became clear that the Unit Block houses had stood the test of time: they were among twelve Dow houses in Midland added to the National Register of Historic Places in 1990 as a thematic nomination stressing the architect's ground-breaking achievement in bringing the International Style to the middle of America.

During the years 1933–34, when Dow's first Unit Block houses were getting under way, Wright was wrestling into being his own new type of house—what came to be called Usonians. A transitional prototype faced in brick, the Willey House in Minneapolis, was designed in 1933 in part with Robert Goodall's involvement and was followed in 1936 by what is considered the first Usonian to be built, the Jacobs House in Madison, Wisconsin. Conceived primarily as "houses of moderate cost," these simple residences—less spatially complex than Dow's Unit Block houses—were based on modular forms designed to be less expensive to build. Wright began with wood, later moved to brick and stone, and only in the 1950s reinvented his earlier textile blocks for what were styled as build-it-yourself Usonian Automatics. Comparing the work of Wright and Dow in this period, it is obvious that some synergy was taking place between mentor and apprentice in one direction or another.

By the time the Smith House was completed in 1942, Dow had discarded his Unit Block system. During World War II the blocks became too expensive to manufacture and too labor intensive to build. The forms were eventually sold to a developer in Florida, sold again to a buyer in Israel, and subsequently lost. "The disappearance of their textural pattern and planning discipline," notes Sidney K. Robinson in *The Architecture of Alden B. Dow*, "removed an important element in Dow's architectural palette." Dow, however, did not forsake his experimental building blocks until he had used them for what became his most important commission: his own Home and Studio.

Dow's 1939 house for Anderson and Dorothy Dow Arbury was designed like a pinwheel centered on the entrance. Four wings hold the bedrooms, a kitchen and dining room, a large living room, and a three-car garage reached by an eighty-foot-long covered walkway.

The Arbury House's exuberant exterior forecasts the fanciful playroom. Plain wall surfaces of white Unit Blocks give way to a symphony of primary colors and swirls of geometric shapes. Patterns in the linoleum continue onto the walls, producing a seamless composition of energy and delight.

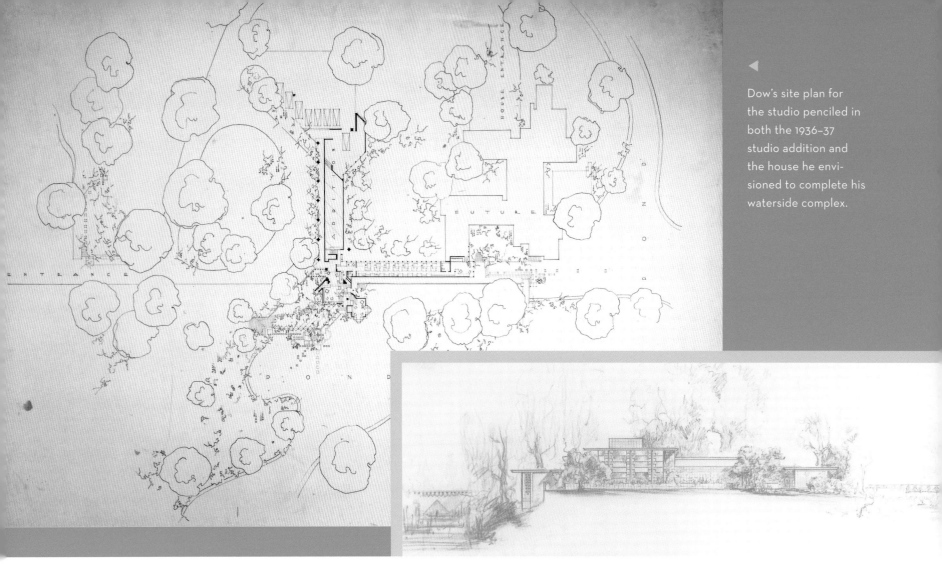

◄

Dow's site plan for the studio penciled in both the 1936–37 studio addition and the house he envisioned to complete his waterside complex.

INVENTION FOR ITS OWN SAKE

Alden Dow began his creative life without one of an artist's key tools: a studio of his own. He created a makeshift work space in the basement of Dr. William Hale's house, where he and Vada spent winters beginning in 1931. Hale (whose wife, Helen—Alden's oldest sister—had died in the 1918 influenza epidemic) returned each summer, so the couple had to move to temporary lodging at the country club. After Dow returned from Taliesin in the fall of 1933, the idea of a studio began to exert both practical and emotional appeal on him. The spirit of the home and studio that Wright had built on his Wisconsin hilltop may have cast a spell on Dow, showing him how a sense of community might arise from an architect's workplace.

A natural site conducive to organic architecture was no doubt on his mind as he searched in 1934 for a location on his father's property. Drawings made for one site, with the help of Robert Goodall, his new draftsman, adapted the flat-roofed, Unit Block style he had begun to build for his clients. Forced to move to another part of Herbert Dow's plum and apple orchards to hook up to existing utility connections, Dow found inspiration in a creek on the property that he diverted to his own site. The seamed copper roofline was raised (unique among his Unit Block projects) and shaped into startling angles. Blocks spilled from the walls in a lifeline reaching out to nature. A prominent stair-stepped chimney—variously likened to a stalagmite and an altar—was all the sign Dow needed to announce the new firm of Alden B. Dow, Architect.

First to come, in a matter of about two weeks, was a long, narrow structure (forty-eight by twelve feet) that Dow likened to a railroad car. This wood-framed building with inset Homasote panels

▲

Dow's original design for his studio continued the flat roofs he was then building on his Unit Block houses, making it seem residential in appearance. After choosing a new site, he settled on soaring roofs.

▶

Dow, photographed about 1937, usually met with clients in the studio's submarine conference room—providing a watery baptism in his daring architectural ideas.

Preliminary elevation drawings for the conference room show Dow's imaginative interweaving of spaces, forms, and textures. As built, the rectilinear chimney became more delicate and randomized, and the roof gained its sheltering, arrowlike shape above the man-made pond.

became his studio in 1934; no Unit Blocks were yet available for the architect's own building. Large windows on what was to become the courtyard side brought in strong northern light for his draftsmen. Next came the exuberant chimney as well as the public areas in 1935, notably a conference room that Dow wanted to place right at the edge of his new pond to merge the man made with nature. The problem was how to meld the two rooflines, which Dow solved ingeniously by sloping a new arrow-shaped roof at a forty-five-degree angle downward to within five feet of the water line. Thrusting away from this room, and completing an open V shape, the roof dissolves into a coppery trellis seemingly suspended above a seemingly random assortment of Unit Blocks that appear to have slipped their mooring from the wall alongside the pond.

In 1936–37 the final leg of the original studio plan was put into place with a second drafting room placed at right angles to the original. With its sawtooth profile and matching triangular windows, it was provocative where the first had been understated—another in the calculated contrasts Dow built into this abstract composition: straight and irregular, smooth and textured, human (white blocks) and natural (tented green roofs), calm and wild, ordered and random.

Talbot Hamlin offered his opinion in *Pencil Points* in 1942: "Its rhythmically-lined slanting roofs, its dynamic—perhaps even exaggerated—varieties in plane, and the sharp staccato of its chimney mass, the richness of color, give evidence of the mind of an artist to whom the important things in architecture are *rhythm*, the play of *plane against plane*, and of *color against color*, and the *relation of building to landscape*, and indicate a temperament that seems to enjoy the process of invention for its own sake."

PILLAR TO POST STREET

Recalling the proverbial shoemaker, Midland's most famous architect and his wife were virtually homeless at the beginning of their married life. "We were knocked around from pillar to post for ten years," Vada Dow later laughed, recounting how they first divided their time between the home of Alden's brother-in-law William Hale and Dow's country club. Four winters following their marriage in 1931 were spent in the gray stucco Hale house on West Park Drive, across the street from the residence Dow later designed for Calvin Campbell (1939). The first two summers of 1932 and 1933 found the displaced couple at home on the golf course and then at Taliesin.

By the summer of 1934, when Dow was working on his own studio, they had come up with an idea "to build some little thing that we could live in," Vada recalled. They picked a site for it on the Dow property beside an old apple tree. "It was made of honest lumber," said Vada of the simple boxlike design sheathed in board and batten—walls similar to the studio's newly completed drafting room. The Dows' later permanent residence would go nameless, but not the one they put up in about two weeks: the couple dubbed it the Shanty. As Vada remembered it: "The Shanty at first had one bedroom, a living room, and he [Alden] built a nice big fireplace; it had no heat otherwise, just a fireplace, and a little screened porch right off the kitchen, and we would eat on the screened porch. We had fun because we could have friends there. The apples would drop on the roof at night. Oh dear, that was fun."

The Shanty was not insulated, but the Dows stayed there until November before trekking back to the Hale house. After their first child, Michael Lloyd, arrived in February 1935, they added another bedroom to the Shanty for the coming summer. "The Shanty was just a great little place," said Vada.

After two summers there, the Dow family relocated to a brick house near the architect's studio

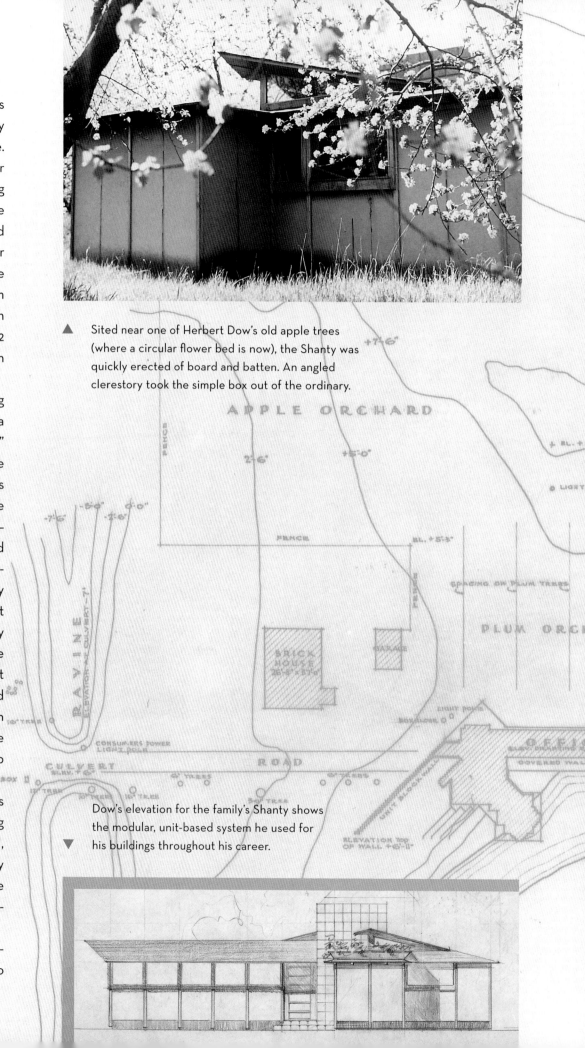

Sited near one of Herbert Dow's old apple trees (where a circular flower bed is now), the Shanty was quickly erected of board and batten. An angled clerestory took the simple box out of the ordinary.

Dow's elevation for the family's Shanty shows the modular, unit-based system he used for his buildings throughout his career.

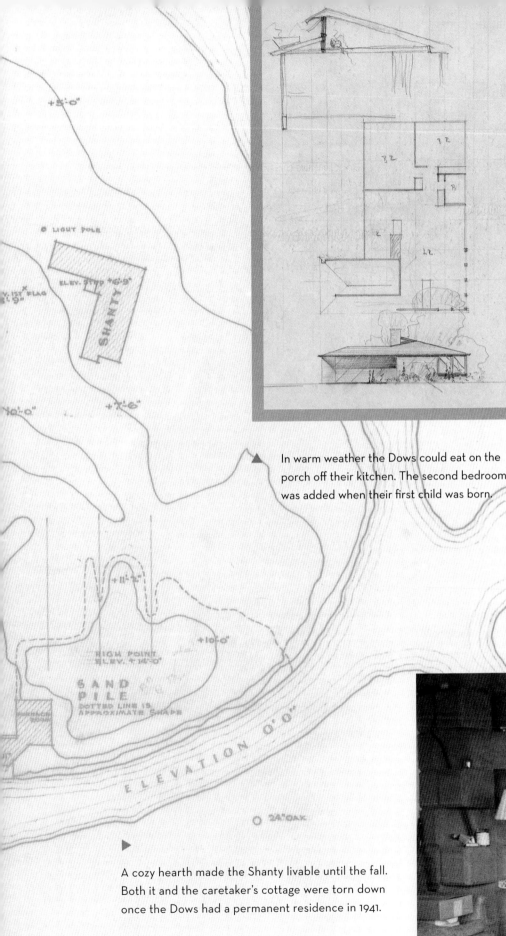

In warm weather the Dows could eat on the porch off their kitchen. The second bedroom was added when their first child was born.

A cozy hearth made the Shanty livable until the fall. Both it and the caretaker's cottage were torn down once the Dows had a permanent residence in 1941.

that had once been the home of the orchard caretaker. "And we were there for five years!" Vada noted ruefully. During this time they began to rent a summer cottage at Crystal Lake north of Midland. "It was a big old house and very pleasant when the children were really little," recalled Vada (the Dows' first daughter, Mary Lloyd, was born in 1937). "So," she added, "when we would get home from there we would sort of sigh about the size of the little place where we lived." On the trips from the lake back to Midland, Alden made a habit of joking with Vada about how much she hated to return to the old brick house. "Well, the third year he made some joke about it," noted Vada, "and I said: 'It isn't funny any more!' I had really lost patience."

Alden had long been trying to decide whether it was indeed a good idea to build a house onto his architecture studio. But the next morning, Vada Dow later recalled, he started on the drawings for a real home for his family. Dow consulted her about areas such as the children's bedrooms, but—unlike his outside clients—"I didn't get to say, I want this, I want that," Vada pointed out. "I was so afraid that he wouldn't build it, I didn't care. I was so glad to get a house." By 1939 Dow began to complete the vision for his Home and Studio that he had originally sketched out in 1934.

59

COMPOSED ORDER

Composed Order is the bouquet placed that it contributes the most up of parts that are free to exp to the creative discussion rather than r Order encourages empathetic thi It calls for st sensiti form. It reco that it but it is not way to based upon facts expressed with

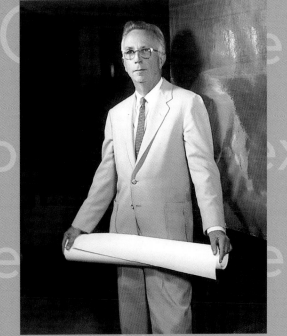

Composed Order is the bouquet of flowers where each flower is so placed that it contributes the most to the total form. Any form is made up of parts that are free to express themselves as long as they contribute improved quality to the whole. Composed Order demands creative discussion rather than reactionary resistance. Composed Order encourages empathetic thinking rather than reactionary reflex. It calls for strong leadership sensitive to the esthetics of the composed form. It recognizes the fact that it is human nature to be reactionary, but it is not the intelligent way to build a decision. A good thing is based upon facts expressed with sensitive and imaginative feelings.

■ During a career that spanned fifty years, Alden Dow approached architecture using a concept he termed "composed order." Unlike mathematical order, in which change is impossible, his philosophy called for the imposition of personal aesthetic choices on the existing "order" of a project. The facts of each commission—site, climate, budget—were to be composed with feelings—creative responses to the facts. In composed order each part, said Dow, is "pleasantly related to every other part," much as in a bouquet "where each flower is so placed that it contributes the most to the total form.... Composed Order demands creative discussion rather than reactionary resistance." ■ The approximately six hundred projects that Dow designed, about 365 of which were built, show anything but resistance to change. Starting out in the early 1930s, he entered an architectural stream that appeared to be flowing toward modern solutions to modern

ARCHITECTURAL BOUQUETS

problems. Dow jumped in with enthusiasm, swimming against the tide with a small band of like-minded designers. "I have never built or designed anything in a traditional style," he asserted in 1946. "My practice has dealt with everything from towns to the smallest house and none of them represents traditional thinking." ■ Early in Dow's career most of his work was done for Midland, but commissions for The Dow Chemical Company, including the chance to design a Texas town from the ground up, broadened his reach. (He was a registered architect in fourteen states from California to Connecticut.) Dow soon concentrated on houses; he eventually produced approximately 260 residential designs, half of which were built. Next in number came more than a hundred commercial commissions and alterations, two-thirds of them executed. School and university projects outside Texas totaled about one hundred, three-fourths of which were constructed. Civic projects numbered about sixty, two-thirds of them built. More than forty churches and several synagogues were designed, all but a quarter of them executed. Some 170 built and unbuilt projects, just under a third of Dow's work, were conceived for Midland—helping change the face of his hometown. ■ Two indicators of Dow's incessant quest for better solutions to living and working are the variety of patents and awards he received. Beyond the Unit Blocks, his inquiring mind also came up with a furlike coat for buildings, plastic windows, a boat steering mechanism, poker cards, and self-choreographing music; imaginative plans for a "readily deflectable vehicle" remained just an idea. Between his first major award, the 1937 Diplome de Grand Prix, and his last, his 1983 designation as Michigan's architect laureate, Dow was showered with honors. In 1944 he won first place in the 36th Division War Memorial competition in Texas. In 1957 he was named a fellow of the American Institute of Architects, in 1960 he was awarded the gold medal of the Michigan Society of Architects, and in 1961 he was honored as a leading Columbia University alumnus. He received honorary degrees from six Michigan colleges and universities. He was feted by architects, planners, landscapers, Realtors, bricklayers, policemen, Boy Scouts, and the Southern Christian Leadership Conference. His work was exhibited numerous times during his lifetime. In 1978 Northwood University, which he designed, founded the Alden B. Dow Creativity Center to perpetuate his commitment to innovation. In 1989 Dow's own Home and Studio in Midland was named a National Historic Landmark. ■

"COMPOSER OF COMPOSERS"

Preceding page: Because people were beginning to live in more modern houses in the 1950s, Dow decided to give them churches that followed suit. For the First Methodist Church (1947) in Midland, he conjured up a ceiling panel that he called the building's "life stream."

From the days when there was room for only five architects in the studio's original drafting room (by 1937 the staff included six), designers relished the opportunity to work with Dow. "Alden had a capability that would have shown through no matter what his background," said William Gilmore, who arrived in 1959 and became one of the firm's named partners in 1981.

When Alden Dow set up his own architecture firm, Alden B. Dow, Architect, in the fall of 1933, he did not attempt to recreate the fellowship he had just experienced at Frank Lloyd Wright's Taliesin. Yet over the years, as more architects joined him in his own bucolic world, Dow ended up gathering a coterie of associates as loyal as Wright's own. "Members of groups inhabiting composed places need to share more than the spaces they move about in every day," suggests the author Sidney K. Robinson, who worked for Dow in 1970. Such proximity, he notes, "expands to a mystic unity."

Dow brought the same thoughtful approach to the running of his business as he did to architecture itself. For him, as one of the heirs of Herbert Dow, the aesthetic mission took precedence over usual needs of earning a living. Although Dow and Wright shared a messianic approach to architecture, only Dow was financially free to pursue his vision so single-mindedly (a cause of some jealously on Wright's part). Dow took only a nominal salary but saw to it that his employees received bonuses.

From the beginning Dow strove to bring out the best in his staff, as he explained in a 1962 interview:

One of the great problems of running an office or business is to inspire those who are working with you to really do their best.... Pride of participation is a must. In architecture, a building is so involved it must inspire as many people as possible. We can't afford to have anyone working on a building who does not feel that he is a very vital part of it.... It is fun working when everyone feels this way. It is like playing a game.... I believe that the boss's relationship to the employees should be understood—and it includes the readiness to assume responsibility.

He described the leader of this band as "really a composer of composers." In this architectural symphony, everyone is encouraged to contribute ideas, Dow added, "and the leader composes the sum total into an empathetic whole. The composers are pleased ... all the ideas harmonize ... and the final result functions in the best possible fashion."

The first of these fellow composers to arrive, in 1934, was Robert Goodall, whom Dow had met during his 1933 stay at Taliesin; Goodall was working for Wright, who acknowledged him to be an extraordinary draftsman. Goodall was eager to move out from under Wright's wing and brought to Midland maturity, a genial personality, and a dry wit. His attention to detail no less than his familiarity with Wright's way of building proved invaluable to Dow. "If Goodall needed control," Sidney Robinson has written, "Dow needed someone whose mastery of facts could make his feelings work." Goodall helped Dow refine his Unit Blocks in the 1930s and until he left in 1950 detailed the architectural concepts that Dow conceived. In the process Goodall also served as a mentor to other staff members and artisans.

Draftsmen who followed also came with experience. They sought out Dow as much as he chose them. As one architect, Francis Warner, recalled later, Dow looked for talents his staff had buried within them. Projects were collaborative. "He never repressed ideas. He tried to bring out ideas," said William Gilmore. "He tried to give you a chance to ask why on your own." Other colleagues remembered a patient man, one who would stop at each desk every day to help with any problems—using "body language" more than words "to get his point across," suggested James Howell, who arrived in 1961. Dow planned coffee breaks twice a day to encourage discussions and even arguments over topics ranging from new technology to how behavioral science could be applied to architecture. Dow, like his father, would turn conversations to humor when necessary. "He never went away upset," said Howell.

The firm was incorporated in 1941 as Alden B. Dow, Inc. By the early 1950s the staff numbered about fifteen persons, but its size grew to twenty-five by the end of the decade as the annual volume of business reached $5 million in construction value; it became one of the largest architecture firms outside greater Detroit. Dow made his staff stockholders, as his father had at The Dow Chemical Company. Employees of the firm during this golden era included Harvey "Cle" Allison, George Austin, Glen Beech, Eldine Crampton, Harry Cummings, Nancy Thomas Fischer, Willard Fraser, Richard Gustafson, Jackson Hallett, Jean Keller, Norman Kline, Robert Kostus, Fumiko Maki, Gloria Jacobus Olsen, Rueben Pfeiffer, and Florence Gartung Wise. Among later additions were Norma Babcock, Jack Feagley, Bill Gilmore, James Howell, Robert Hynes, Dick Knopf, Jack Lee, Theodore Maniatis, Otto Parrish, Robert Paulsen, Dick Schell, Larry Sweebe, and Mary Jane Williams. Ted Gwizdala, a superb woodworker, worked exclusively for Dow

For a while Dow also provided design-build capabilities through the Alden Dow Building Company. The emphasis in both design and construction remained on quality and integrity. If the work or even the design were not to Dow's satisfaction, such as windows installed on the Irish House (1941), he would personally pick up the tab for redoing it.

By 1963, as the work turned more toward larger public commissions, he changed the studio's name to Alden B. Dow Associates, Inc. By then, in contrast to the earlier decades, Dow let his staff make many of the client presentations. In 1974 James Howell followed Cle Allison as president; Dow served as chairman of the board from 1972 to 1982. In 1981, to ensure the firm's perpetuity as it neared the half-century mark, it became Dow Howell Gilmore Associates, Inc. As William Gilmore later reflected, working in Dow's office "was like getting a doctorate in design."

In a 1949 caricature of his boss, Ralph Appleman drew Dow with a haircut that seemed to grow from his own Unit Blocks. Many people commented on Dow's fine head of hair. "He just didn't like to be bothered going to get it cut," said his wife, Vada. Midland's First Methodist Church was one of the commissions on which Appleman worked.

▼

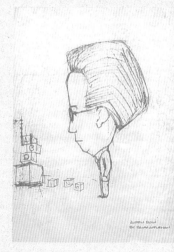

On the First Methodist Church, the steeple disappeared in favor of new symbols of worship.

◄

A WAY OF LIFE

Alden Dow was one of the few architects who built his principles not only block by block but also in words. Unlike most of his peers then and since (exceptions being the likes of Robert Venturi and Rem Koolhaas), Dow was a verbal architect. It is a trait he shared with Frank Lloyd Wright; in fact, this desire to explicate his own philosophy through writings and lectures is perhaps what links him most closely to Wright. When asked late in life what he wanted to be remembered for, he answered, "my philosophy."

Architecture in the 1930s, in Dow's opinion, was a "ship without a captain." Reaching for the helm, he became a prophet of modern architecture—of natural, livable buildings and well-planned communities. As his fellow modernist Richard Neutra was later quoted by *Time* magazine, "In our profession you must be an evangelist as well as an architect." Dow did what he could to further the midcentury tenet that Good Design should be available to everyone. In November 1933, shortly after returning from Taliesin, he began to lecture, often using his own slides or movies; he wrote voluminously, from professional and popular articles to his own book; he eventually drew his own philosophical map for achieving individual creativity along the road to human progress.

Dow liked to quote several eminent thinkers from Ralph Waldo Emerson to Louis Sullivan and Frank Lloyd Wright. In essence, however, the architect composed his own homegrown philosophy, following his father's advice to think for himself. James Howell, who became a partner in Dow's firm, viewed him as "a very spiritual man because he tried to understand the true meaning behind everything he did."

One of Dow's strongest beliefs was that architecture mattered. "I am a firm believer in the old idea that architecture is the mother of all the arts," he wrote in 1960. In this statement lay Dow's abiding optimism about both his profession—its

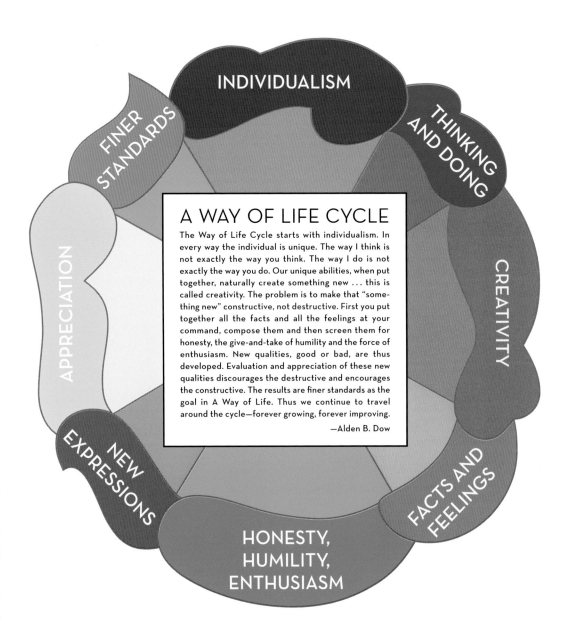

A WAY OF LIFE CYCLE

The Way of Life Cycle starts with individualism. In every way the individual is unique. The way I think is not exactly the way you think. The way I do is not exactly the way you do. Our unique abilities, when put together, naturally create something new ... this is called creativity. The problem is to make that "something new" constructive, not destructive. First you put together all the facts and all the feelings at your command, compose them and then screen them for honesty, the give-and-take of humility and the force of enthusiasm. New qualities, good or bad, are thus developed. Evaluation and appreciation of these new qualities discourages the destructive and encourages the constructive. The results are finer standards as the goal in A Way of Life. Thus we continue to travel around the cycle—forever growing, forever improving.

—Alden B. Dow

It was natural that Dow, as an architect, wanted to give actual form to his philosophical principles just as he did to his architectural ideas. This diagram of his Way of Life Cycle was the result. "This is a graphic picture of a process of thinking about quality," he wrote. "There seems to be a logical sequence in developing an expression of quality."

INDIVIDUALISM

The Way of Life Cycle starts with a person's individualism. In every way the individual is unique. When this uniqueness is coupled with time and place, there can be no duplicates. Even the atom exhibits individualism . . . no two atoms are excited the same way, at the same time, in the same space. As atoms combine into higher forms, even the human being, this individualism grows. The theme of individualism is universal.

THINKING AND DOING

The way I think is not exactly the way you think. The way I do something is not exactly the way you do it. When you put these two unique producing qualities together, the result is a one-of-a-kind effort. This effort can never be duplicated exactly by either the originator or anyone else. No two creators, try hard as they will, can create absolute identicals.

CREATIVITY

Our unique abilities, when put together, naturally create something new . . . this is called creativity. The process of creativity involves conscious thought, subconscious feelings, plus the skill to put ideas together. Each of these activities has its own individualism. Creativity provides human expressions that can aid the progress and welfare of mankind. The products of creativity help satisfy man's ever-increasing needs.

FACTS AND FEELINGS

Facts are the realities of life, feelings are the realities of the imagination. When all the facts are arranged, through feelings, into a satisfying form, the result is a composed order expression. These results, consciously or subconsciously generated, can be subject to reason or logic. Facts are the science of the subject; feelings are the art of the subject—when both are utilized, the resulting expression has real value.

HONESTY, HUMILITY, ENTHUSIASM

The expression, then, may be screened for honesty, humility and enthusiasm. Honesty is compatibility to everything known about the subject. Humility is the balanced give-and-take between people and their environment. Enthusiasm is the quality that generates excitement and the force that gets things done. If the idea meets these conditions, in the eyes of the creators, it is on its way toward establishing finer values.

NEW EXPRESSIONS

New expressions, good or bad, are thus developed. In the opinion of the creator, the new expressions are always constructive. They have received maximum creative input of facts and feelings. They have been personally screened for basic values. The end result should be a new expression of finer quality.

APPRECIATION

Evaluation and appreciation of these new expressions by both the individual creators and society in general discourages the destructive and encourages the constructive. The new expression must be considered beneficial by both individual creators and society before it can be properly appreciated. The ability to appreciate and evaluate the good and bad is a most constructive human attribute. Without appreciation there can be no awareness, beauty or love in this world.

FINER STANDARDS

The end result of this Way of Life Cycle is the accomplishment of finer standards. Man's major objective in life is to progress in as many directions as possible. Progress toward higher quality in all areas is a never-ending process. The accomplishment of finer standards becomes a continuing purpose of life.

ability to change the world—and life itself. He retained a faith in the future nourished during the decades in which he came of age, the 1920s and 1930s.

Pulling him along was a quest for perfection. As he said in 1977, "I am convinced that future great human expressions will result from one basic effort . . . that of a constant striving toward perfection." Quality—knowing when you have a good idea—was one component, but for Dow the source of perfection was individualism.

When in his last decade he broadened his architectural principles into a full-fledged philosophy with creativity at its core, what he called A Way of Life Cycle, Dow placed individualism at the top. He had been trying for years to give a physical form to his ideas. At one time he prepared diagrams balancing moral values on one side and aesthetic values on the other, beneath attributes of social rightness (a passive trait) and individual rightness (aggressive). In 1959, inspired by "the most romantic kind of dream while listening to Richard Strauss on the phonograph," Dow even proposed that his ideas be synthesized in a multifaceted drama-opera-dance-music-poetry performance involving Paul Tillich, Robert Frost, and similar creators. (He continually yearned for this added dimension to his thoughts, whether music, dance, colored lights, or a combination of these.) By 1976 Dow had translated his thoughts into a colorful, circular graphic symbolizing an infinite, interconnected life cycle (shown opposite).

Writing about the architect in the *Midland Daily News* shortly after his death in 1983, Michael Roberts adroitly captured Dow's struggle to convey his Way of Life: "In his philosophical musings he tried to find that formula [for how creativity worked and how it could be cultivated], but, I believe, fell short as most philosophers do. Words are fragile and imprecise and usually fail reality. Better was his ability to be creative, to teach by example, to play, to toy, to follow his wondering, to *be* what it was he sought to propagate."

THE TAO OF DOW

Designed over fifty years and ranging in size from modest houses to imposing civic buildings, Alden Dow's architecture is too varied to be characterized by a generalized set of features. Yet his aesthetic and philosophical tenets can be read clearly in his buildings. Given the influence of Asian cultural values on his work, Dow's guiding principles—his quest for composed order and individual creativity—can be viewed in terms of an oriental philosophy:

Architecture should inspire its users

Dow resurrected the Arts and Crafts ideal of the House Beautiful: that a beautiful structure can instill beauty in the hearts and minds of its occupants, challenging them to mold their behavior to its own model. "The real objective of architecture," suggested Dow, "should be to inspire constructive creativeness in those that use our buildings. This means that our buildings must aim for something more than pure utility." He spoke of "furnishing soil in which the individual can take root" but noted, "It is everyone's obligation to make his surroundings more beautiful."

The outside is part of the inside

Dow's designs strove to be organic: to rise from nature, to coexist with the natural world, to reflect it. Architectural inspiration might come from a spider web, a snowflake, a flower, a butterfly, an orchid, a rock formation. Generous windows brought nature indoors, trellises and terraces reached outward, and water splashed reflections on walls and ceilings, all blurring the distinction between outside and inside. To cement this relationship, he often used the same materials indoors and outdoors, such as his Unit Blocks or brick, and repeated some of the same forms and rhythms.

Gardens never end and buildings never begin

Reinforcing the interconnectedness of outside and inside, Dow professed that "gardens never end and buildings never begin." In an organic design based on nature, there should be no obvious dividing line between the built and the natural. One lends its qualities to the other to create something greater than the parts. Connections can take many forms: from terraces to bridges to building blocks that tumble into nature, appearing to have merely fallen free of a man-made structure. "Nature relieves architecture. Architecture relieves nature," Dow postulated.

Style is the result, not the objective

Rather than resurrect historic styles of architecture, Dow sought to meld contemporary needs with true creativity. "Never copy" was his mantra. Style was an "insidious thing" to him. "When style, itself, becomes the objective," he declared, "nothing results but a copy. For style is a process pattern, and fine style, real character, develops only when you have an objective beyond obvious utilitarian requirements. So there is never a fine thing unless it is original." Some architects keep "rebuilding historical buildings," he suggested, only because they "cannot imagine anything else." Good architecture will stand the test of time.

A building should reflect its function

To fulfill its occupants' needs, a plan should be approached not from any preconceived style but from its intended function—from inside out, rather than from the facade in. While reflecting its structure's purpose, the form should also enhance its use. "Beauty needs function," Dow said. "Function needs beauty." He favored "constructing with the nature of the materials for the nature of the human being." Because a house, for example, is made for the individual, its highly personal nature calls for a small scale. Of his own buildings, Dow said that "no two ... resemble each other in any way, for the possibilities of form in building are infinite." He did not forget humor, asking, "Isn't fun a worthy goal, a kind of function?"

Each structure must have honesty, humility, and enthusiasm

Honesty—a straightforward, truly creative expression of design and materials to meet specific needs—is the most important quality. Humility is "the balanced give-and-take" between a design and its environment: a building fits into the land, contributes, and collaborates, while the land in turn contributes to the building. Enthusiasm for Dow was "the real life-giving property ... the quality that makes a building more than a box"; for him it meant "the accent on the extremities": the playfulness or genius that generates excitement, "the quality of not being completely understood at first glance."

Adding composition to order produces quality

"Any form is made up of parts that are free to express themselves as long as they improve the quality of the whole," said Dow in comparing his concept of composed order to a bouquet of flowers (an analogy that came to him when he remembered his mother's floral compositions). Order harmonizes facts—the realities of life—and feelings—intuitive artistic expressions—and from order arises strength and a sense of repose. "A pile of rocks is a pile of rocks," suggested Dow, "but when man composes them, it becomes a balance, a thing of beauty."

Space is not confined within four walls

A building in which a person can see everything from one position lacks the vital sense of mystery. Never make a room "a simple rectangle where all is seen and understood at the first glance," he instructed. "Lines become fascinating when, like meandering rivers, they seem to have no end but lead the eye on and on." Space in his structures flows dynamically around corners; sightlines are not confined by blocky walls but end at an attractive feature such as a door or a window. Half walls or steps subtly divide functions or rooms, making spaces appear larger and less confined. Ceiling levels change, from low over intimate areas (because too much open space "is frightening") to higher in more formal areas. Mirrors extend the sense of space while adding the element of surprise.

One thing is part of another

"You can't think creatively without letting one thing grow from another," Dow suggested. The parts of a structure must be compatible: "the exterior part of the interior; one space part of another space. Only through this point of view can a building become part of the people that use it, a path for their inner growth." A desk juts out from shelves, a sofa emerges from a wall, a trellis grows from the roof, stepping stones wander away from a building to demonstrate interrelatedness.

Texture is to architecture as rhythm is to music

"Textures must offer … balance with plain surfaces," said Dow. "There must be intricate patterns balanced with plain surfaces. There must be colored patterns balanced with plain patterns." Roof balances siding, glass balances brick, fabric balances concrete, softness balances hardness, smoothness balances roughness, plainness balances pattern, horizontal lines balance vertical lines. "The play of light and shadow, perhaps from the sunshine filtering through a tree or bush, creates motion and constant change in texture."

Bright colors are uplifting

Dow's buildings are known for their use of strong primary and secondary colors, from red, yellow, and blue to contrasting green, purple, and orange. He used them for specific purposes: for function, to divide spaces; for stimulus, to create pleasure and drama; and even for safety, to distinguish components of industrial structures. He stressed the use of opposites on the color wheel because the "physiology of the eye dictates the balanced use of several, rather than a single color…. Too much of any one color upsets the human equilibrium."

All senses should be stimulated

According to Dow, "That old saying, 'Variety is the spice of life,' does not go far enough. Variety is essential to life." He attempted to activate all senses—from sight and touch to smell and sound, playing off the contrasts like musical counterpoint. Ledges to sit on, railings to lean over, artwork to see, trellises to walk under, flowers to breathe in, water to hear all added up to human balance in his buildings.

Organizing clutter is essential

Taking his cue from Japanese and colonial American kitchens, Dow remarked, "I think we all like to live with organized clutter." Collections personalize a space but should be artfully organized to provide a pleasant contrast to the lines of the furnishings and the architecture itself. To streamline interiors, furniture was specially designed or chosen to be an extension of the architecture. Built-ins such as sofas, tables, and counters seamlessly integrated building and furnishings, yet Dow warned that too many attached pieces would give an institutional look to a home. Because people are movable, they like flexible, movable arrangements. Dual-purpose objects such as the stools in his own living room eliminate duplication and allow pieces to be rearranged as needed.

A good building is never finished

"A finished house is a dead house," proclaimed Dow. He liked to leave room for expansion—for example, by putting bedrooms in their own zones to make residential additions easier as families grew—as well as for changes that personalize a building. "The home," he said, "is made by those who live in it."

DESIGNS FOR LIVING

In the early 1930s most Americans who could afford an architect-designed house set their hearts on a Tudoresque lodge or a Spanish hacienda—something from the past instead of a house of the future. Alden Dow countered that a house should be "of such a character as to reflect that of its owner and not that of his great-great-grandfather." He joined a select cadre of visionary architects—European immigrants such as Rudolph Schindler, Richard Neutra, Walter Gropius, Ludwig Mies van der Rohe, and Marcel Breuer as well as native talents from Frank Lloyd Wright to Bay Area architects including William Wurster and Harwell Hamilton Harris—who took a different path. In reinventing the idea of what a house should be, Dow and his peers rejected historical styles and, in fact, the traditional concept of architectural style itself.

Dow built his reputation on houses. "I almost prefer houses and churches to anything else," he announced. "Houses want to be playful, churches want to have significance." Designing residences allowed him to build on his belief that "the individual is supreme." With five dozen of them erected in Midland alone, his houses formed little enclaves of modernism; architects who had worked for Dow and went on to their own practices also extended this design legacy in Dow's hometown.

The terrain was lonely in the 1930s when Dow began to introduce Midlanders to modern architecture, showing them first the products of the machine—his Unit Block solution for efficiently building homes (see pages 50–55)—and then gradually adapting his ideas to Americans' increasingly casual ways of living. His early forays were sometimes described in the Michigan press as different, strange, or, damning with faint praise, functional. Dow houses were said to look like garages, sheds, factory buildings. Even fellow architects were diffident about them, and the FHA was reluctant on occasion to grant mortgages for such unconventional living spaces. But by 1948 *Life* magazine was calling Dow's houses "thoroughly livable" and "some of the most satisfying residences in the U.S.," noting: "His style grows out of a deep conviction that man's emotional requirements in architecture are as vital as his material ones." In 1961 the magazine *House and Home* avowed that Dow's houses are among "the least stereotyped being built anywhere today."

That was because of the care Dow took to shape each structure to the client as well as the site. "Dow never begins a house," *Life* noted,

■ SPACE OR INTEREST IS NEVER CONFINED WITHIN FOUR WALLS. ■

▶

Originally planned to use Unit Blocks, the MacCallum House (1935) in Midland was constructed of brick. The exuberance of the rear contrasts with the dignified simplicity of the front.

Appliances in the original MacCallum kitchen give it away as a 1930s design, but the cabinetry and layout lend it a contemporary appearance. High windows ensure privacy while bringing in sunlight.

▼

"without making an unusually painstaking study of the needs and personalities of the family that will occupy it." He approached each plan not from the standpoint of style but from function—the needs of the occupants. His first clients, many drawn from the Dow Chemical community and his family, had both money and a sense of experimentation emanating from the company's own mission. When Louise and Donald Irish (he was a noted biochemist and toxicologist at Dow Chemical) met with Dow in 1941 to discuss a house for themselves, the architect came with "a pocket full of colored pencils," remembered Louise Irish. "And the whole time he talked to us, he was drawing and sketching out his ideas. He very much wanted to understand your viewpoint."

While continuing to design Unit Block residences in the 1930s, Dow simultaneously began to try out freer house types, substituting brick for block and sloped for flat roofs. Houses in Midland for the Cavanaghs (1933), MacCallums (1935), and Diehls (1935) reprised various features from his first commissions, for the Towsleys (1932) and the Steins (1933). One Dow hallmark became a low,

subdued appearance streetside that cascaded into two or three glassy levels at the back. In the Greene House of 1936, he departed from an L shape to angle the living and dining rooms at forty-five degrees, as he had done in his own studio's sunken conference room. That building's watery surround was also adapted in Bloomfield Hills for the startling Saunders House (1936; demolished 1999), its sunken living room a foot below the water line proving perfect for gliding out the door on ice skates.

Neighbors also took note in Grosse Pointe Park when Dow's textbook International Style Pryor House (1936) went up, but a legal fracas over an extended trellis ended in the architect's favor. "The more we live in our house," Mrs. Millard Pryor wrote to Dow, "the better we like it, and even those of our friends who started out to feel sorry for us are coming around to the realization that there's nothing like a modern house for really living." In 1942 *Architectural Forum* saw this Dow tour de force as "one of the most striking he has done to date, and in many ways the most successful."

Once he was no longer relying on the Unit Blocks, Dow tried other materials and forms to achieve variety and economy. He played with hipped and asymmetrically gabled roofs, mixed materials (brick and Homasote panels), and raised living areas to take in the best views. The Rood House (1937) in Kalamazoo and the Campbell (1939)

The Riecker House (1961) in Midland, designed for Dow's niece Margaret, hugs the ground with a mature assurance. Its varied roof levels add a dynamism that contrasts with the quiet horizontality. On the sun porch, rustic ceiling beams help create a woodsy space that seems both indoors and out.

and Irish (1941) Houses in Midland each gained such a *piano nobile* because of their sloping sites. The Penhaligen House (1941) in Midland was one of the first residences that Dow both designed and then built through his decade-long experiment with design-build projects; at a time when the typical Michigan house cost from $8,000 to $12,000, this one came in at a little under $20,000.

As a nationwide housing boom heated up after the shortages of World War II, Dow was joined by fellow modernists who carried a similar message from coast to coast. Charles and Ray Eames and architects of the Case Study Houses on the West

Coast, Paul Rudolph in Florida, Eero Saarinen in the Midwest, and European émigrés in the East all sought to persuade Americans to think modular; Joseph Eichler, a California developer, and Charles Goodman, an architect outside the nation's capital, created whole communities that Dow must have applauded.

With houses designed in the 1950s and 1960s, Dow crossed new frontiers. Some examples include his refined "timber tepee," the A-framed Ashmun House (1951) in Midland; swimming pools in living rooms, skylighted interior gardens, sunken living rooms; and a tripartite residence–guest

In the Defoe House (1941) in Bay City, Dow took the midcentury penchant for casual living a step beyond. Having a swimming pool indoors, lighted by a partially transparent ceiling, must have been a delight in Michigan's winters.

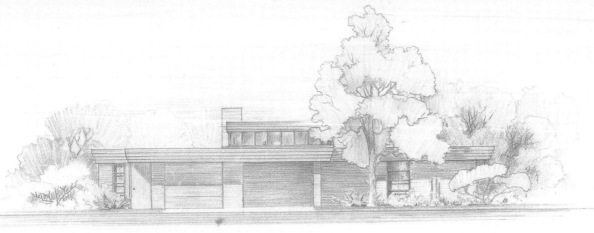

A HOUSE FOR MR & MRS C. S. COMEY
ST CLAIR SHORES MICHIGAN
ALDEN B. DOW ARCHITECT
MIDLAND MICHIGAN   MARCH 1951

Like a northern hacienda, the plan of the house Dow designed for the Comeys in St. Clair Shores in 1950 wraps around an interior courtyard that brings light and nature indoors.

house-and-entertainment center (1963) for Duke University's president. Dow continued to number among his clients captains of industry (Lynn Townsend of Chrysler and Leland Doan of Dow Chemical, to name only two) as well as family members (his children and also a niece ensconced in the elegant Riecker House of 1961 in Midland). By this time his reach extended well beyond the hometown he had done so much to house so stylishly.

Over four decades Dow's devotion to the principles of organic architecture remained unchanging. From the outside his houses hewed to the earth with strongly horizontal lines, fit into—or seemed to grow from—sloping sites, used bold chimneys as vertical counterpoints, contrasted materials and textures, controlled sunshine with wide eaves, secluded entrances for mystery, and integrated the garage or carport with the house via a breezeway. Trellises and water features linked residences with nature. A calm public face was matched with a more open private side at the rear.

Inside, spaces grew from geometric modules into open plans in which space was divided not by walls but by changes in levels and ceiling heights. Space was borrowed visually from adjacent areas to increase vistas; angles added surprise. The dining alcove became part of a larger family room. Built-ins conserved space and provided aesthetic continuity. Playrooms for children were located near the kitchen and Mother's watchful eye. Broad and tall windows brought the outside in,

aided by clerestories and skylights. The hearth remained the heart of the home. Plans were flexible enough to change as families grew or condensed. Details were not missed: door knobs, for instance, were placed high to avoid catching on pockets. A sense of delight infused all these spaces. "A home," said Dow in 1944, "is the place where the individual's creative instinct has a free rein."

Today one can look back at Dow's residences from the 1930s and 1940s and see the outlines of the split levels and ranch houses that became so popular at midcentury as well as the asymmetrical constructions that defined the 1960s. But more than fifty years later, the modernity of his residences has never been matched by any other mainstream American house form. "Dow brought to that scale of design a level of sensitivity and insight that will stand against anybody," Sidney K. Robinson has observed.

In 1988 the Midland businessman Donald Smith, testifying to the timelessness of Dow's work, decided that an adaptation of one of the architect's 1959 residential designs would make a perfectly sized home for himself. With plans modified by Dow Howell Gilmore Associates, the house finally came to life not far from the architect's own Home and Studio. Another Dow latecomer, Joan Raulet, who purchased the former Anderson House (1948) in East Lansing, took time to write the architect in 1972: "We have all been uplifted by the privilege of living day by day in a Dow creation."

DREAM HOUSES

Contemporary efforts to develop a new breed of prefabricated house share a long history with similar endeavors to design more cost-efficient residences, but few eras were as active as the mid-twentieth century. The Great Depression, shortages of building materials during World War II, high labor costs, and veterans with government housing subsidies all underlined the pressing need for living spaces that average people could afford. Like a number of his own contemporaries, Alden Dow spent much of the 1930s and 1940s searching for dream houses on a budget.

As an optimistic Dow said in 1945: "Anything is possible if we put our minds to it.... Ownership of a home is the only way to build a happy nation.... It stimulates creativeness, which I feel is also essential to happiness." To produce a low-cost house, he advised, architects would have to "abandon all standards of present-day building." Simpler construction methods, units that "inexperienced hands" could put together, and small but flexible plans were at the top of his list of requirements. Flexibility trumped standardized prefabrication: "I do not believe that a standard house in a world that was made for individuals will ever create a happy solution," Dow said. In 1947 he challenged his fellow Michigan architects to propose model "dream houses" costing less than $6,000.

After the Lewis House (1933), a hybrid clad in Masonite that used Unit Blocks for the chimney and fireplace, Dow realized that his patented blocks would be too expensive for an economical project. In 1938 he stepped in to help The Dow Chemical Company fill a housing shortage for its growing staff, offering two approaches. His three-bedroom "functional house," built for the family of John Best in Midland, was advertised at $4,577. It used Homasote panels over conventional frame construction and featured a flat, cantilevered roof and a projecting picture window. The design's moderne asceticism, lacking traditional trim and a gabled roof, helped lower costs.

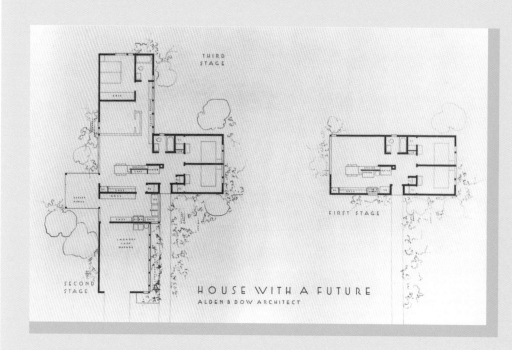

HOUSE WITH A FUTURE
ALDEN B DOW ARCHITECT

In Dow's outward-leaning proposal for the 1945 Ingersoll housing project, the ceiling rose to follow the roofline; the rafters were exposed for both economy and novelty. Red and green as well as blue and yellow contrasts added cheer.

Dow's more provocative solution, named the House with a Future (1938), was to be built in three stages to stretch out the expenses. Stage one included two bedrooms; stage two added a porch, a garage-laundry-shop wing, and an expanded kitchen; and stage three, growing with the family, appended two bedrooms and a bath to complete a T-shaped plan. "Everybody who ever lived has had a dream house," Dow acknowledged, but he suggested that these imaginary homes were too nebulous and "if they ever come true, usually run into money." He insisted that the goal of having a home of one's own should not be put off for lack of funds.

In 1939 Dow was a participant in the Ingleside Housing Project, which called for five hundred homes to be built in Detroit. He designed eight prototypes priced from $3,800 to $4,800, offering flat or pitched roofs, all finished in wallboard with battens like his own studio. A variety of financial and regulatory problems, added to the fact that Dow did not like selling homes in the abstract, led him to pull out.

Another industrial housing project in 1945, nicknamed the "World's Fair of Postwar Housing," had a more felicitous outcome. Borg-Warner's Ingersoll Steel and Disc Division came up with the idea of an all-in-one utility unit that could be dropped into a house to provide furnace, water heater, plumbing, electrical circuits, kitchen, bathroom, and laundry ready to use. Dow was one of a handful of noted architects—along with Edward Durell Stone, George Fred Keck, Harwell Hamilton Harris, Hugh Stubbins Jr., and Royal Barry Wills—asked to provide envelopes for what Dow impishly called the LAUNKITCHEATOIL unit. Two of his one-story, asbestos-sided designs were built in Kalamazoo (a choice of two or three bedrooms). Dow sloped the windows outward front and rear, ingeniously increasing the real and perceived feeling of spaciousness without having to enlarge the footprint. "Few people buy a minimum house, or at least, few want to buy minimum," he noted. "They are looking for ideas, and the more we can show them in this house, the happier they are going to be."

In these years other low-cost housing ideas never got off the drawing board—from a 376-unit project in Midland to an embassy compound in the Philippines—but Dow's persistence paid off with a trio of houses specifically created in 1950 and 1952 to use Dow Chemical materials. Midland was his laboratory for lightweight "sandwich" panelized walls he had first tried in 1945. Styrofoam® panels were glued to fir plywood facings for use on load-bearing walls as well as interior partitions and the roof. The unit system used for these houses on a cul-de-sac was three feet, six inches, rather than Dow's more typical four-foot grid. The first house was built by two carpenters in three months; the third was ready in six weeks.

In the end, Dow was not much more successful than his peers in erasing the nationwide deficit of good-looking, low-cost houses. Too many would-be homeowners, then and since, have been all too willing to settle for cookie-cutter Levittowns. Yet by striving to put everyone in a rewarding home, Dow developed ideas—from inventive sandwich panels to residences designed for expansion—that helped point the way to more lasting solutions to our perennial housing problems.

BOOMTOWNS

Frank Lloyd Wright could only dream about turning America's suburbs and exurbs into his visionary Broadacre City, but in the 1940s it was Alden Dow who actually got to build a model city. The locale was not Michigan, as one might expect, but Texas.

Even before Hitler's armies marched into Poland on September 1, 1939, Willard Dow had sensed that The Dow Chemical Company would need to increase its output of chemicals, especially magnesium to make British and American airplanes as light as possible. Chemists and engineers sent to scout the Gulf Coast of Texas for plant sites where the wonder metal could be extracted from seawater reported back with two choices: Corpus Christi and Freeport. The latter, a sleepy coastal hamlet founded in 1912 about sixty miles south of Houston, won out as the site for the company's $15 million investment. The two thousand acres it amassed for its Texas Division along the Gulf of Mexico and the Brazos River pioneered the petrochemical industry for which the Gulf Coast soon became known. Willard Dow offered an eloquent description of his company's marathon in marshy coastal Texas to outrun America's enemies: "There is an epic quality involved in the peopling of a flat, narrow, tongue of waste land with strange shapes of structures and having them combine to take a ladle of gleaming metal out of a curling, white-capped ocean wave. Not even the old alchemists, in their wildest fancies, ever got that far."

While Dow Chemical's plant in Freeport and another it built for the government in nearby Velasco were rushed to completion in 1941 and 1942, a housing crisis loomed as workers converged on the area. Freeport's population of 3,100 shot up 140 percent to 7,500 in three months. Using Texas hyperbole, *Collier's* magazine in December 1940 recounted the state's worst housing shortage: "Rough board shanties sprouted like mushrooms after a rain, and trailers clustered around water hydrants like cows around a water hole."

Alden Dow's ideas about modular construction and low-cost residences were put to the test when his brother called on him to help solve a sequence of housing problems around Freeport. First he designed a one-story motel-like hotel with twenty-three guest rooms; thanks to simple detailing and materials, it went up in three weeks' time in 1940. Working from Midland, Dow also developed plans for modular three- and four-bedroom houses that could be adapted to include maid's rooms, porches, and garages. Fifty-three of these streamlined, low-slung frame homes were built on Freeport's flat, treeless landscape. Dow developed a basic square plan and stretched, reversed, and otherwise molded it to fit a variety of family needs. He also contributed a hospital, a school, and a six-family apartment building similar to the hotel.

As workers arrived to build the Velasco plant, the housing crunch worsened. "Within a matter of weeks, Alden Dow had plans drawn for a workers'

▶

With its frame skeleton, Dow's streamlined hotel in Freeport, Texas, was conceived for fast construction. White asbestos shingles served as siding. The interior—with its brick fireplace in an airy lobby, open to the dining room—offered a comfortable residential feel.

Freed from the need to build for a winter climate, Dow was able to design houses for Freeport, Texas, that could be assembled quickly. Siding was variously stucco, asbestos, or wood. Broad eaves on the asbestos-shingle roofs ▼ served as sun shades.

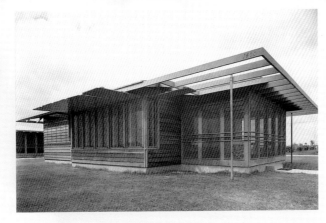

One of Dow's wooden variants in Freeport, Texas, this home featured a dramatic trellis as well as hurricane shutters that could be raised to form a canopy. The porch provided needed cross-ventilation in the humid Texas air.

community dubbed Camp Chemical," Don White-head reported in *The Dow Story,* calling it "a triumph of planning." This company town big enough for as many as twenty thousand residents bloomed in the Texas salt marsh. Fitting together prefabricated walls, roofs, and floors, some two thousand carpenters turned out one cottage every ten minutes, six every hour, sixty each day. Roads paved with oyster shells covered a modern water and sewer system. Construction began February 20, 1942, and just a month later, on March 23, a new town was open for business.

Dow had begun commuting between Midland and an office he set up in Houston in 1941. In March of that year, just three weeks before the Dows' third child, Barbara Alden, was born, the family had moved into its new residence adjacent to Dow's studio. With three young children, the separation was especially difficult for Vada Dow. But by early 1943 a three-bedroom house became available in Freeport, and the Dows took it. At

first Michael and Lloyd did not want to go, and for Vada the move meant leaving the home that was so long coming. "We weren't even used to it yet," she later recalled. Dow himself spent four years in Texas (1941–45), including about a year each in houses in Freeport and Houston with his family, who returned to Midland in fall 1944.

Alden Dow next found himself carving an entire new town out of a Texas thicket of brush shaded by graceful moss-strewn live oaks, pecans, magnolias, and cypress. The Dow Chemical Company wanted to attract permanent employees to its Freeport operation, but many families shared the Dows' reluctance to relocate to storm-prone coastal Texas. Dow was thus sent in late 1941 to find more fertile territory on higher ground. He rode on horseback into a jungle that had grown up around the antebellum Jackson Lake Plantation northwest of Freeport and came back with a vision for a garden city to equal Frederick Law Olmsted's Riverside, Illinois (1869), one of America's

Dow allowed for wide expanses of windows and opened the combined living-dining room to the porch for more air and light. A built-in window seat and ledge beneath the window show the same attention to detail he gave his clients back home.

earliest planned suburbs. The five thousand acres soon purchased by the company, bordered by the Brazos River and winding Oyster Creek and holding the crescent-shaped Jackson Lake and three other lakes, were chosen not just to fill a need for housing. The dream was to create an ideal residential community where a rewarding home life would be separate from industrial labor.

In sketching out the town of Lake Jackson, using an orange pencil, Dow followed several guiding principles. One was to set residential and commercial areas apart in their own spheres. Another was to ensure that neighbor did not intrude on neighbor. And, paying heed to that new modern necessity, the automobile, streets were carefully laid out in meanders recalling the area's creeks. These curves, Dow explained, would give each roadway more personality while producing irregular, seemingly larger residential lots: "Traffic hazards have been avoided as much as possible. Through traffic by-passes all areas used by pedestrians and no residences face these through streets. They are lined with one-hundred-foot parkways on each side. These park-bordered through streets also separate our commercial area from our residential area." This thoughtful plan offered physical and social order while it enhanced the site's natural beauty.

Lake Jackson's plan also gave Dow a chance to show off his puckish wit. Through streets were designated as drives, while roads leading to the commercial area were called ways. To Winding Way, Center Way, and Circle Way, he and Vada cleverly added This Way and That Way and Any Way. Streets and courts merely had floral names. "Newcomers and visitors to Lake Jackson may sometimes find our winding streets confusing," Dow admitted. "However, they will always find them interesting."

Bulldozers and mule teams began taming the jungle in 1942, and by April 1943 Lake Jackson was open for business. All it lacked was the monotonous, government-issued look of other wartime housing. Dow made sure that buildings

Dow eventually opened an office in Lake Jackson's shopping center, operated by the Lake Jackson Company. He finished it in his typically bright colors: a brilliant green ceiling topping blue-gray walls, magenta doors and trim, and yellow touches, with a mobile overhead. The picture window rose almost to the eaves.

▼

▲

Alden Dow fell in love with a horse when he was living in Texas in the 1940s and later had it shipped to Midland by train. Named Anaconda Rebel, it was the horse on which the actor Leslie Howard (as Ashley Wilkes) rode away in *Gone with the Wind*. Here Lloyd Dow accompanies her father on her pony.

Dow's Lake Jackson houses nestled under a canopy of live oaks and other tall shade trees. More shading came from thoughtful devices such as the trellis and the screened carport shown here. This home is typical of the five hundred built in the new Texas town.

▼

here were as architecturally honest, humble, and enthusiastic as his other work. In all about fifty house plans in Dow's signature clean, modern style were offered to buyers. Most had in common functional frame construction with clapboard siding, wide eaves, generous windows, a living room with a dining alcove, two or three bedrooms, ample closets, a screened porch, and a carport. Lots were a minimum of 78 by 140 feet, with homes set back 25 feet from the front property line and 10 feet on each side, allowing plenty of breathing room between neighbors. About five hundred single-family homes and another two hundred duplexes were built in a garden setting of trees, parks, and lakes. Private developers put up the houses, while the federal government subsidized the duplex apartments and offered FHA loans for homeowners. Residents vied for prizes for their landscaping and wartime victory gardens. Dow dubbed it "an ideal home town."

Within two years 2,800 persons were enjoying Lake Jackson's comfortable homes, its shopping center with convenient parking, its Dow-designed schools, churches, recreation areas, nearby airport, and, this being Texas, a riding club. When the time came for Dow Chemical to turn over the reins to residents, the town obtained a charter and elected a mayor and a council. By 1950 it had grown to a population of 3,500 in 850 houses and boasted that it was a dream town lacking not only pretentious homes but also slums and mosquitoes.

In 1963, during Lake Jackson's twentieth anniversary, Dow added city founder to his list of honors, as the town unveiled a monument in tribute to him. That year he also showed a color movie he had made to record the town's birth. By 1999, when Lake Jackson had grown into a sprawling city of 28,000, the local museum displayed an animated mannequin of Dow during its celebration of what would have been his ninety-fifth birthday. Lake Jackson, Dow had declared, was "designed to work right." His hopes that it would be a model of postwar living were outweighed by the reality of subsequent suburban development in America.

STRIVING TO INSPIRE

In describing an American church-building boom that exploded in the 1950s, *Time* magazine noted in 1955 that many churchgoers "found American Gothic phony, dark and depressing." Alden Dow was surely among them. Religious architecture, long based on the perpetuation of tradition, reflected its clients' inherent conservatism. As these institutions changed to include more social and community activities, a new architectural response was called for. Dow answered this call, transforming Midland from merely the "City of Beautiful Churches" into a "City of Beautiful Modern Churches" and Michigan into a mecca of his new style of worship.

Next to houses, Dow most relished the challenge of church building. In addition to their "significance," he noted that they offered the most potential for originality. Although these structures, like houses, are relatively small in scale, the chance to design such public buildings marked a change in his career in the late 1940s and the 1950s. Of his more than forty religious projects, Midland received ten.

Dow searched for new architectural forms that would inspire the concept of growth: "growth beyond ourselves . . . beyond this time." In a 1950 statement heralding the opening of the First Methodist Church (1947) in Midland—a writer at the time called it Dow's "cathedral"—he explained the palette of materials and metaphors he devised to replace "blind conformity":

The transparent doors and walls tell us that beliefs must not be concealed from any man. Nor inside does the building care to confine itself within four walls, for growth cannot be confined. . . . The pointed ceiling panel running down the center of the church is the life stream of this building, and it serves as a source of light and air and transmitted sounds for the church, and ends in the sky window. This sky window is the steeple of this church turning our eyes to the highest Heavens. . . . The luxuriance of growing plants beneath the sky window reminds us that man does not grow alone. . . . Above [the cross], light and clear glass in the sky window tell us man's possible growth is infinite.

Dow began by helping congregants translate their aspirations into brick and mortar while, as Sidney K. Robinson has observed, "expanding their own powers of imagination by his suggestions." Dow recounted his first church design in 1941, Midland's Reorganized Church of Jesus Christ of Latter-day Saints: "Grouped around the drafting board, the building committee and I designed the church as it is today, each member

The gentle upturn of the roof of Midland's First Methodist Church (1947) is the only remnant of a traditional steeple. Beneath it, Dow inserted a "sky window" of stained glass. Toward the courtyard, colorful glass in a Mondrian-like pattern proclaims the modernity of Dow's vision.

contributing his share." This simple rectangular structure of brick lined with expansive windows and entered through doors sculpted with light and shadow was followed by a trio of successively assured churches for Midland.

The First Methodist Church, opened in 1950, replaced the traditional steeple with views of the sky and was symbolically opened to nature through garden courts and pools. At St. John's Episcopal Church (1949), windows also pulled the outdoors inside; its dramatic narthex end, a glassy ship's prow, calls to mind Wright's Unitarian Meeting House (1947) in Madison, Wisconsin. For St. John's Lutheran Church (1953), Dow relied on Martin Luther's saying "Go out and build a fortress." Concluding that the fortress should be the people of the church, the architect put them in seats surrounding the pulpit on the altar. The church fans out into a dynamic octagon under an exceptionally complex roof—likened to the petals in the Lutheran rose. "The altar is at the center of the plan," said Dow, "and everything radiates from it: congregation, preacher, choir, social rooms, study rooms—even the openings to the sky and the garden outside." For him, this was his most significant church, the one that spoke most clearly on its own.

More churches, three synagogues, and structures such as a rectory and a parsonage joined these landmarks. Several of the most notable are the ground-hugging Christ Episcopal Church (1958) in Adrian, oriented inward around a courtyard; the First Presbyterian Church (1960) in Dearborn, with its intricate triangular plan; and the Roscommon Congregational Church (1960), clothed in redwood inside and out in the best Craftsman tradition. One of his most unusual projects was the Indian River Catholic Church (1948–59), dedicated to a spiritual Indian maiden known as the "Lily of the Mohawks." Beyond Dow's simple church, serendipitously found later to resemble an Iroquois long house, stands the world's largest crucifix, carrying a thirty-one-foot-high, seven-ton bronze of Christ sculpted by Dow's friend Marshall Fredericks.

While stripping away congregants' preconceptions with new materials and shapes—plain glass chosen for economy and tented designs for their ease of expansion—Dow blended old and new. Some key traditions were kept intact, such as the location of the choir, but new ones, such as more integrated Sunday schools, were initiated. He considered all of these structures living beings, never entirely finished.

St. John's Episcopal Church (1949), also in Midland, points skyward using a sloping roof that simulates hands poised in prayer. This triangular motif reappears inside in simple glass and intersecting planes.

RETHINKING THE SCHOOLHOUSE

The son and husband of teachers, Alden Dow "thought it would be fun to build a school," recalled his wife, Vada. His first chance to design a new one came in 1938, with his Parents' and Children's School in Midland. Alden had been encouraging Vada to make use of her education in early childhood learning by opening a progressive nursery school. Her school moved from one rented house to another until Alden's residential-style design was finished. Plans were made in 1942 to add more classrooms in the basement, but teaching was put aside once World War II intervened. In 1943 Alden easily converted the schoolhouse into a private residence, after which it was rented until it was sold in the late 1960s.

The postwar baby boom led Midland and communities across the nation to rethink how they could educate the coming influx of new students. Gone for the most part was the iconic little red schoolhouse as well as the elaborate revival styles of the 1920s and 1930s, and in their place—using the ideas of architects such as Dow—came forward-looking buildings in which to teach space age children. His belief that architecture holds power to enlarge the human imagination and enrich people's lives, not to mention his own childlike playfulness, made him eminently suitable for the task. Dow's schools and college buildings totaled about eighty projects, eleven of them in Midland.

His first public schools, constructed in coastal Texas in the early 1940s as part of his Freeport and Lake Jackson developments (see pages 76–79), grew out of the region's sunny, humid climate. Covered walkways and verandas brought needed shade as well as broad play areas. With the

At the enclosed Delta College (1957) outside Bay City, Dow (working with Paul Brysselbout and Frederick Wigen) arranged the buildings around a one-acre landscaped court featuring a pond, paths, and stepping stones. Paul Tono, whom the Dows had met in 1922 on their voyage to Japan, came to Michigan to aid in the placement of the landscape features.

Northeast Intermediate High School (1949), Dow introduced Midland to his evolving ideal of the modern schoolhouse. This L-shaped, two-story brick structure used ribbons of windows to bring light into classrooms and hallways. From the broad entrance foyer, a library—viewed as "the heart of the school"—a theater, a gymnasium, and offices radiated outward, some filling dual school-community uses. The board of education lauded its "modernistic beauty."

More elementary, intermediate, and high schools followed around Midland and south to Ann Arbor, where the private Greenhills School was designed in 1966. All radically changed the traditional look of American schools to a campus-like plan with a ground-hugging profile and economical cubistic forms. By 1961, with Midland's North (Jefferson) Intermediate School, Dow was using movable walls for open teaching but clustered classrooms away from exterior windows; amenities included a swimming pool, air conditioning, and ramps for the handicapped. The Midland High School that he had designed in 1953 became seriously over-crowded within a decade; in 1965 he was called back to design the Herbert Henry Dow High School, named to honor his father.

During the last decades of his career, in the 1960s and early 1970s, Dow increasingly found himself working on education projects. His town planning experience in Texas inspired him to pro-duce campus plans entwined with nature. The In-terlochen Center for the Arts near Traverse City, including a year-round academy and a summer school for musicians and artists founded in 1928, combined everything that stirred Dow's creative juices: an idealistic program centered on music and the arts in a rustic, lakeside setting. Beginning with a dormitory in 1958 for the Arts Academy, he went on to serve as Interlochen's campus planner. Dow's legacy there ranged from a star-shaped language arts building and science and fine arts facilities (1961–62) to a gymnasium (1961), Kresge Auditorium (1961) at the water's edge, and the Grand Traverse Performing Arts Center (1967).

Brand-new colleges gave Dow carte blanche to paint a new campus with his modern brush—lack-ing existing architectural context, there was no need for collegiate Gothic or other stylistic com-promises. Two of his earliest plans, for Delta Col-lege near Bay City and Hillsdale College, both begun in the late 1950s, featured linked assem-blages of buildings that reserved space for natural features. Dow's aim was "a sense of spacious-ness," to make "the form and space of one [struc-ture] contribute to the form and space of an-other." Covered walkways provided shelter and fostered "a more sociable relationship between parts of the college."

Plans and buildings were also designed in the 1960s for Muskegon County Community College, Saginaw Valley State College, Mid-Michigan Com-munity College, Kalamazoo Valley Community Col-lege, Wayne State University, and Northern Michi-gan University, with brick and stucco a standard palette and water features wherever possible. The University of Michigan's Administration Building (1964), notable for its Mondrian-like "cut stone trac-ery," had the misfortune to open at the height of the student protest movement: it became the site of sit-ins, and for years afterward, the building was regarded by students as a fortress.

Thinking that Midland would be "a great college town," Northwood Institute decided in 1961 to lo-cate its business college there. Land was pur-chased from The Dow Chemical Company, and Alden B. Dow, Inc., was commissioned to get stu-dents into its buildings in five and a half months. Dow helped the school grow over the next decade, fitting new structures into its 176 wooded acres. In 1973 the institute, now a university, opened its petal-like Griswold Communications Center. Dow's close ties also brought about courses in creativity and later the launching of the Alden B. Dow Creativity Center in 1978. A dozen years earlier Dow had reflected that his campus buildings, blending the built with the natural, tried to call on architecture to say something to stu-dents that could not be said any other way.

TENDING TO BUSINESS

Alden Dow believed that it was "dangerous to do too many schools or similar type buildings one after the other," as he wrote in 1959. "It means filling your mind with the facts of one particular problem and then by force of habit applying the same ideas without reason to the new problem." To prevent the ensuing creative void, he interspersed places for business and industry among his houses, churches, and schools.

Beginning in the 1930s, about three dozen projects for The Dow Chemical Company allowed Dow to flesh out architectural theories such as the importance of color. The first, also his first major nonresidential building, was a 1937 remodeling of the company's main office in Midland. Two existing structures were joined with intersecting cubistic volumes of brick, divided by rivulets of stairs illuminated with inset glass blocks. The company also tapped Dow to design its exhibit at the 1939 Golden Gate International Exposition in San Francisco, where he had a chance to use plastic building blocks that he had

developed based on Dow Chemical technology. More company commissions followed: corporate offices in landmark New York buildings (1940 and 1947), research laboratories (1940 and 1950s), a hotel and buildings for the Texas Division in the early 1940s, headquarters for the new Dow Corning Corporation (1943 and 1960), administration buildings in Midland (1950s and 1960s), and offices in California and Canada (1940 and 1946).

Dow defined architecture as an arrangement of form and color that produces a satisfactory effect on the optic nerves. For a St. Louis branch office of Dow Chemical that opened in 1945, he showed just how satisfactory that effect could be in the modern workplace. Here he substituted glass partitions for solid walls to make the office seem more spacious, even using a mirror in the reception area to fool the eye. "One space seems to develop into the next space," he noted, "like one bend in a river develops into the next." Most shocking was the rainbow of colors on walls, floors, and furnishings: burnt orange balanced by blue, reds by greens, with yellows mixed in to create the feeling, in Dow's words, of "a cool morning after a good night's rest."

Dow, who served on Dow Chemical's board of directors from 1941 to 1965, also took his color palette into the company's chemical plants, starting a new trend in the 1940s. Before then, pipelines might be color coded for safety reasons, but the architect theorized that brightening up drab processing units and chemical exchangers would bring other benefits. Chief among these was a reduction in worker fatigue, which not incidentally was viewed as a boon to increased productivity. Dull gray and black parts were replaced by spring green tanks emptying into white, orange, and red pipes. Conduits painted blue contrasted with others in yellow, opposites on the color wheel. Light hues provided relief from darker ones, all in the name of safety, vibrancy, and sheer pleasure. Although widely adopted for a time, Dow's industrial color system was eventually abandoned as the bright paints required frequent repainting and altogether more effort than many companies were willing to devote.

The reception area of Dow Chemical's 2040 Plastics Building (1963) exemplifies Dow's strong belief in color's vital role in the workplace.

SCIENCE IS THE MATERIAL FOR CREATING. ART IS THE CREATOR.

Among the startling design departures observers noticed in the reception area of Dow Chemical's 1945 office in St. Louis were its solid blue carpet and the recessed fluorescent lights. Orange and yellow accents added unusual cheer.

Tethered by corner pillars that seem to strain to hold the twenty-seven-foot-tall roof in place, Dow's experimental Bay Service Center (1961) has undergone a variety of uses but remains a Midland landmark. Styrofoam® was used for the roof framing, covered with a thin concrete layer, and waterproofed.

Surely few industrial workplaces could rival this Dow Chemical plant, colored by Alden Dow, for unexpected beauty. The architect liked the "clear, clean colors that Walt Disney might take pride in using in one of his most fanciful movies."

Helping launch a savings and loan association in the Great Depression led to a series of modern bank designs over four decades. In 1946 he remodeled a space for Midland National Bank that was heralded for the privacy it afforded patrons as well as for its experimental Dowmetal doors. Rising from a red floor, triangular planters separated transactions, making the bank a "friendly place," said Dow, where "aloofness won't be necessary." The following year he designed an office for Midland Federal Savings and Loan, whose board he had joined in 1933, and then turned out more banks in subsequent years, including for Chemical State Savings Bank (1947 and 1951), New Midland National Bank (1954), Midland National Bank (1946 and 1961), and New First National Bank and Trust (1963), all in Midland, and People's National Bank and Trust (1962) in Bay City. For their more suburban locations, Dow included drive-in windows and a covered walkway from the parking lot.

His other commercial commissions ranged from flower shops (1946 and 1954) to the Consumers Power Company headquarters (1955) in Midland, from a Holiday Inn (1966) in Traverse City to the Laboratory for Macromolecular Science (1967) in Midland, from a bakery's garage (1934, unbuilt) to the law office of his son-in-law Peter Carras (1974), as well as stores forming a shopping center in the new town of Lake Jackson, Texas, in the 1940s. With commercial buildings often in the path of progress, a number of Dow's designs have been lost variously to new construction or in at least one case—LaPelle's Flowers (1946) in Midland—to a fire.

One of Dow's commercial structures that brought the most public scrutiny when it started to emerge in 1961 was a model gas station in Midland for the Bay Refining Company, a Dow Chemical division. With its uplifted hyperbolic paraboloid roof shaped from Dow Chemical's Styrofoam® and covered in concrete, this small gem seems poised for flight. Here feelings merged with facts. Even in places of business, said Dow, "The creative spirit should soar. It should touch the unknown."

CIVIC PRIDE

Designing public buildings is an opportunity, Alden Dow said in 1970, to instill pride in each user: "pride in his own individual integrity and personal accomplishment, the heritage of his country, and in the buildings and public facilities he is privileged to use and misuse as he sees fit." Dow likewise invested considerable pride in his civic buildings beginning in the 1940s, bringing to them the same thoughtful design solutions he used for his residences and religious structures. As the cost of producing custom houses rose and the sizes and budgets of other buildings exploded in postwar America, the residential scale at which Dow excelled vanished, replaced by larger programs that challenged the best of the nation's architects.

Fittingly, some of Dow's earliest and most experimental public structures were designed for his hometown of Midland. In 1938 he started work on a municipal band shell that was less shell than a sound reflecting board. A concrete slab roof was hung from cantilevered concrete beams, the vertical form counteracted by an inclined ceiling of horizontal plywood baffles concealing lights and capturing undesirable sounds. That same year he designed a streamlined bathhouse using an open soffit for ventilation and translucent plastic eaves to direct light inside.

By 1938 Midland needed a modern hospital center, a commission that allowed Dow to put his color theories to work. More than a decade earlier he had specified that a hospital "should have a restful and open feeling and not a serious and forbidding character, which seems to be so common." His mother, Grace Dow, donated a forty-acre wooded site that inspired the architect to give patients peaceful views of nature. Inside there was no gray or brown or dull white to depress spirits. Instead Dow used color as a therapeutic agent: red nurses' stations atop a red linoleum floor, calm blue in the waiting room, even calmer pink and green in the operating arena. Brilliant corridors segued into more restful palettes in the patient

The unusual shape of Dow's bandstand (1938) in Midland, still in use, made it low in cost while eliminating the tendency of sound waves to dissipate over the audience. It accommodates large and small orchestras. The design was copied in 1949 by the town of Ashland, Oregon, with Dow's assent.

In Frank Lloyd Wright's own bailiwick, Dow won the bid in 1949 to serve as master architect for the Phoenix Civic Center. The complex of library, museum, and theater was centered on a pool and a garden—an oasis in the desert. Associated architects designed individual buildings.

Framing ribbons of glass, contrasting stucco bands on the Ann Arbor City Hall (1960) step outward with each ascending floor. To keep the costs low, Dow made 84 percent of the space usable by avoiding excess corridors.

▼

rooms. "It's a beautiful place to be sick in, if you have to be sick," said an employee.

In the 1950s and 1960s, Dow continued to add to Midland's architectural stock. Returning to the thirty-year-old courthouse that his father had sponsored, in 1955 he designed a jail and office addition that was probably unique among his work: anything but modern, its stone walls and gabled roofs perfectly fit Bloodgood Tuttle's original Tudor-style conception. Next came a fire station in 1955; the King's Daughters Home (1956), a residential-looking home for the elderly; and the Tri-City Airport (1961) serving the region.

What worked in Midland was applied to his out-of-town buildings as well. "Industry is not interested in coming to a community that is interested only in industry," he said in 1958. "Industry wants to know: Does the community provide facilities for the individual to grow?" The subject at hand was the Phoenix Civic Center (1949), the job he won over the protests of Frank Lloyd Wright. Dow created the comprehensive plan for this civic complex that within a decade housed a library, a theater, and an art museum. After the personal acrimony had abated, Wright telephoned, said Dow, "to tell me that he was delighted with the building and wanted me to know first hand that he thought it was a very good building. As I recall, I was speechless!"

For Ann Arbor's new city hall (1960), Dow almost literally turned the idea of municipal architecture on its head. He rejected the concept of a "traditional marble monument"—a building designed to be an impressive symbol of city government instead of one that operated efficiently and wisely used taxpayers' money. Wide stucco panels on his upside-down ziggurat were designed not for visual impact but to conceal the ventilating ceilings; a dramatic central spine encloses the mechanical units. One of several of the firm's nature centers was built in Kalamazoo in 1961. A dome fifty feet across holds the Sun-Rain Room, whose curved panels of gray Plexiglas bring nature up close; the Glen Vista Room puts visitors at eye level to a forest.

The two-story central space of the Midland Public Library (Grace A. Dow Memorial Library) (1950) in Midland captures the residential feeling at which Dow excelled. To the side, expanses of glass make nature part of the learning experience. The building was a gift to Midlanders from the Herbert H. and Grace A. Dow Foundation.

Theaters held a special appeal for Dow, who put a small one in his own home and designed a number of public venues over the years: in high schools, in his winning entry for an army memorial auditorium (1944, unbuilt), in the Phoenix Civic Center, and for the McMorran Memorial Auditorium and Sports Arena (1956 and 1957) in Port Huron. A theater, he said, should "play on our imaginations." Ideas he had used in his churches were adapted to break down the demarcation line between actors and audience and to make the action "fascinating from all angles." Dow incorporated movement, such as having the orchestra rise from below, to turn the building into a living mobile.

All of these ideas culminated in what became for Dow the crowning achievement of his career:

the Midland Center for the Arts. The city's new cultural complex, a place Dow dubbed "a discovery center," was launched in 1950 with a public library named to honor his mother, who served as chairman of the library board for thirty-two years. A pinkish brick was used for walls outside and in, a soft canvas that Dow speckled with bright colors such as yellow (linoleum floors) and green (seating). Innovative features including a children's reading room, a storytelling amphitheater, an exhibition hall, a local history room, and an auditorium made the modern three-level library a magnet for community activities.

For a site between the library and the Dow Gardens, Dow began in 1966 to give form to a place where science and art, facts and feelings, could work

Dow's far-reaching ideas of how architecture, art, music, theater, and history should interact came to fruition in the Midland Center for the Arts (1966). In the main auditorium, colorful reds and greens, punctuated by a geometric-patterned curtain, enliven the senses.

together—music, sound, light, dance, drama, art, sculpture, film, and history all interacting to stimulate in visitors their own creativity. The Center for the Arts became a manifestation of its architect's broad-ranging ideas on the intersection of art, science, and life. As Dow explained: "The Center was conceived not only as a facility to enhance and encourage arts involvement in a basically scientific community long devoted to the intertwining of science and art, but to provide a setting in which the arts can grow and experiment without fear of failure, so detrimental to any creative impulse, and in a highly stimulating interpersonal environment similar to the atmosphere in scientific research laboratories."

Except for his Home and Studio, no other commission so clearly reflected Dow's personality or captured his imagination. Under one roof he brought together six Midland institutions that promoted music, theater, art, and history, providing personal financial support to supplement contributions from his parents' foundation as well as from the community. When the Midland Center for the Arts opened its doors in December 1970, Dow termed it a "balanced creative ecology."

The center's three stories are disguised on the exterior by a tall mansard roof of standing-seam metal that ranges across brick walls and piers. Over a broad stucco cornice, a filigreed pattern serves as a marquee. The heart of the center is the Great Hall of Ideas, a four-level exhibition area emphasizing through circular forms the interrelatedness of human endeavors. Light comes into the hall through translucent skylights atop pyramidal coffers of plaster. The bob on a Foucault pendulum—round like the earth and the space that holds it—is made of silicon to represent one of Midland's key products.

The Center for the Arts contains both an auditorium-concert hall seating 1,500 and a "little theater" with a revolving stage. In contrast to the center's subdued exterior, bright colors such as red and green add excitement to the theaters. Art and sculpture galleries, art studios, a lecture hall, a shop, and offices help fill the 200,000 square feet of space (enough, claimed Midland's newspaper in 1969, to provide standing room for every resident).

Dow viewed the center as "a place to *produce* new things, and not just reproduce what has been done before." Toward this end, a commissioning series undertaken to honor Dow brought in innovative new plays, music, and dances. This emphasis on creativity helped make the center Dow's philosophy fleshed out in brick and mortar.

A NEW LANGUAGE

For an architect who loved to dream about the possibilities of modern materials, Alden Dow was fortunate to have a chemical company within arm's reach. His palette tended toward the organic—concrete, brick, glass, wood, and copper, for example—but grew to include a heady wash of the miracle plastics being developed by Dow Chemical. As the company released new products, someone there might ask what it could be used for. And then the wonder material ended up in Dow's studio for some brainstorming. "We were sort of the architect's architect," recalled Francis Warner, one of Dow's staff members in the 1950s.

It is not surprising that Dow viewed the architect as "a professional inventor." His was an exceedingly inventive mind, nourished in a climate of invention, so he did not recoil from "the thought of science invading the field of the fine arts," as he said in 1936. Rather than produce standardization, he believed that science would speed the way to greater individualism by opening the doors to more creative, flexible buildings.

Hardly out of architecture school in 1931, Dow began prognosticating about the house in America's future. In the 1930s he saw building blocks molded from leftover cinders. In the next decade, as he wrote in 1946 to Eugene Masselink, Frank Lloyd Wright's secretary, "The more I see of them the more I am convinced that the future of building lies in plastics." Dow's visions conjured up materials varied in texture and color (always bright), translucent walls and roofs to turn houses into "lanterns glowing outside from the life within," temperature-sensitive roofing, self-insulating walls, windows that would roll up like a screen or change from clear to crystalline depending on the temperature, floors resilient enough for both dancing and sitting, wiring and plumbing that would be pleasing to look at (through those translucent walls), all finished off with plastic paints and plastic draperies.

Dow invested considerable hope in a skinlike covering of transparent, translucent, and opaque plastic panels made in the late 1930s from two Dow Chemical products, Ethocel® and Styron.® An adaptation of his earlier Unit Blocks, these thin units were a foot square with a flange that could be nailed to a wood frame for walls and roofs. Air space was left between interior and exterior walls of the same material, which was lightweight, easy to handle, and clean; eliminated the need for paint, plaster, glass, and wallpaper; resisted fire and decay; and repelled insects. With no defined market, a high cost, and lack of promotion, however, these structural units failed to carve out any niche in the bulding industry.

Components of the new architectural language that Dow the architect was inventing with Dow the chemical company, these plastic building blocks debuted in the addition to the company's main offices in Midland (1937), its exhibit (1939) at the Golden Gate International Exposition in San Francisco, and the skylight over Midland's municipal bathhouse (1938). Finding someone to live in a house of plastic proved an impossible dream (think of heavy rain pounding a plastic roof). Dow's Ethocel House (1937) never made it beyond the drafting table, nor did a sensuous Circle House (1943) with phosphorescent walls that changed colors with the time of day. A later plan incorporating circular pavilions connected by covered walkways was designed for an Ohio site but was cancelled once its price rose to $200,000 because of wartime scarcities.

The firm tackled other cutting-edge products. From 1945 to 1950, Dow and his staff searched for the right glue to make a sandwich of Styrofoam® panels between plywood. They succeeded in creating a lightweight, economical, prefabricated building system used on three Midland houses in 1950 and 1952. Similar sandwich panels were devised in 1961 for the Dow Test House, which became the Midland home of Dow's daughter Barbara Carras, as well as for the Riecker House. Styrofoam® was also used for its acoustical properties in the domed lecture room of the Language Arts Building (1963) at the Interlochen Arts Academy and the

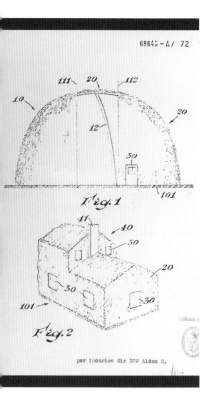

▲

One of Dow's most provocative proposals, in a patent application dated 1971, called for a furlike coat used as insulation. First discussed for the University of Michigan's Administration Building (1964), the fuzzy material was meant to be self-cleaning and usable for cooling as well as heating. Animals, however, replace their coats, but Dow to his great regret could not find a way to make a building grow a new coat.

In 1944 Dow adapted his Circle House design of the previous year for the Donnell family in Ohio. He chose this shape because "in curved lines there is a sense of spaciousness not achieved by straight lines."

Dow's 1945 proposal for a solar house, one of forty-eight designed by notable architects for each state, designated a "berth" to hold the car at night; by day it was to be a playroom, workshop, or laundry.

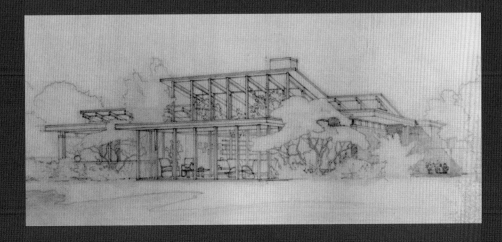

domed library of the Laboratory for Macromolecular Science (1967) in Midland. Styrofoam® eventually proved too expensive because it required considerable fire retardants.

Typically, for simplicity's sake, Dow relied on a small group of materials dressed up with the occasional glass block, patinated copper, edge-grain fir, or bright linoleum. "You would have the composition of repose," said his associate William Gilmore, "and yet a lot of rich color going on at the same time." Saraloy, a rubber product from Dow Chemical, was experimented with to solve Michigan's perennial roofing problem of temperature extremes. And, because waste was never discarded without asking what it might become, the company's plastic extrusions were recycled as sculptures. The architects also turned experimentation into a two-way street. For help in creating workable thermopane windows, for example, they went to Dow Chemical and returned with a technique using a metal part to dehumidify the air between double panes of glass.

Dow also joined with notable peers in trying to pinpoint what the house of the future might look like. In 1945 he was called on by Libby-Owens-Ford to visualize a solar house for Michigan, which he did with a double-height glazed porch to capture sunlight. That same year *Pencil Points* published his entry in a competition cosponsored with Pittsburgh Plate Glass seeking A House for Cheerful Living. Dow's Design for the Southwest featured broad banks of outward-leaning, operable windows to catch the breeze. For a demonstration village of fifty houses in Grand Rapids sponsored by the Homestyle Center Foundation, Dow in 1955 produced an intricate two-story, flat-roofed $50,000 residence that visibly contrasted with Buckminster Fuller's nearby Geodesic Dome home.

"Today, all we can do is dream about these things," said Dow in 1944. "But these are dreams that can come true." A few did, but the house of the future he envisioned continues to remain somewhere in America's future.

For a site near Midland's Central Park, Dow designed a residential-style structure to welcome seniors to the King's Daughters Home (1956). In 1965 he was called on to design low-cost rental housing for the elderly at Cleveland Manor in Midland.

OUR TOWN

No other town or city benefited more or longer from Alden Dow's attention than his own hometown of Midland. A reporter for *Time* magazine who followed him around in 1947 observed that he seemed to relish small town life: the bridge parties, potluck dinners, and school festivals as well as the country club get-togethers. "He's the sort of person who would never look or act out of place in J. C. Penney's, the Waldorf-Astoria, or Schraffts," noted Helen Douglas, "and he'd be equally at home presiding at a meeting, watching a circus, praying in the local church, or laughing at a corny vaudeville act."

One of the small American towns that Dow most admired was Disneyland. Its "two-block-long Main Street," he told the Midland Art Association in 1965, "is the most pleasant little town I've ever seen.... Obviously quality is praised here and lack of it is not acceptable.... Disney controls quality." Fresh from designing his own picture-perfect town of Lake Jackson, Texas, Dow sought to bring that same quality control to his birthplace. He urged that his fellow Midlanders consider covered walkways along Main Street, bright colors for commercial buildings, hidden parking, flowers on balconies and window ledges, creeping vines, and canopies of trees. "I hadn't realized until lately, when I've been away so much, what a swell town it really is," he said in 1944. "The river winding through is beautiful. We ought to use it as much as we can."

Compared to building in virtually virgin territory in Texas or California, reshaping a historic place of work and business required more than a Disney-like suspension of disbelief. Yet over a half century Dow changed the face of Midland with more

As he did with school buildings, Dow reinvented the archetype of a firehouse in 1955 with his Fire Station no. 1 for Midland. Broad and low like his innovative schools and colleges, this fire station easily conveys a sense of security.

than one hundred homes, schools, religious structures, commercial and office buildings, and civic landmarks of his own design. A latter-day Johnny Appleseed, the architect sowed the seeds of modern design from one end of town to the other. It remains a testament to what a single-minded architect and willing clients can create together.

Dow did more than replenish and refine Midland's architectural stock, however. In his quiet, unassuming manner, he went about taking care of his town in myriad ways: serving on boards, offering financial support, lecturing, providing advice (bidden and unbidden), teaching in a continuing education program, even judging snow sculpture at the new farmers market. From 1935 to 1941, Dow served on Midland's planning commission. In 1956 he helped found the Midland Art Association and served as its director two years later. In 1957, to create a workshop for practicing artists, he renovated the Post Street School near his home, where his mother, Grace Dow, had taught. Then he provided grants for artists in residence, sponsored exhibitions, and supported education programs. He was a presence at the county historical association, the Midland Little Theatre, and the Chippewa Nature Center. As president of the Herbert H. and Grace A. Dow Foundation in the 1960s, he supported local needs and endeavors, supplementing this largess with personal contributions of his own for activities from musical composition to pee-wee football. Few pursuits appealed to him as much as the Midland Center for the Arts, where a commissioned art series was named to honor him and the building he designed.

Dow also gave his time to regional and state activities, particularly from the 1940s to the 1960s. He was president of the Saginaw Valley Chapter of the American Institute of Architects in 1948–49 and of the Michigan Society of Architects in 1949–50. A partial list of other organizations in which he participated, representing the breadth of his interests, includes the Michigan Cultural Commission, Michigan State Council for the Arts, Michigan State Capitol Commission, Michigan

Society of Planning Officials, Michigan Engineering Society, Historical Society of Michigan, Keep Michigan Beautiful, Michigan Library Association, Michigan Music Teachers Association, and Michigan Foundation for Advanced Research. Dow was even a card-carrying member of the Sleepy Business Men's Breakfast Club in Midland. In 1968 the Greater Midland Area Chamber of Commerce recognized him for his "outstanding contribution to the business growth and economic development of the Greater Midland Area."

What he tried to develop in Midland, said Dow in 1971, was more than just a community. It was "a

good ecology"—a relationship between humans and their environment: "It's a *house* you want to go back to … a home. It's a *neighborhood* where you like to visit with neighbors. It's a *community* where everything is pleasantly related.... The future of this community, or any other, depends on its ability to constantly improve the relationship between its environment and its citizens. In the final analysis, it is not size-of-community but quality-of-community that counts."

As Vada Dow recalled later in life, her husband loved Midland. To him, it was the center of the world.

In his innovative approach to the design of the Midland Hospital (1938), Dow focused on the use of color to both separate functions and provide a cheerful environment. Nurses' stations featured a red-and-white desk, as did the entrance lobby. Bright green walls contrasted with red orange floors.

REFLECTIONS

To musical accompaniment and with the architect himself manning the controls, Dow's Somnophonics shone floodlights on dancers behind a polyethylene screen. "Music becomes a picture painted in sound; a picture becomes music played in color," he explained. Somnophonics, which recalled his high school decorations of lights and crêpe paper, was hailed as a new art form following several performances in Midland in 1956.

▼

As a boy Alden Dow developed a fascination for the motion and rhythm of the world around him—a sense of play that never left him. Grace Dow made sure that her younger son got to do what he wanted to fulfill his own talents and passions. Childhood loves of trains, puzzles, and photography were carried over into adulthood, with dozens more interests and hobbies acquired en route.

What didn't he like? Dow took fun seriously: model trains, mechanical toys, motion pictures, music and dance, jokes, spirited discussions on controversial subjects, inventions, Japanese art, ceramics, mobiles, cars, travel, figure skating, sailing, ping pong, croquet, costume parties, children, dogs, and especially family and friends. One of his greatest joys was seeing other people have fun and watching them develop their own potential. "The creative personality seems never to grow old ... but

rather simply grows," he offered by way of advice.

Friends and relatives remember Dow as personable, gracious, and generous yet humble; calm and seldom angry yet spontaneous; ethical rather than religious; quiet and discreet yet fond of boisterous humor; tender rather than dramatic yet a playful tease. He did not read so much as attempt to think things through on his own, following the advice of his father, Herbert Dow. "He was always trying to do something just a little different and a little better," noted Dow's nephew Herbert H. Dow II.

A sense of humor ran through the extended Dow family. According to Vada Dow, her husband took after his mother and his sister Dorothy in this respect. He loved the Marx Brothers—Harpo best of all; for fun Dow even had a Harpo wig made for himself out of wood shavings. His theatrical sense spilled over into costume parties and seasonal rituals at the family's vacation home on Higgins Lake north of Midland. On New Year's Eve, he would lead a line of barefoot revelers outside to

Dow liked to manipulate wooden blocks—pieces of his own design that permitted hands-on tests of his modular construction ideas. He regularly allowed himself time for this purposeful play.

▼

make a circle in the snow while singing in the new year, holding a big frying pan aloft as a drum.

If one had to single out Dow's preferred pastimes, they would no doubt be trains, photographs, motion pictures, and music. He dated his first interest in trains to the age of four, when he watched a man in London climbing between train cars at a station. From this grew a boyhood passion for model trains, which he continued to collect as an adult and viewed as anything but mere toys. His O-gauge engines pulling a ribbon of passenger cars or a colorful circus train would steam out of the master bedroom, chug above his office, and circumnavigate the house's sitting room. Over the winter holidays, at least three model trains would occupy the living and dining rooms, his daughter Barbara Carras remembers. Dow also supported efforts to preserve several of Michigan's last working standard-gauge steam locomotives.

Taking pictures was another pursuit carried over into adulthood. Wherever he was—with family or friends in Europe, at Taliesin, around his home or studio, at Higgins Lake, in Japan, on fishing trips, viewing his construction sites, at family events— Dow had a camera with him. In the 1930s and 1940s, he began bringing his own "colored movies" and other homegrown pictures to illustrate his lectures. Later he took motion pictures using an advanced anamorphic (wide-angle) lens. A listing of Dow's films beginning in 1925 runs to a dozen pages. Standouts include his 1933 documentation of the Taliesin Fellowship during its first year, panning from workers in the field to Vada sketching and Wright directing. In the dream-sequence *Little Beach Blossom* (1953), Dow spontaneously filmed his friend Pat Oppermann at Higgins Lake dressed as a Japanese woman. *Pat's Bath* (circa 1955) was similarly light hearted. *The Four Seasons*, made in the mid-1960s, evocatively traces his Home and Studio as the landscape changes from green to orange and yellow to white. Nature, captured as reflections on the surface of ponds and streams, was also the subject of a 1970 exhibition of his photographs, work that inspired the title of his 1970 limited-edition book, *Reflections*. This large-format volume, conceived as artistically as any of the architect's buildings, set out Dow's personal philosophy and surveyed favorite accomplishments.

Like his mother and his sister Helen, Dow was musical. He enjoyed Beethoven and Brahms, but opera was not his cup of tea, except for the most lyrical arias. "I prefer to hear only the highlights … like the sextet from *Lucia,*" he admitted in 1978. He was a stellar dancer, a skill that led in 1956 to Dow's most provocative creation after his own architecture. His likely inspirations were Walt Disney's *Fantasia* (1940), an innovative film melding images and music, as well as the way he was able to make light dance within his earlier walls of plastic panels. What he called Somnophonics (dream music) was Dow's way of allowing a live audience to "see" music through a picture painted in sound. After trying it out at home with the children, he took it to Broadway, as it were—the stage of the Midland Public Library. Behind a forty-foot-wide wood frame with a translucent polyethylene screen specially made by The Dow Chemical Company, modern dancers interpreted classical music played by a pianist. Their motions were turned into a rainbow of shadows produced by floodlights behind them beaming three primary colors. The result was a visual abstraction illuminated by sound: "a perfect medium for fantasies," noted Dow.

Inspired by his first hearing of a Moog Synthesizer (which he found too monotonous), Dow by 1971 had devised yet another musical form in which the body became an instrument. This was his Moodical, a patented cagelike wooden cylinder in which a person—a real-life Wizard of Oz—was to stand or move about to activate various sets of keys, bars, switches, panels, and rods using hands, feet, or the whole body. "The idea," said Dow, "is that when you step into it, you can dance a form of music." The Moodical, patented in 1973, was meant to pick up an artist's every mood, to be "exquisitely sensitive to every feeling in the soul of the player"—fact and feeling synthesized.

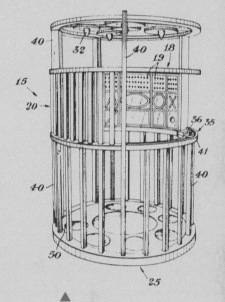

In 1973 Dow received a patent for his Moodical (Self-Choreographing Musical or Luminescent Appliance). It may have been another of his ideas that were ahead of their time, as it failed to generate excitement to match his own.

THE LIFE AND WORK OF ALDEN DOW

1904   Alden Ball Dow is born on April 10 as the fifth of Herbert and Grace Dow's seven children.

1911   Starts schooling at home with his younger sisters, Margaret and Dorothy. At age eight, glasses improve his eyesight.

1918   Begins public high school. His older sister Helen Dow Hale and his Aunt Helen Griswold die in the influenza epidemic.

1922   Graduates from Midland High School.

1923   Visits Japan with his family, including a stay at Frank Lloyd Wright's Imperial Hotel. Enters the University of Michigan to study chemical and mechicanal engineering.

1925   The Dows travel to Europe and Algiers; Alden flies on his own from Paris to London.

1926   Leaves college in February. After working for The Dow Chemical Company, he moves to New York City in the fall.

1927   Enters Columbia University School of Architecture. Two of his bridges are built in the Dow Gardens and at the Midland Country Club.

1929   Takes a Grand Tour of Europe with friends, experiencing the continent's "new architecture" first-hand.

1930   Begins to design the Midland Country Club. Herbert Dow dies and is succeeded by his son Willard Dow as president of The Dow Chemical Company.

1931   Graduates from Columbia University after the country club opens to rave reviews. Marries Vada Bennett on September 16. Begins eighteen months with Frantz and Spence architects in Saginaw. The Dow Gardens open to visitors.

1932   Designs the Towsley House for his sister Margaret as well as several speculative projects. *Architectural Record* features the Midland Country Club.

1933   Spends six months with the Taliesin Fellowship, where Dow revises the Stein House plan. Obtains architecture license in June. Opens practice as Alden B. Dow, Architect at his brother-in-law's house. Develops his Unit Blocks and completes the Cavanagh and Lewis Houses and the Heatley House (unbuilt).

1934   Begins a drafting studio that becomes the nucleus of his Home and Studio. Other designs include the Shanty for his family; the Heath, Hanson, and Whitman Houses; and Ethyl-Dow house prototypes in North Carolina and Oviatt's Bakery (unbuilt).

1935   Alden and Vada's son, Michael Lloyd, is born and named for Frank Lloyd Wright. Designs include his studio conference room and reception area; the Ball, Diehl, and MacCallum Houses; the Mitts House (unbuilt); and the Frolic Theater in Midland. Dow begins a six-year tenure on the Midland City Planning Commission.

1936   Starts addition of a second drafting room and fills the pond around his studio. *Architectural Forum* introduces Dow's studio and four of his houses. Commissions include the Pardee, Mary Dow, Greene, Charles W. Bachman, Koerting, Saunders, and Pryor Houses.

1937   Receives Diplome de Grand Prix from the Paris Exposition. *Life* magazine features Dow's Midland work and returns in 1948. The Dows' first daughter, Mary Lloyd, is born. Residential work includes the Rood House and the 1940 Ethocel House.

1938   Designs include the Midland band shell, bathhouse, and pool; Midland Hospital; the Hodgkiss House and the low-cost Best House; the House with a Future (unbuilt); and the Parents' and Children's School for Vada. Dow's Unit Blocks are granted a patent.

1939   Begins to design the family home attached to his studio. Residences include the Arbury, Campbell, and Wells Houses; the Leland Doan Beach House; the Ingleside Housing Project (unbuilt); and the Dow Chemical House 101.

1940   Designs Dow Chemical offices around the country as well as housing and plant facilities for the company in Freeport, Texas. Receives commission for the Reorganized Church of Jesus Christ of Latter-day Saints in Midland, his first church. Houses include the LeRoy Smith, Dreisbach, and Robinson residences.

1941   The Dows' second daughter, Barbara Alden, is born after the family moves into its new home in March. Dow's firm is incorporated as Alden B. Dow, Inc., and he joins the Dow Chemical board of directors. Houses include the Butenschoen, Penhaligen, Reinke, Irish, and Boonstra residences as well as unbuilt experimental and low-cost proposals. The plan for Lake Jackson, Texas, begins to take shape.

1942   Talbot Hamlin reviews Dow's first decade of work in *Pencil Points*. A fire damages the studio entrance.

1943   The Dows move to Freeport, Texas. Lake Jackson opens following a rushed construction. Designs, except the proposed Circle House, are focused on Texas projects.

1944	Wins the competition to design the 36th Division War Memorial in Texas (unbuilt).
1945	The Dow family moves again, to Houston. Designs include A House for the Southwest and the Michigan Solar House (both unbuilt).
1946	Designs a new Michigan governor's mansion (unbuilt). The Midland National Bank renovation is the first of several banks.
1947	Designs the First Methodist Church in Midland. Spearheads a Midland tree-planting program. Rents a cottage at Higgins Lake and buys it for his family two years later. Named by the governor to Michigan's Capitol Building Commission. Closes his Texas office.
1949	Becomes president of the Michigan Society of Architects. Willard Dow dies in a plane crash with his wife, Martha. Commission for the Phoenix Civic Center causes a rift with Wright. Schools, churches, and other civic buildings become an important part of the firm's work.
1950	Designs include the Midland Public Library (Grace A. Dow Memorial Library), the Ballmer House, and the first of several low-cost sandwich-panel houses in Midland.
1951	Designs the Josephine Ashmun House as his first A-frame residence, attracting wide press coverage.
1953	Grace Dow, Midland's "First Lady," dies. Designs include St. John's Lutheran Church and Midland High School.
1956	Wins an AIA Honor Award for the First Methodist Church. Designs King's Daughters Home and McMorran Memorial Auditorium.
1957	Named a fellow of the American Institute of Architects. Creates master plan for Delta College near Bay City.
1958	Designs the University of Michigan Botanical Gardens and the first of numerous buildings for the Interlochen Arts Academy.
1959	*House Beautiful* features Dow designs as part of "Your Legacy from Frank Lloyd Wright." Creates a master plan for Hillsdale College.
1960	Receives a Gold Medal from the Michigan Society of Architects and an honorary Doctor of Fine Arts from Hillsdale College. Named by the governor to the Michigan Cultural Commission (later State Council for the Arts). Designs include the Ann Arbor City Hall and Roscommon Congregational Church.
1961	Receives the second president's award from the Columbia Architectural Alumni Association. Designs include the Riecker House and Tri-City Airport.
1962	Creates the site plan and buildings for Northwood Institute in Midland.
1963	Named an honorary Doctor of Architecture by the University of Michigan. Changes his firm name to Alden B. Dow Associates. Designs include house for Chrysler Chairman Lynn Townsend and the president's house at Duke University in North Carolina.
1964	Designs the University of Michigan Administration Building. Designated an honorary Doctor of Fine Arts by Albion College.
1965	Begins work on the Midland Center for the Arts. Retires from the board of directors of The Dow Chemical Company.
1966	Designs a Holiday Inn in Traverse City and a house for Michael Dow. Named an honorary Doctor of Laws by Michigan State University.
1969	Awarded honorary doctorate degrees by Northwood Insitute and Saginaw Valley College.
1970	Dow's book *Reflections* is published. The Michigan Association of Nurserymen honors him.
1971	Named Community Leader of the Year by the Midland Board of Realtors.
1974	Develops a master plan for revitalizing the Dow Gardens and begins a series of new bridges, a greenhouse, and a visitors building.
1975	A Way of Life exhibition at the Midland Center for the Arts pays tribute to the architect.
1978	The Alden B. Dow Creativity Center is founded by Northwood University to honor Dow's commitment to innovation.
1981	The architecture firm name is changed to Dow Howell Gilmore Associates. The Michigan Fraternal Order of Police honors Dow.
1982	Receives the first Frank Lloyd Wright Creativity Award; Olgivanna Wright calls him "the spiritual son of Frank LLoyd Wright."
1983	The Michigan Senate names Dow the state's first architect laureate in May. Dow dies at his home on August 20; services are held at the Dow Gardens with interment at Midland Cemetery.
1988	The Alden B. Dow Archives opens in the Home and Studio to preserve Dow's papers and interpret his legacy.
1989	The Alden B. Dow Home and Studio is named a National Historic Landmark and other Midland houses designed by Dow are added to the National Register of Historic Places.
1991	Vada Dow dies on October 8.
1992	The Alden B. Dow Home and Studio opens to visitors for regular tours.
2000	The American Institute for Conservation of Historic and Artistic Works and Heritage Preservation recognizes the Home and Studio for the care of its collections and the building itself.

Good architecture stands the test . . . the structure must stand the attacks . . . . . whether it be far . . . best designs are timeless. In the w . . . different forms and functions pleas . . . are performed smoothly without . . . ev . . . other in natural . . . is . . . se practical and . . . lo . . . ture stands. Re . . . he . . . or their quality o . . . its own style . . . . its own way of . . .

THE STUDIO

Good architecture stands the test of time. Physically, this means that the structure must be built with materials and workmanship that will stand the attacks of nature and usage for its planned life expectancy … whether it be fifty or two hundred, or more, years. Aesthetically, the best designs are timeless. In the well-designed structure, all its many different forms and functions pleasantly relate to each other. Functions are performed smoothly without interfering with each other. Forms evolve from each other in natural and beautiful ways. The end result is a structure whose practical and aesthetic qualities work together as long as the structure stands. Really well-designed structures lean heavily on style for their quality of timelessness. Every structure has its own style … its own way of satisfying its purpose or function.

■ With his Home and Studio, Alden Dow wrote a new chapter in the history of the American country house. It followed no style but his own, no form but what the functions required, no plan but what nature (artfully shaped) dictated. The structure and its site are intensely personal statements, representing an order composed Unit Block by Unit Block, tree by tree, and almost drop by drop. ■ Dow regarded his waterside complex as one of the best examples of modern domestic architecture. Others have shared this judgment. Michigan's architects named the Home and Studio one of the state's most significant structures, noting, "The Midland residence of Alden Dow is an exceptional example of the harmony of building with site. Its every aspect of both exterior and interior design and expression is characterized by richness of detail, a sense of scale, and of the relationship of the spaces to each other and to the whole.... Its lakeside setting, its landscaping, and

EARTH, AIR, FIRE, AND WATER

its total ambience mark it as one of Michigan's all-time great residences." The National Register of Historic Places called it "visual poetry using contrasting colors and planes that flow together like the water visible from many windows." On being designated a National Historic Landmark in 1989, the Home and Studio was termed Dow's "most clearly acknowledged masterpiece." *Architectural Digest* called it "one of the two most beautiful contemporary homes in America." Writing about the work of Frank Lloyd Wright's Taliesin apprentices, Tobias S. Guggenheimer declared that Dow's creation "remains one of the most moving, if undiscovered, architectural treasures in the United States." ■ When he set out in December 1933 to design a workplace for himself, Dow visualized his studio as one branch of a sylvan retreat that would include his home. The studio as originally planned was essentially completed in 1937, but the house was not begun until 1939 and finished two years later. For a time Dow wrestled with whether or not he really wanted to tie his home so closely to his place of work, but when Vada Dow gave him an ultimatum about their housing situation the initial concept was the quickest to set in motion. Together the original Home and Studio filled nearly twenty thousand square feet and took seven years to build; the cost is unknown. (The studio occupies about six thousand square feet, the residence fourteen thousand.) ■ This extraordinary complex at 315 Post Street—in Midland but occupying a place apart—was built on family land virtually next door to the homestead in which the architect grew up. It was crafted of natural elements: Unit Blocks molded from recycled cinder ash, space enclosed in highly imaginative ways, undulating roofs of fire-tempered copper fashioned into undreamed-of planes, and life-giving water to frame and reflect Dow's conception. Both nature and architecture were brilliantly manipulated to heighten the relationship between the natural and the built or, as Dow would say, between science and art, fact and feeling. *Architectural Forum* recognized in 1936 that the studio had "grown out of a setting instead of being forcibly inserted into it." ■ When construction of the studio got under way, the Unit Blocks were not yet in production, so Homasote panels with wood battens were used innovatively to clad the first drafting room; by the time the house was built, Dow was moving away from the blocks, so it became one of the last residences built with them. In between came a series of essays in the visual possibilities of Dow's geometric blocks. The sixteen variants were used for both exterior and interior walls—

▶

A photograph taken at night when the studio was new captures the magic of its shapes and textures. The evanescence of the glass acts as a foil to the solidity of the Unit Blocks, just as squares and triangles play a game of contrasting geometric forms.

◀◀

Pages 100–101: The Home and Studio rises like an island in the pond Dow created. The water's constantly changing reflections add dynamism to the site, expanding the evocative power of the buildings. Tall and straight like a tree trunk, the playful chimney recalls nature, while the conference room roof swoops down to touch it. Tentlike, these roofs seem to float on the secure base of Unit Blocks.

◀

Preceding page: On the studio's front door, red and clear glass triangles reinterpret the exterior's geometric motif. Angles formed by the copper straps hint at what lies inside.

stressing the interrelatedness of the natural and the man made—as well as for chimneys and fireplaces, retaining walls, garden walls, planters, terraces, steps, sculptures, and other decorative elements. Some walls were straight, some serpentine or zigzagged or interrupted by a stairway; some were solid, others perforated to intensify the rhythm of the blocks. On the south side of the original drafting room along the pond, a 100-foot-long wall of blocks was later built to the water line; here the blocks vary from standard (one-foot square) to half size (six inches), providing visual relief on what might otherwise have been a stark bulkhead. Against the mirrorlike pond or the feathery trees, Dow's Unit Blocks added an earthy element of texture while demonstrating the almost unlimited sculptural dynamism possible from simple rectilinear blocks.

The most fanciful of Dow's block constructions, the first to catch the visitor's eye from the driveway or across the pond, is the brilliant white studio chimney. With the studio's two wings seeming to rotate outward from it, this playful pile of blocks visually anchors the spreading, horizontal building to the earth. Its setbacks recall the Art Deco skyscrapers that Dow would have watched rising in New York City while he was at Columbia. Part altar to modernism, part stalagmite growing in the moist environment, it was designed to be fun as well as functional. Its stair steps, like a jungle gym, invited Dow's children to climb aboard for youthful play. With a fire lighted at its heart in the reception room fireplace, the chimney fulfilled its chief purpose on a cold Michigan day.

In every way the blocks also provide a counterpoint to the Home and Studio's second major architectural element: the standing-seam copper roofs, whose shape and material are unique among Dow's Unit Block projects. These eminently sheltering coverings reach downward on the pond side to mimic the gentle banks on the opposite shore. Elsewhere they unfurl in a frenzy of angles and upturned finials, all conceived no

doubt for pure delight outside and in. Their intricacy, designed before AutoCAD and Frank Gehry, is astonishing. The Dow scholar Sidney K. Robinson has found hints of their picturesqueness in Wright's Oak Park Play House projects of 1926: "When these play houses were published in the *Architectural Record* in December 1928, Dow saved the pages for his files." He had admired copper roofs in his European travels and had used them already on his sister's house in Ann Arbor and the Stein House in Midland. The seams' rib lines, as Robinson has pointed out, "are an effective means of tying the roof planes into the orthogonal grid of the blocks." Flat roofs would have been more in keeping with the modern aesthetic, but once again Dow opted to do it his way and chose the organic solution. Although executed in costlier copper, the tented roofs on the Home and Studio pay respect to Wright's favorite idiom of shelter during his Prairie period. Dow liked copper because it oxidizes to an organic green patina—a natural process returning the material to nature, one he helped along with chemical treatment.

Although counterintuitive based on first sight, the overall site plan inscribed by the Home and Studio is nearly square in deference to the unit system created by Dow's building blocks. One L shape is formed by the studio's two wings, even though its corner spills out into the pond via the sunken conference room. A looser ell, including a waterfront terrace, is formed on the residence side. However, with the help of connecting devices, the space enclosed by these almost abstract wings is more complex. The angled wall of the family's bedroom wing, a covered walkway to the house, and a serpentine wall of Unit Blocks all serve to hint at a parallelogram within the rectilinear form. Shape unfolds within shape to embrace a courtyard at the heart of the combined Home and Studio. The manicured courtyard—a man-made paradise—is of course a masterful Japanese architectural device, one that Dow surely admired. Such an inner sanctum offering views from most windows peacefully turns the gaze inward, away from the world, to simulate an alternative universe.

Few elements of the Home and Studio are as breathtaking or pleasing as its watery bed. Dow harnessed this symbolic life force to create an obvious symbiosis between architecture and nature. Ringing half of the complex with water allowed his creation to appear to rest more lightly on the land, to double its beauty through reflections outside and dancing patterns inside, to blur the line where building ends and garden begins. In deference to the water, the studio cascades gently from its spiked chimney to a conference room actually submerged into the pond itself. Connections between the two worlds of land and water are emphasized by a wooden bridge here, there a copper trellis dipping down to the water's edge, and blocks that seem to break away into stepping stones fording the pond. Although windows in the Home and Studio provide more direct views of land than of water, from the outside it is the sinuous pond that sets the design apart and creates its romance. Dow's enthusiasm for this incomparable frame of water led him in 1936 to try it on the handsome Saunders House outside Detroit, where he similarly set the living room into the water.

Surprises abound in the Home and Studio complex. Here a door to the courtyard is virtually hidden in the notch where the studio meets Dow's office, located in the residential part of the structure. It allowed quick egress into the natural world.

The canopied walkway along the 1936 drafting room wing of the Dow studio provides shelter as well as decoration from patterns stencilled by sunlight onto the ground below. Planters shield the cars parked at the front.

▲

Befitting its watery location, Dow's conference room, now known as the Submarine Room, was designed as tightly as a ship. Steps flow downward and walls undulate inward to make a sense of motion almost palpable. Dow met with clients in this space.

▶

An early color photograph captured the scene that awaited clients inside the studio's front door. Unit Block walls made a seamless transition from outside to inside. Nature was brought indoors to soften the edges.

▶

The triangle became the motif of the loft area Dow added above his studio reception area in 1942. Exaggerated brackets direct the eye to the elevated work space. Triangles are also the dominant element in the adjacent second drafting room.

◀

Dow's office, completed along with the residence in 1941, featured furniture of his own design. The curving forms of the chair and the table, covered in linoleum, contrasted with the rectilinearity of the Unit Blocks.

▶

Guests waited in the reception area to meet with Dow, warmed in the winter by the imposing hearth. Being here gave them a chance to learn his architectural vocabulary in a few glances—from his preferred textures to his favorite colors.

Soon after Dow began shaping his own work and living environment, Wright embarked on his design for Fallingwater (1935) in Pennsylvania. Both were romanticized attempts to control nature. The author Sidney K. Robinson, who was briefly a Dow employee and in his 1974 dissertation compared Dow's work with that of Wright, has described closer similarities between Dow's Home and Studio and Wright's own home at Taliesin (1911–59) in Wisconsin, where Dow spent a half year in 1933 as an apprentice. Their predecessors were idealistic, utopian communities from monasteries to the nineteenth-century Brook Farm and societies of craftsmen promoted by William Morris and his American Arts and Crafts followers. As Robinson suggests: "The composed places created by these two architects are closely related representatives of the desire to concentrate beauty and harmony in a place intimately related to nature. They are both ground-hugging houses of the north, trailing along natural features of hillside or stream. Their uncomplicated construction is supported by a technological world at some remove. Aesthetics linked to morality governs life inside these settings. They are examples of the attempt to compose an enduring relationship between architecture and life."

Robinson notes that one characteristic of the charismatic personality is its sense of freedom. "To revalue the expected, the ordinary, to fuse it into a new form can only be undertaken by one who is free of constriction," he has written. The architecture critic Talbot Hamlin recognized this aspect of Dow in 1942, when he wrote of the architect's work that "there clearly speaks a personality which is individual, which is thinking imaginatively—not in terms of style but in terms essentially creative—and which is seeking *aims quite different* from the aims of the usual modern designer." In Dow's search for an orderly world, he felt free to experiment with his own studio and home. He typically had progressive and engaged clients, but for his Home and Studio the client was a uniquely creative personality.

THE SITE

Just as a meandering stream withholds its full glory until it is conquered bend by bend, so does this most liberated of all Alden Dow buildings unveil its snaking rivulets only hook by crook. The architect tantalizes with a glimpse here, a peek there, until the entire complex unfolds completely. The site plan reflects Herbert Dow's approach to his own gardens, as his son recalled it: "If you can see all of a thing from one position, it lacks appeal, or in other words, lasting expression."

The stream, dammed into a tranquil pond, is the backbone of the five-acre site. Like the little island city that hovers along its edge, however, the pond is artifice. Seemingly natural, and representing nature, it began when Herbert Dow first redirected Snake Creek and dammed several streams nearby. His son further rerouted and dredged it on his building site to produce an irregular shape about 60 feet wide by 150 feet long.

When Dow began to build here, the sloping, square-shaped property (once more than five times larger) still bore the fruits of his father's labors. Apple and plum trees, lilacs, flowering crab apples, and a red maple dotted the land. Mounds of earth dug up for the pond were planted with pines and spruces, birches, weeping willows, maples, and wisteria—Midwest natives chosen for their contrasts with the buildings. As Dow liked to say, "Nature relieves architecture. Architecture relieves nature."

As important as the views from inside the structure were the views of it from outside. When Dow looked at his work from the Dow Gardens across the pond, he called it a "beautiful picture." He enjoyed waking before sunrise to photograph the lily-filled pond as the sun began to send down its reflections and the air agitated the cattails dotting the water. Evening parties would bring rafts, floating candles, and loud music from a phonograph in the Submarine Room, giving guests a chance to experience Dow's concept of composed order in a meticulously composed setting.

An aerial photograph helps capture the complexity of the Home and Studio's interlocking pieces. Extending from the entry, the original 1934 drafting room (partially hidden by the courtyard trees) runs parallel with the pond. Built at a right angle is the sawtooth 1936 drafting room and the adjacent workshop. Beyond the curved wall is a 1965 studio addition (since removed). The residence is found at the end of the driveway at the far left. Hidden in the crook of another ell is the front door, shaded by a covered walkway. The projecting wing at left holds the guest room and the kitchen. In its cross wing are the dining room and the porch, and at the top of the cross is the living room, overlooking a terrace and the pond. Angled off to the right, completing the courtyard, is the bedroom wing, which terminates in the dramatic sitting room marked by a tall chimney. On this side of the property, opposite the Dow Gardens, the pond is a treat reserved for those who enter the studio or the home, as the buildings shield the water from immediate view.

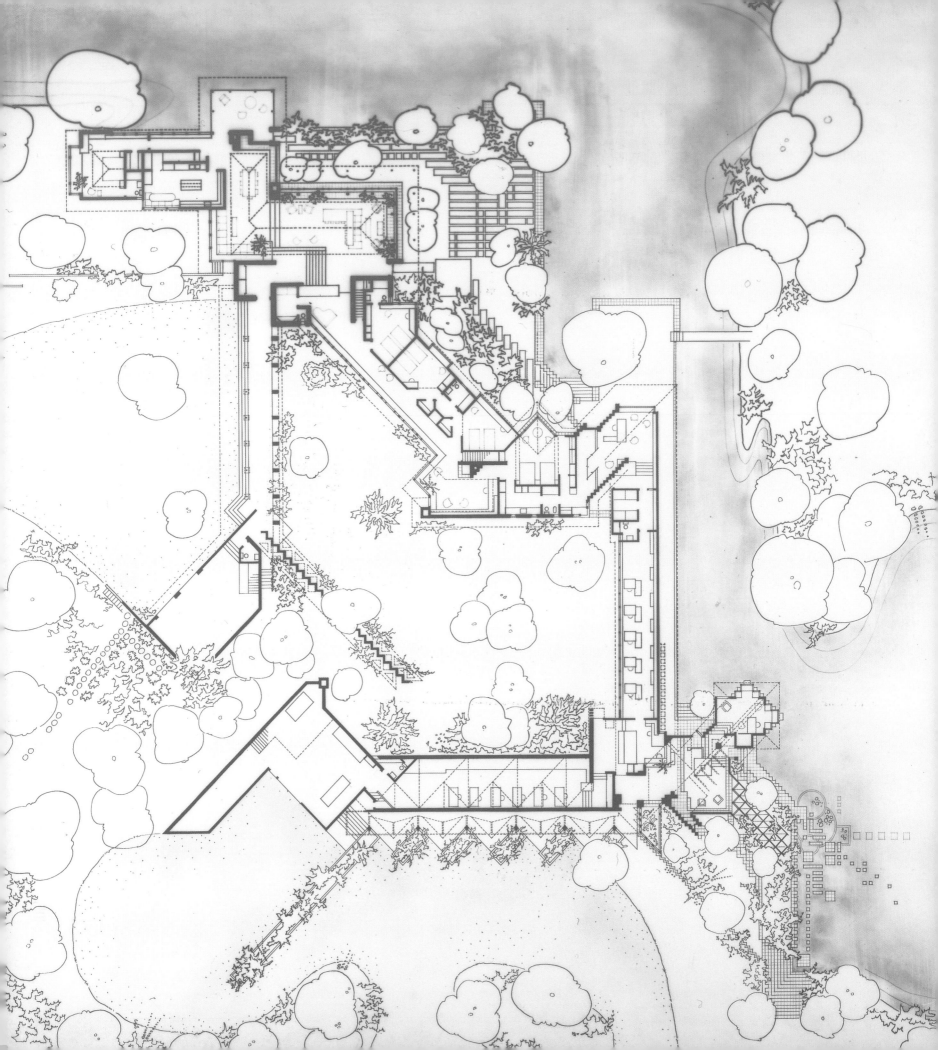

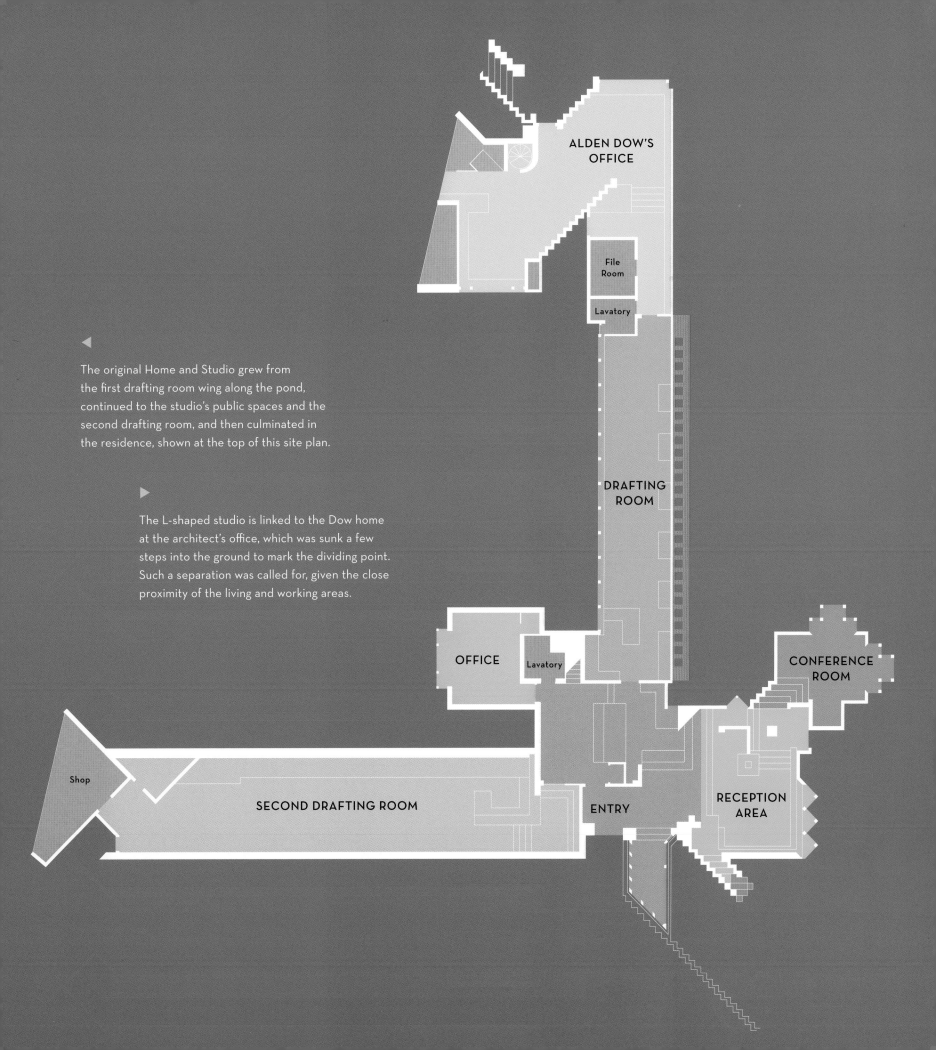

The original Home and Studio grew from the first drafting room wing along the pond, continued to the studio's public spaces and the second drafting room, and then culminated in the residence, shown at the top of this site plan.

The L-shaped studio is linked to the Dow home at the architect's office, which was sunk a few steps into the ground to mark the dividing point. Such a separation was called for, given the close proximity of the living and working areas.

ALDEN DOW'S OFFICE

File Room

Lavatory

DRAFTING ROOM

OFFICE

Lavatory

CONFERENCE ROOM

Shop

SECOND DRAFTING ROOM

ENTRY

RECEPTION AREA

THE ENTRANCE

Post Street remained a gravel road until the late 1960s, making it one of the last unpaved streets in Midland. Alden Dow wanted it that way, as a transition space between town and his private world. Turning off Main Street and traveling the hundred yards to the cul-de-sac, a visitor's sense of arrival is heightened. Through the trees a white apparition—the tower of a modern castle perhaps?—slowly makes itself visible but gives few hints as to what is inside or behind.

To the left rectangular planters advance forward under the shelter of a trellis and the saw-tooth roofline of the second drafting room. To the right a low wall of two stacked Unit Blocks undulates toward the pond. Rising above them is a symphony of overlapping triangles, with shed roofs to the left and right dipping down toward the center and a triangular monitor roof peering out over the green copper sea. Through the lower windows, outlined in burnished cypress, can be seen what the architectural historian Talbot Hamlin called a "sharp staccato" note: the imaginative chimney, signifying a warm welcome inside. This entrance to the Dow studio serves as a sign calling out "inventive mind at work here." As Hamlin advised in 1942, "Whoever approaches the office of Alden Dow ... need be in no doubt as to the kind of architecture to be expected from it."

The triangles part to reveal a door framing a triangular concrete entry pad. Deeply recessed to increase the sense of mystery, the big slab of cypress is 4½ feet wide and just 6½ feet tall but is as playful as the entire studio it encloses. Copper straps angle downward toward the copper escutcheon to emulate the roof slopes. The metal lines—bisecting triangles of clear glass that permit the merest glimpse inside—form rhomboid shapes recalling the hidden sides of Dow's Unit Blocks. At four points, inset triangles of red glass accent the composition just as apples once dotted the former Dow orchards.

No threshold exists to create a division between outside and inside. The first step into the studio

▲

Dow wrote an architectural symphony to greet visitors to his studio. Triangles, squares, and rhomboids provide a peek, literally and figuratively, into the wonders within. This detail of the massive cypress door was taken from inside.

◄

Although the door to the studio is sequestered, no such inhibitions hinder the architectural enthusiasm of the entrance area. The topmost clerestory at left brings light into the balcony work area added by Dow after a 1942 fire.

drafting room. Clients waited for him in the sitting area, and until the house was completed in 1941, he and Vada often annexed the space to entertain family and friends in the evening. On October 25, 1935, Vada's sister, Grace Bennett, was married here to Charles F. Reed and serenaded by a string quartet playing in the sunken conference room on the studio's waterside level below.

Throughout the space nature beckons. From the entrance the floor levels step down toward the pond in three stages. A simple glass-paneled door on the middle level leads outside and down a short flight of steps to the pondside terrace. But even from the inside, the overhanging roof points the way to the water. At the juncture where triangular bay windows reach out into the eaves, the roof dissolves into a triangulated trellis. A matrix of open copper work and alternating panels of red glass—color opposites again—directs a ruby glow indoors while it sifts patterns onto the plantings underneath; the geometric motif is picked up in red glass

◄

Dressed in the colors of spring, the spaces of the reception area unfold like a tender shoot opening according to natural law. The fireplace, raised on a Unit Block hearth, is the raison d'être for the chimney first encountered on approaching the studio.

entry reveals a low-ceilinged space, as compressed as the exterior is expansive. One is meant not to linger here but to move toward the more open reception area at right, where the ceiling explodes upward in an exceedingly complex series of levels and angles. Steps lead down into a sitting area, which pivots around a hearth served by the iconic entrance chimney. Overhead the ceiling's wood banding and strong slope echo the diagonal straps marking the front door. Originally the ceiling was white and the carpet purple, as in Dow's earlier country club, but this palette was changed in 1937. Today smooth surfaces in delightful tones of raspberry and moss green emerge from cool white walls of Unit Blocks. Like a budding blossom against a spring branch, the pink areas add balance and contrast to the restful green. Red, green's opposite on the color wheel, covers the room's chairs.

The reception area, including an office Dow used to the left of the door, was part of the original studio construction, finished in 1935 after the first

Casting changing shadows onto the floor, the roof's lacy fretwork can be seen through the reception area windows as it reaches toward the pond. The ceiling panels echo the downward slope, merging outside and in.

The copper trellis stretching from the roof to the pond is the second tour de force to be found in the studio. Here solidity has vanished in favor of intricate variations on a triangular theme. It is as audacious as the Submarine Room itself.

triangles lining the bases of the bay windows. The continuum from inside to outside is virtually seamless, as if the building had grown organically from natural elements. With nature intertwined in the trellis, building and nature become one.

The trellis has a practical purpose as well: to serve as an umbrella for a walkway leading out to the pond. Along the water's edge, groupings of Unit Blocks gradually taper off until they disappear into an underwater garden, as if they had been scattered on the pond's surface. Did they slide away from the building, or did they emerge from the landscape? It is a playful conundrum cleverly designed to engage visitors in the architecture. As they jump from one block to another, they have a rare chance to walk on water. The way back inside can be found by ferreting out a hidden path under the trellis.

On July 24, 1942, a fire from a smoldering cigarette caused $15,000 in damage to the studio's entrance area but gave Dow an opportunity to reshape the space. After the maid discovered the

fire about 9:30 P.M., firefighters arrived and, thinking the door locked, tried unsuccessfully to axe their way through the solid cypress and copper cladding. The fire gutted the reception area; the original drafting room was only partially burned but was damaged by water and smoke, which also seeped into the residence.

Soon Dow set about changing a sitting area in the reception room into the glassed-in garden nook still maintained today. Expanding upward, he added a loft above the entryway; in retrospect, Dow worried that the change created some awkwardness outside in the roofline between the door and the second drafting room. To structurally reinforce the studio, the architect later replaced the wooden ridge beam running from the chimney to the conference room. Although he would occasionally rub his hand over the three holes in the front door, Dow never repaired it, however, preferring to keep the firefighters' marks as a reminder of the building's fortitude.

THE CONFERENCE ROOM

Arriving to see their architect, Alden Dow's clients were ushered—perhaps steered is a better word—into what he called his studio's floating conference room, known today as the Submarine Room. Here they were baptized in the tenets of organic architecture. To step down into the snug space is to abruptly cast off from the man-made world and glide slowly into nature. With the floor sunk eighteen inches below the surface of the surrounding pond, visitors are made to feel marvelously adrift, eye level to the mirrorlike surface when seated, plying an inland sea. Some Midland citizens were said to have been shocked by the room and hesitant to entrust their schools and civic buildings to a man who put visitors' noses practically in the water.

Angled dramatically forty-five degrees away from the studio entry, the cruciform-shaped room anchors the building to its natural surroundings. In its siting, its form, its materials, its colors, and its total sensibility, this shipshape space reflects an architectural vision exceedingly mature for a beginning designer. It is a case study in the ideas that guided Dow's career. The Unit Block walls project into nature while large windows, zigzagged like

▲

The conference room acts as a punctuation mark for the complex studio roof. Its own V-shaped roof is the mirror image, in miniature, of the inverted V formed by the copper trellis. From roof to water is just five feet, as if the building were dipping into the pond for a cool drink. ▶

▼

To descend into the Submarine Room is to feel the draw of the water. On sunny days sunlight reflects off the pond to dance on the ceiling, producing integral art. The Unit Blocks offer the solace of solid ground.

Just as Dow built in patterns cast by the sun, he integrated artificial light into the wall itself. The wooden latticework shielding the light fixture hints at the copper trellis that reaches outward toward the pond.

glassy folding screens, invite the outside in; no mesh screens disrupt the connection with nature. The eye is drawn outward, then upward from small clerestory windows to the billowing sail of a ceiling. Green carpeting and matching built-ins (once topped with linoleum, now laminate) merge subtly with the tones of the pond; Louisiana red cypress accents recall the trees visible in the gardens beyond. This cool serenity is shocked awake by the ceiling's raspberry pink, balancing the color wheel. The ceiling flows without interruption past the windows to form a seamless soffit, extending the ceiling line with the same pink to eliminate typical barriers between inside and outside. Ripples on the pond stencil shimmering patterns onto the ceiling, incorporating light and shadow— an ever-changing landscape painting—right into the architecture; shadows cast by the blocks add their own counterpoint. Dow also liked the way light could be reflected through extruded plastics he found at the Dow Chemical plant; the amor-

phous shapes of these serendipitous sculptures further balance the space's rectilinear geometry.

Below the water line Dow used concrete blocks rather than his Unit Blocks. The walls and floor are two shells of concrete more than one foot thick. Sandwiched in between are several layers of asphalt-impregnated felt. Any buoyancy is prevented by the structure's weight, which holds the room in place. A spillway helps keep the water in the pond just below the window level. Well sealed against moisture, the Submarine Room has never leaked or flooded since it was completed in 1935.

Both stimulating and playful, it was a perfect spot—his public pilothouse—in which to meet with clients. Dow would ask couples to tell him what they wanted to do with the rest of their lives, including how many children they planned to have. Some were even asked to write an essay so he could shape a home around them. He did not have to advertise his services. His own studio was advertisement enough.

THE FIRST DRAFTING ROOM

The original drafting room was the heart of Alden Dow's studio. This was, after all, the space in which the firm's first buildings were fleshed out, and it was the complex's first component to be built. The rest of the Home and Studio grew around—and from—it.

Had Dow actually built the flat-roofed studio he originally envisioned, his drafting room would have been the lesser for it. Redesigned with sloping panels of copper, the roof, now coaxed to a mossy lichen green patina, recalls the pond's own sloping banks. Organic inspiration carries over inside, where sturdy, angled beams of Louisiana red cypress create the illusion of a wooded bower—an indoor forest. These great trunks rise from the south, as if growing from the pond, and branch downward only on the opposite wall. There a long ribbon of four-foot-square windows invites northern light to spill onto the drafting tables directly below.

In the days before widespread air conditioning, these casement windows were designed to naturally cool the studio as well as light it. Hinged at the top, they could be propped up with a pole when opened to catch the breeze. The copper roof retained heat, however, necessitating one of numerous refinements Dow made to his workplace. On the ledge along the narrow part of the twelve-by-forty-eight-foot room, he added thirteen small, screened window openings, each one foot square. They lift out, creating air currents that cross-ventilate the space without ruffling the draftsmen's work. Flitting patterns on the white ceiling reflect movement in the pond below.

Dow's trainlike drafting room was outfitted with five drafting tables and work stations; cabinets and storage space for drawings were built into the opposite wall. Red panels in the row of cabinets echo the legion of red posts that undergird the ceiling beams; originally the panels were green and the posts were unpainted wood. Dow liked to walk down this aisle, stopping at his draftsmen's tables to help them with any problems or penciling in revisions to plans after hours. With water views foreclosed by the nearly solid wall to the south, excessive daydreaming apparently was not encouraged.

Over the years cubicles were added for privacy and linoleum was laid atop the diagonal floor boards, but the space has since been returned to the way Dow first conceived it: intimate yet open, workmanlike yet uplifting—a rustic tent pitched alongside a bucolic stream.

▶ One of a number of changes Dow made to his first studio was to add overhead lighting above the drafting tables to supplement the room's natural light. A floating deck with these integral fixtures bisects the rugged ceiling beams.

▶ In Dow's first drafting room, the chairs are original but the draftsmen's desks are reproductions. By making them flat, Dow could more easily assist his staff architects as he walked through the room.

◄

In the 1930s only the rare architect would dare to use pressed-wood panels outside, especially in a climate as harsh as Michigan's. But because the Unit Blocks that Dow wanted were not yet manufactured, he used Homasote sheets with wood battens on a wood frame to clad the first drafting room. Birdlike copper details with red "tails" channel water away from the building.

▶

Large windows on what was to become the Home and Studio's courtyard side at left brought in strong northern light for Dow's draftsmen. On the opposite wall are built-in cabinets that held the architects' work. At the room's far end, just outside the architect's own office, is a model for Dow's W Frame House (1955), adapted as a summer home by his daughter Mary Lloyd Mills in 1992. It is the last Dow house to be built.

The jagged roofline of the second drafting room is a subtle complement to the studio's complicated entry. By folding the roofs on this new wing, Dow masterfully segmented what might have been a long, straight roofline.

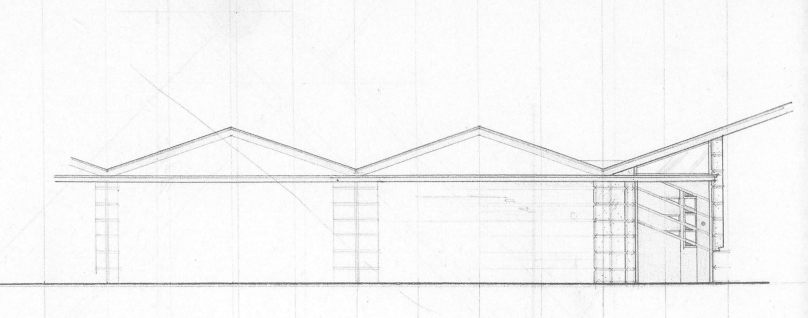

THE SECOND DRAFTING ROOM

By 1936 the firm of Alden B. Dow, Architect, was solidifying its reputation: adding clients, perfecting the Unit Blocks, and using them for residences such as the Pardee House in Midland. It was time to increase the staff. Work started that November on a second drafting room to the west, as Dow had planned from the beginning. Built at a right angle to the entry and the original drafting room, the new wing began the process of enclosing the inner world that would hold the Home and Studio.

Where the first drafting room rested under a simple pitched roof, the new work space took its cue from the folding planes and steep inclines that characterize the studio's public spaces. Along the front the structure's profile hugs the earth. Dow sunk the room about six feet below the entry level to follow the contours of the sloping landscape, letting the wing rise just seven feet above ground. A complex plan based on parallelograms and equilateral triangles is telegraphed by angled Unit Block planters that zigzag outward to mark parking areas. Their blocks rise to hold aloft a trellis perforated with triangles, linking the new building to the original studio.

The triangular motif is reprised in sawtooth projections of the copper roof that echo the canopy sheltering the entrance. Inside, the narrow drafting room (sixteen feet wide by sixty feet long) comes to life under its own canopy of light. Illumination was built into the folds of the roof, which carry large triangles of glass filtering natural light from the north onto the work areas below. Translucent electric-light panels—triangles on a smaller scale—interlock with them to softly fill in the spaces.

The wing is punctuated on the north by a copper mountain: the firm's original garage-workshop and heating plant. A striking conception, its form mimics the studio rooflines and its color their green patina. Triangles appear at the rear in peek-a-boo openings leading to the heating plant, whose roof looms above. Towering over all is a tall chimney of Unit Blocks that anchors a small greenhouse where seasonal plants were grown for use in the residence.

A trellis along the drafting room walkway extends the triangular motif of the wing's sawtooth roof, painting the walls and ground with an ever-changing array of patterns. Dow purposefully kept the building's profile low: "A small scale tends to be highly personal, made for the individual," he said.

ALDEN DOW'S OFFICE

At the far end of the original drafting room are five steps that mark the transition from Alden Dow's studio to his home. On workdays he descended the residence's back stairway to come to his studio. For a man who worked where he lived, a demarcation line was important in separating the two spheres of his life. The nexus point between these worlds was the architect's new office, completed with the house in 1941. Here he could meet with clients around a table he designed himself, work quietly at his white laminate desk, or keep in touch with his staff just a half level above. Or he could peer up into the ceiling's triangular layered "skylight" to watch his model trains chugging by. For Dow work and play were never far removed.

Befitting its role as a semipublic space, his office continues the architectural playfulness of the sunken conference room. Because it was Dow's own space, it is even more personal and idiosyncratic. Planes intersect and then rush off in different directions. Vibrant colors draw the eye upward to take in the ever-rising vertical layers. In the seating nook, by contrast, the ceiling is low to convey a sense of security and privacy. Partitions of Unit Blocks zig and zag in and out of formation, while a gently curving wall hides circular stairs up to a balcony outside the master suite. The rotundity of a hanging lamp and round objects take the edge off rectilinear lines. Walls were essentially bare of pictures, except for the sketch of Vada drawn in 1931 to accompany their engagement announcement. The room, observed Carol Coppage, a former director of the Home and Studio, "is a study of balancing opposites, areas exciting and stimulating, areas calm and restful; soft textiles and hard architectural forms; bold bright colors and plenty of white to keep them from becoming overwhelming."

Dow's desk mediates between indoors and outdoors. A broad picture window just beyond it makes the pond and gardens part of the interior landscape—the boss allowed himself a good view.

A short flight of steps brought Dow from his office to the original drafting room. He kept his professional library here, the books intermingled with some of his favorite objects.

Contrasts are everywhere in Dow's office: high ceilings and low, straight edges softened by round objects, smooth surfaces against rough, one color abutting another. Joy is palpable in this highly individualistic space. The playful cutout ceiling, lighted by a raised level of clerestory windows, is a simulated reach to infinity. Gourds grown by Dow were strung together and hung from the balcony. Contrasting with the recessed lighting in the conference area, George Nelson's 1952 saucer pendant lamp hangs over Dow's desk like a glowing sun.

The perimeter wall outside Dow's office parts to allow an inconspicuous stairway down to the water. From here he and the family would launch their boats to glide off into the pond.

Dow scattered his organic lanterns around the property as much to entrance the eye as to illuminate the landscape. This trio calls to mind flower petals cascading down a stem.

While the window pulls one's gaze outward, the conference area across the room draws it inward. Guests and staff would sit there, on the built-in sofa encircling the double-deck round table, to discuss projects. Combining form and function, the table is large enough to hold spread-out drawings on top; coffee cups went on the bottom shelf to keep them out of harm's way. Dow's appreciation for new materials can be seen in the table's green linoleum covering, which was prone to spotting and had to be waxed; loops of a Dow Chemical polymer used in the company's Saran resin technology wrap around the edge.

Many pieces of furniture here and throughout the Home and Studio were designed by Dow and were manufactured to his specifications by the noted furniture maker Herman Miller. Some of the linoleum tops have been replaced by laminates, and the floor, also originally of linoleum, was changed to carpeting with similar yellow tones. In the late 1960s Dow altered the room's colors to the green, purple, red, and mustard yellow combinations seen today.

On many days the architect set aside time to play with items in the office, a break designed to keep his mind fresh. Chief among his architectural toys were blocks and puzzles that he could combine into pleasing forms; one of them was a Chinese puzzle that Dow made himself and then adapted as a pull-apart table. One result of this purposeful play can be seen around the property in a series of abstract wooden lanterns that seem to have grown organically from their garden settings. Designed in 1962, some take the shape of tree trunks inset with lights shining through plastic panels, while others resemble pagodas assembled from diamond-shaped "leaves" of redwood. A trio of the tall "trunks" stands across the bridge visible from Dow's office, and a miniature pagoda keeps watch outside the master suite above the office. Each was built from a kit of parts—duplicated geometric shapes—much as Dow's Unit Block structures were. "They do what most garden lanterns do not even attempt: use the power of light to evoke emotion and mood," observed the June

1962 *House Beautiful* in a feature on Dow's lanterns. "Lighted or unlighted, they are striking works of art." Dow created variations for some clients and invited *House Beautiful* readers to send him two dollars for complete working drawings for six of these garden lights.

Using the door near his desk, Dow could easily move out into his man-made landscape, stepping into the office's secluded courtyard. The roof's broad eaves, visible from inside, provide shelter even in a drizzling rain. A natural umbrella is offered by a rare Camperdown elm tree (a weeping elm grafted onto a scotch elm). Not far away, steps down to the pond link the worlds of work and play; Dow and his family or visitors could float off in a rowboat, kayak, or raft often tied up here. Around the office corner a gravel path stretches

alongside the original drafting room, providing photogenic vistas of the Submarine Room.

The most entertaining route is across the pond—up and over and down a stairstepped wooden footbridge spiced with oriental red accents. When the studio wall was built, a space was left for a bridge. Before it was finally built in the early 1950s, however, the Dows trod on wooden planks to cross the pond when they wanted to visit his mother or enjoy the gardens. Said Dow of his creation, faintly evocative of Japan: "I have indulged myself in architectural humor. That bridge is not functional just as a bridge but because it also makes people want to climb it . . . for fun. But isn't fun a worthy goal, a kind of function?" This bridge of delights is one of a handful that link Dow to the Dow Gardens.

As *House Beautiful* magazine declared of Dow's red-tipped camelback bridge in June 1962, "The purpose of crossing a garden stream over a bridge like [this] is not to get to the other side so much as it is to savor the pleasure of crossing."

THE HOME

Just as the clothes we wear, so should a building be dressed to suit its function and its function is to produce the right character for its social requirements.... If it is a house, it should be a background for the social activities of its owner and of such a character as to reflect that of its owner and not that of his great-great-grandfather. All buildings in their simplest form are machines. Every mechanical appliance available which will reduce manual labor is now found in the best built homes. Even so, the house as it is today is a very crude machine, comparatively speaking, but improvements are coming fast.... Around this improved machine will develop a new style of architecture which will be a logical design and have more character and beauty than any style yet developed.

When asked to name his favorite among all the buildings he designed, Alden Dow typically responded that it was his own home. The residence into which he and his family moved in spring 1941 was more than just a house. It was the final leg of his masterful studio, an intimate community embracing drafting rooms, offices, a workshop, gardens, and an outdoor playground centered around the pond—and at last a real home for the Dows, who that year numbered five. ■ "We just got squeezed in in time for Barb to be born," recalled Vada Dow, noting that their move came barely three weeks before the birth of the couple's younger daughter. Barbara Alden Dow joined sister Mary Lloyd (called Lloyd) and brother Michael Lloyd, the oldest of the Dows' three children. Construction had begun in 1939, after Vada's prompting that it was time for the architect's family to have a proper home and after Dow persuaded himself that attaching his home to his studio was

A MACHINE FOR LIVING

a good idea after all. Unlike Frank Lloyd Wright (the namesake of two of the Dows' children) at Taliesin, Dow was too modest to give his own home a name. ■ The residence, compared to the willfully complex studio, is less playful and has a less intense relationship with the pond. Raised up high and protected by a stepped-back bulkhead of Unit Blocks, it appears to glide through the water like an ocean liner. The plan, as in the studio, is difficult to describe in words, except to say that it is generally a branching L shape or more specifically a small Z atop a recumbent L angled 120 degrees. The house is two stories, with the public spaces and bedrooms above and the entertainment and utility spaces at pond level, including a two-bedroom apartment for the household staff. It encloses a courtyard whose opposite boundaries are formed by the studio; alongside the pond a terrace offers serene views from inside and places for the family to relax outside. ■ One of the last of Dow's thirteen Unit Block houses, the residence for the most part continues the hipped, standing-seam copper roofs seen on the studio—setting it apart from the preceding Unit Block houses, whose flat roofs more clearly reflected the new European style. However, one flat roof over the family bedrooms served almost as the house's third story and provided endless opportunities for play. Lloyd and Michael would go out onto the roof to fly kites or watch for thunderstorms with their father. The family also placed deck furniture there for unobstructed sunbathing. The roof's original surface of poured concrete and slate pavers has been replaced several times, variously with gravel over tar, rubber, and a continuous membrane. ■ Inside the house he used steel beams and columns to create interior spaces that are larger and more open than in his studio, which was built on a wood frame that restricted the length of spans. The highly irregular plan produced rooms in a variety of sizes and shapes, some intimate and others grand in scale but each flowing seamlessly into the other. Windows, framed in edge-grain fir and custom made in the studio's workshop, vary from nearly floor-to-ceiling screens of glass in the living area to broad picture windows in the bedrooms to scaled-back clerestories where more privacy was desired. With the white Unit Blocks forming a quiet backdrop for interior walls, Dow let his imagination roam freely in the choice of colors, textures, and decorative objects for his home. Surprises can be found around every corner in this meandering composition, just as in the pond that envelops it. ■ The house was an extraordinary conception for its time, as it still seems today. Dow and his few

In this photograph from the 1940s, the long bulkhead defines the house's reach. To contrast with the standard, foot-square Unit Blocks forming the base of the wall, Dow sculpted a tapered frieze at the top using six-inch blocks to vary the rhythm. At left are the family bedrooms and at right the living room and the porch; at the time it was screened in at the pond level but was later enclosed with Unit Blocks.

Preceding page: The building's complexity is immediately visible from the pond. Major features—the chimney, the projecting eaves over the master bedroom, and the undulating bulkhead wall—each stake out a different plane, inviting shadows to enliven the mix.

forward-thinking contemporaries were struggling to nudge homeowners out of their traditional boxy houses. The average person would hardly have known what to make of such a residence that paid homage to no known style and no standard floor plan. In some ways less daring than other residences he was designing (such as the Whitman and Pardee Houses), in others more spectacular (the living and dining area), the house above all excelled in filling Dow's own prescription for a home that was "a background for the social activities of its owner and of such a character as to reflect that of its owner and not that of his great-great-grandfather." Or even that of his father. Although the Dow house was designed in the 1930s, noted a writer in the *Detroit Free Press* in 1967, "it might have been torn off a drawing board the day before yesterday—or the day after tomorrow."

Even before the house was ready for occupancy, Dow had begun working in Texas on the Freeport and Lake Jackson projects. The family hardly had time to adjust to their new home when he found a house for them in Texas. Off went Vada and the children in early 1943 to join him for almost two years, returning in the summers because of the everpresent threat of polio in the South. When the Dows finally made the Midland house their permanent home, it proved to be an ideal playground for the children. They variously describe playing hide and seek on the roof and games in the Dow Gardens, clambering over the chimneys, and taking ballroom dancing lessons and putting on performances in the game room.

The pond invited a multitude of activities. Inspired by Dow, himself a figure skater, the family hosted skating parties there in winter, gliding onto the ice from the lower porch. They also made forts along the pond's perimeter, skimmed the water in a Styrofoam® boat built by Dow or on a heavy wooden raft, and had contests to see who could venture out the farthest onto the studio's stepping stones.

One of the children's secret places was the

Like the studio, the Dow residence was well photographed in the 1940s by noted photographers of the day, such as Bill Hedrich of the firm Hedrich Blessing. Black-and-white photography captured the sculptural quality of Dow's architecture, as can be seen in this view of the trellis wall that distinguishes the house's entrance.

▼

tunnel running between the house and the garage, an eerie place for a Halloween maze (complete with a bubbling cauldron stirred by the housekeeper) and also just for inching along the wall in the dark with friends. Dow's children did not regularly go to his studio, to avoid interrupting the work there, except to walk through his office on their way home from school. But on weekends he might take them to the Submarine Room, the balcony over the reception area, his office, or the workshop to stoke the furnace.

"At the house we had activities that my friends and I could not do elsewhere," remembers Dow's daughter Lloyd Mills. "These were exciting spaces that my friends later told me expanded their lives. Because our home was unlike anyone else's, I was sometimes embarrassed. But the fun we were able to have there was far more important." Dow loved to travel "to meet new people, see new places," his daughter Barbara Carras recalls, "but he always really loved returning home."

The Dow living room is dominated by its sheltering ceiling, which was designed to glow from within. Beneath it, a ribbon of tall windows links the house to nature. The open room annexes space from the dining area and the hallway.

Separated from the living area by a few steps, this cozy nook lends a casual tone to the dining space. High windows provide a viewing platform for the entrance and the old Dow orchards beyond. The bilevel table is a Dow design.

Keeping watch over the dining table is a set of *Saints and Sinners*, quarter-scale bronzes based on Marshall Fredericks's sculptures for the Cranbrook Academy of Art. The raised Unit Block hearth puts the fire at the tabletop level, where it can warm hands and food at the same time.

In the game room on the ground floor, a custom-designed sofa curls around to embrace the fire. Here a niche carved out of the Unit Blocks provides display space for some of the objects in Dow's collection.

The Dow family and friends gathered around the screen at the far end of the game room to watch home movies and other films, which Dow delighted in bringing home for their enjoyment and edification.

Built-in cabinets such as these marking the way to the guest room can be found throughout the house. Lighted shelves show off the Dow pottery collection.

A cantilevered desk beneath built-in shelves adds a practical feature to the guest room. One of Dow's curved-arm side chairs is reflected in the mirrored wall.

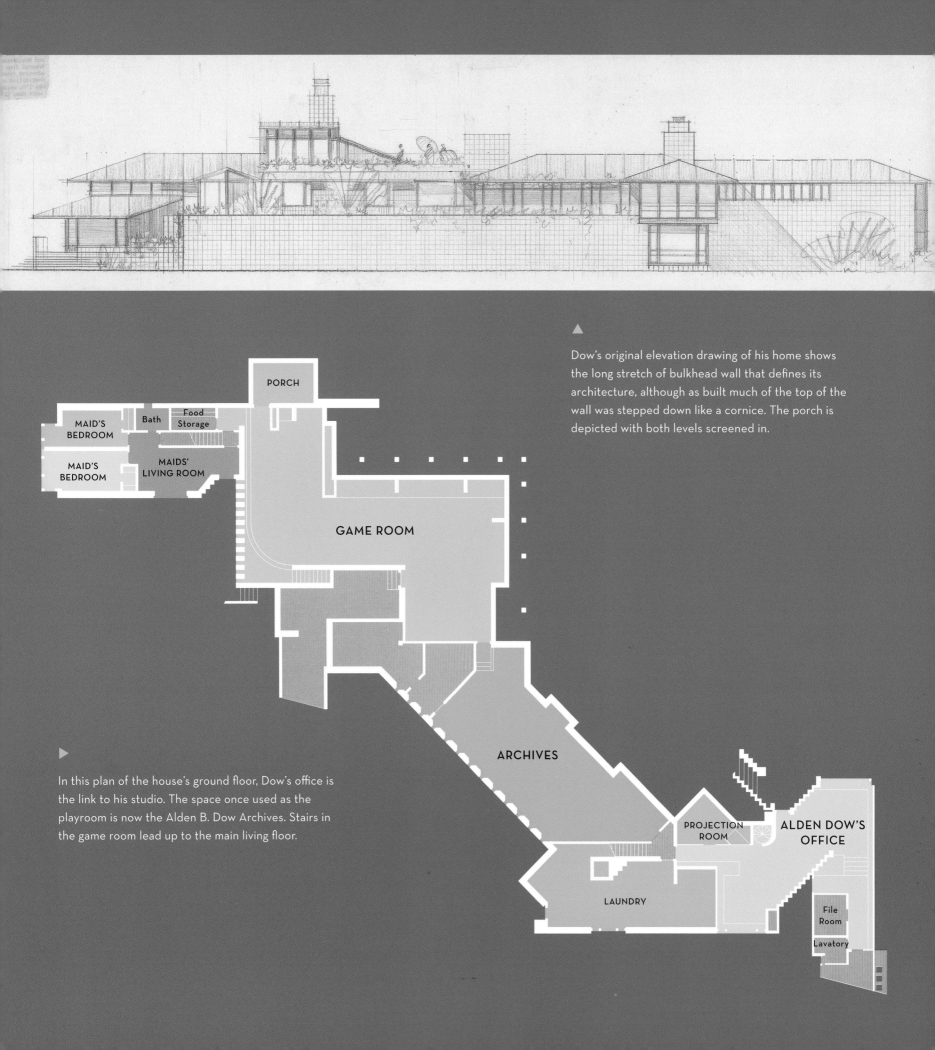

PORCH

MAID'S BEDROOM

MAID'S BEDROOM

Bath

Food Storage

MAIDS' LIVING ROOM

GAME ROOM

ARCHIVES

PROJECTION ROOM

ALDEN DOW'S OFFICE

LAUNDRY

File Room

Lavatory

Dow's original elevation drawing of his home shows the long stretch of bulkhead wall that defines its architecture, although as built much of the top of the wall was stepped down like a cornice. The porch is depicted with both levels screened in.

In this plan of the house's ground floor, Dow's office is the link to his studio. The space once used as the playroom is now the Alden B. Dow Archives. Stairs in the game room lead up to the main living floor.

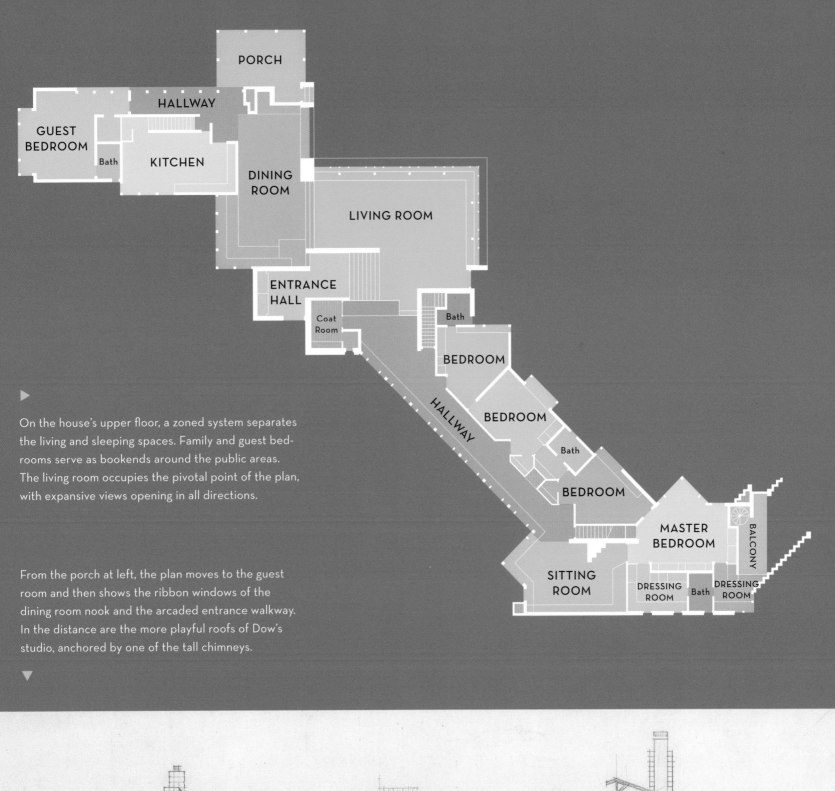

PORCH

GUEST BEDROOM

HALLWAY

Bath

KITCHEN

DINING ROOM

LIVING ROOM

ENTRANCE HALL

Coat Room

Bath

BEDROOM

BEDROOM

HALLWAY

Bath

BEDROOM

SITTING ROOM

MASTER BEDROOM

BALCONY

DRESSING ROOM

Bath

DRESSING ROOM

▶

On the house's upper floor, a zoned system separates the living and sleeping spaces. Family and guest bedrooms serve as bookends around the public areas. The living room occupies the pivotal point of the plan, with expansive views opening in all directions.

From the porch at left, the plan moves to the guest room and then shows the ribbon windows of the dining room nook and the arcaded entrance walkway. In the distance are the more playful roofs of Dow's studio, anchored by one of the tall chimneys.

▼

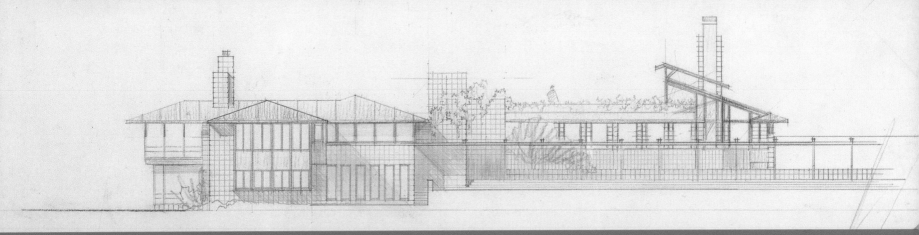

THE ENTRANCE

Although Alden Dow could easily slip from his studio to his home by using a stairway off his office, he did not deprive his family of a formal entrance to their home. Welcoming family and friends, rather than clients, it did not have to be quite as impressive as the one announcing his workplace. A circular driveway skirts the studio complex to arrive at a secluded but nonetheless dynamic front door to the residence.

On the left a peek-a-boo trellis wall of Unit Blocks begins just steps from the doorway to snake into the landscape. In contrast to the solid expanse of blocks on the wall behind it, this lattice screen forms a lacy veil intervening between indoors and outdoors. Alternate units were left out of each course, revealing the blocks' normally hidden angles and symbolizing the freedom of nature.

Perpendicular to this fence, another trellis defines the entrance to the house itself. Wide-spaced columns of Unit Blocks march between the doorway at left and the garage at right to support a covered walkway. Delicate pole lamps balance the sturdy pillars on the opposite side, where the roof overhang provides some shelter for arriving and departing drivers and passengers. "The automobile is a member of the house," declared Dow in 1943. (From the time he ran around town in his homemade childhood buckboard, Dow loved cars almost as much as trains. He progressed to a red Thunderbird that was notorious in Midland. Later he became fascinated with the Mazda rotary engine; he talked about it for months at the office, showing his staff pictures and diagrams.)

The entrance arcade serves to shield the bedroom wing while it closes the last gap in the Home and Studio's courtyard. The columns wend their way off into this inner landscape, segueing into a long zigzag wall topped by a triangular filigree that points toward the studio. At the Dow residence these architectural tendrils embrace nature like the vines and plantings that mark the transition points between the built and the natural worlds.

◄

Starting beneath the dining room's high windows, the trellis wall marks a private zone while forming a picturesque backdrop for Herbert Dow's remaining apple trees. The broad hipped roof over this wing conveys a welcoming sense of shelter (although Dow later wondered if he should have used a more elaborate roof design over the living space).

▶

Dow was adept at shaping his Unit Blocks into delicate forms. To frame his residence, he created a lattice screen by dropping a block from each row in a wall that sits on a low base of two regularly stacked blocks.

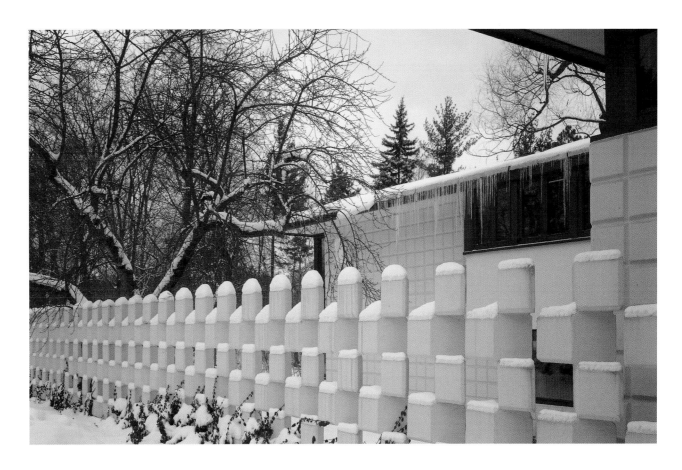

Parallel with the bedroom wing, a zigzag privacy wall divides the Home and Studio's courtyard. An exaggerated pierced trellis sets a triangular motif that recalls the sawtooth roof of the second drafting room.

Unit Blocks were paired and stacked into columns to form a covered arcade leading to the house's front door. Illuminating the way for cars and visitors approaching the house, slender poles hold aloft square light fixtures.

143

Standing at the top of the entry stairs, one can look down toward the game room or up into the living and dining areas. The patterns and colors of the Navajo blanket on the wall, which Dow purchased in New Mexico, complement the decorative elements in the house.

THE ENTRANCE HALL

One is gently shepherded into the Dow home, through the short, wide door of edge-grain fir, with its six horizontal slats of glass (simpler and more private than the studio portal). Without a threshold, the concrete walkway flows smoothly into the floor of the entrance hall. The Unit Block wall opposite the door also repeats the exterior materials to further relate indoors and out. Space is compressed under the low ceiling, pushing one to move forward, where a change in ceiling height suddenly releases the sense of protection. The pull is all upward here—skyward toward the architect's sanctuary.

Drawing the eye to the high ceiling is a brightly colored mobile—a reminder that life, as opposed to architecture, is in a constant state of motion. Dow was fascinated by the mobiles of Alexander Calder he saw in a 1943 exhibition at the Museum of Modern Art, so he came home and tried out his own ideas. Both the shapes and the colors act as counterpoints to the angular blocks behind. Graduated disks and strings of rectangles descend from a solar system of green, blue, yellow, and white orbs, all framed by a quartet of red squares. This abstract universe sways gently with any breeze, creating shifting patterns.

The mobile's primary colors and geometric motifs introduce the architectural palette to come. Thanks to a low wall on the left and the forward momentum to mount the short flight of stairs, the interior landscape soon unfolds. Five levels make themselves known at one glance: the entry, the game room on the ground floor, the living area, the dining area, and the bedroom hallway, separated by a half wall with stair-stepped wooden handles. All the spaces flow naturally from one to the other, channeled by changing floor levels, unobtrusive dividers, and varied colors. Dow made walls vanish in favor of natural ways of signifying different domestic uses. Each area borrows space from its neighbor, making the whole feel much greater than the sum of its parts.

THE LIVING ROOM

The Dows' living area is a garden room in just about every sense. On two sides a band of nearly floor-to-ceiling windows and a door bring the outside in, offering expansive views of greenery and eliminating any desire for competing pictures on the walls. A few of the windows open to allow natural ventilation. Branching overhead is the room's most impressive feature: a cathedral ceiling that diffuses light as a leafy bower might stencil sunshine and moonbeams onto the forest floor. Dow put new technology to work here, specifying that strips of Dow Chemical's Ethocel® plastic be woven into panels and fitted between edge-grain fir ribs; hidden fluorescent tubes supplied the light. Phosphorescence in the yellow-green basket-weave sections made the ceiling glow at night. According to Vada Dow, "You left the lights on for a little while and then turned them off, when the ceiling became bluish. But you didn't really enjoy it unless you just laid down on the floor." It was like watching the moon in the sky, she said. Two men installed the ceiling in just two days, less time than plastering would have taken. Red-tipped handles were added in the mid-1940s to allow the panels to be pulled down. In 1988, after nearly a half century, the ceiling's plastic panels had to be replaced; it is now a slightly different color and has lost its original glow.

The ceiling's spine carries the eye across the full living space and into the raised dining area. Adding to the room's energy, the wood strips change direction at each end. With their common canopy, the two areas are firmly tied together above even though they occupy different levels below; these are signified by carpeting that changes from green in the "garden room" to a red orange in the dining area.

Altogether the combined L-shaped space is about 1,500 square feet. Yet the room feels comfortable because more intimate areas are set apart within the larger environment by furniture groupings in addition to the varied levels. Arts

The combined sofa and two-level, L-shaped table divides the living room into separate conversation areas. Overhead the light-filled ceiling links all the living and dining spaces into one unified composition. Pottery dots the surfaces with rich color and texture.

▲

Seen from the raised dining level, the living area embraces the outdoors with corner walls of windows. With its integral lighting, the ceiling adds cheer even on gray days; its ribs recall the standing seams on the hipped copper roof outside. Tables and chairs were designed on a square motif to mirror Dow's Unit Blocks.

■ NEVER MAKE A ROOM A SIMPLE RECTANGLE WHERE ALL IS SEEN AND UNDERSTOOD AT THE FIRST GLANCE. ■

as a subtle room divider, creating an intimate nook by the window corner and a more open and casual area beyond. Like an island in the room, the two-level table multitasks: as a low end table for the sofa, as a higher buffet board for dinner or cocktail guests, and as an enclosure for pull-out stools that offer extra seating as needed. Its cantilevered planes of wood mimic the room's stairs and add to the overall dynamics. Inset linoleum surfaces reflect the space's rainbow of strong colors. Textures vary as well from hard to soft.

The largest space in the house, this living area was planned for formal entertaining. The Dows could host sixty persons here, spreading up to the built-in seating corner on the dining level. A built-in cabinet for the record player and speakers at the end of the living room showered guests with sound. Among others, these included Fred Waring, the bandleader, and Dave Garroway, the television host. The Dows also entertained their bridge club members for potluck suppers. Vada Dow invited women friends in for tea and welcomed Midland's Monday Club for an annual luncheon, a tradition still being continued. At Thanksgiving and Christmas, her family, the Bennetts, took up two tables in the combined space.

Dow began a lifelong interest in pottery in 1916, when as a boy he became fascinated with the design of a cup and saucer in a gift shop in Ann Arbor. Over the years he collected midcentury American and Scandinavian works, many of which are scattered around his living room like colorful leaves. In shape, color, pattern, and texture, they strike contrasts with the white walls, solid-hued fabrics, and rectilinear forms of the room and become "a natural part of the building." To Dow these sculptural objects added the crucial element of balance, taking care of intellectual needs the way the building took care of the family's physical needs. As he wrote in 1948 to Hillis Arnold, a ceramist at the Cranbrook Academy of Art, "These intellectual needs in their highest form should be inspirations to do more on the part of those that use the building."

and Crafts designers first began to use such flexible, multipurpose spaces at the turn of the twentieth century, and Dow adapted this type of plan for his own residential commissions, even his low-cost houses.

He refined this multiuse approach here by using a built-in sofa and table combination to serve

◀ The living room projects onto a broad terrace overlooking the pond. Here the roof's large overhang metamorphoses into a wooden trellis, blending into nature while adding a link to the wood-lined ceiling inside. "Gardens never end and buildings never begin," said Dow.

▲

Dow's collection includes a Japanese box at top, a clear glass bowl at center, and pottery, at bottom, including three pieces by Harrison Macintosh, an elliptical bowl and a perforated jar by Otto and Gertrude Natzler, and a tall gray vase—all contrasting in size and texture.

THE DINING ROOM

Three broad steps signal the transition from the living area to the dining room. On its high platform, the space is a stage for dining served up on a theatrical red orange carpet. Although the ceiling continues seamlessly at the same height from the living area, the raised level pushes floor and ceiling closer—providing more intimacy for the dining experience.

The dining table is tucked away in its own alcove, affording views of the seating nook and the entrance hall and, in the opposite direction, the terrace outside. The existing teak table is the third designed by Dow and was made by Herman Miller; it expands to seat sixteen. The current upholstered chairs with barrel-shaped arms were most likely designed by Dow. With the lighting integrated into the ceiling, Dow's typical solution, there was no need for a chandelier.

At the diners' eye level is a raised fireplace inserted into a wall of Unit Blocks; wood was stored below. On the ledge, warmed by the embers, is an array of seven quarter-scale bronzes by Dow's friend Marshall Fredericks. Called *Saints and Sinners,* they are smaller replicas of the sculptor's installation at the Cranbrook Academy of Art; among the figures are *Warrior Saint, Temptation, Knowledge of Good and Evil,* and *Saint of the Church.* Nine-foot-tall versions were placed in the Dow Gardens in 1977 and 1978 as a tribute to Alden and Vada Dow.

Where a mirror might have been, on the wall opposite the window, in the 1940s Dow instead installed something unexpected: a map of the world. This makes it easy to guess what the family discussed during mealtimes—to warm up one winter, it was South American countries. (Geography was also on the agenda when they lived in Texas, where Dow likewise had a map on the wall.) The family would often eat lunch here together until the children's school schedules prevented it, even when Dow's business guests were invited to the house.

When Dow spoke during meals, the children listened but were encouraged to share his excitement over new ideas. To this day the three remember lessons about "Honesty, Humility, and Enthusiasm." Conversation ranged over some of their father's precepts, from pursuing constructive rather than destructive ideas to balancing individual and social rightness. Son Michael Dow recalls the positive tone he set, whether talking about a new highway that was not all straight lines, a building he had liked, a visit to the Interlochen Arts Academy, or Karl Haas's music program on the radio. Says Lloyd Mills, "I was drilled by my dad on multiplication tables, which I enjoyed." She adds that her father related that some of his friends' children were allowed to bow out of table conversation if they were not interested in the topic. The Dows' children, however, did not get off so lightly. "Any time I'm tempted to take the easy way out," says daughter Barbara Carras, "I can hear him say, 'Oh, you don't want to do that.' He was first and foremost a philosopher, and his houses and buildings reflect his philosophy of how people should live and work." To this end, the dining room was designed for more than just dining.

◀

A generous built-in sofa fills a corner on the dining level. An end table and a taller shelf running behind the sofa all boldly cantilever from the wall. The glass plate changes the mood from rectilinear to spherical.

▶

The dining alcove, with its world map and *Saints and Sinners* bronzes by Marshall Fredericks, comes into view from the top of the entrance hall's stairs. To the left of the raised fireplace is the door to the porch. The cantilevered ledge in the foreground serves as the end table for the sofa in the nook.

As if picnicking in a forest, feelings of leisure and openness pervade the raised dining area. With few walls, it borrows space from the seating corner, the entrance hall, and the bedroom hallway. On the free-standing bilevel coffee table, books were stored below while the top surface was used for guests' drinks when it was not filled with puzzles or magazines. A bank of elevated windows turns the corner to offer views out to the front driveway.

155

THE KITCHEN

Just behind the dining room's map wall is the
house's spacious and airy kitchen. With its original metal Geneva cabinets, it is a time capsule of
an efficient, upscale midcentury kitchen. Dow in
fact renovated it in 1959, adding the center island
and its inset cooktop.

Rows of gleaming white baked-enamel cabinets
line three sides of the room, above and below
countertops of sleek white laminate. At the far end,
wood paneling around the built-in refrigerator adds
a note of warmth. The wood motif continues in the

frames of the corner windows as well as in a wood
deck that encircles the space. This rectangular feature carries concealed fluorescent lighting over the
sink and counter while serving as a perch for oversized serving dishes. In doing so, it underscores
the complexity of the peaked ceiling here, as in
most of Dow's rooms. On the floor, the yellow
linoleum glows like sunshine.

A breakfast table and its built-in bench use the
windows' light to good advantage, but the family
did not view this as an eat-in kitchen. It was the
province of the family's cook. She could use the
adjacent stairway to reach the food storage area

A bright yellow floor
introduces one of the
primary colors that
Dow preferred.
Windows above the
breakfat nook look
out onto the front
entrance of the house.

on the ground level. Next to it downstairs is the staff apartment where the cook lived, including two bedrooms, a living room, and a bathroom.

Dow's daughter Lloyd Mills recalls that sometimes her father would give the cook just a five-minute warning that he was bringing someone to lunch. For meals he would contribute fresh provisions from his vegetable garden, harvesting peas, radishes, and lettuce; the corn was picked just before everyone was ready to sit down, the pot already set to boil. Dow relished his chances to get in the kitchen—to make hollandaise sauce for broccoli and asparagus, to broil steak, or, on

the cook's night off, to swirl chocolate frosteds in the blender. He was a light eater but had a wide range of favorites: chicken Kiev, oysters (in stew, fried, or Rockefeller), peach and strawberry shortcake with lots of whipped cream, and anything with chocolate. And frog's legs. As recalled by Fern Thomas, who was the family's cook for many years: "There was a place down in Flint that he used to go to get frog's legs with a friend. I tried doing it, and I would either get them not crispy enough or they'd be too crispy. I never could master that one. He said they were good, but not quite like the place in Flint."

Seen at the right from the living room trellis, the simple woodwork of the screened porch off the dining room replicates this delicate arbor. A door leads down two steps to the terrace, which visually enlarges the living area and the bedrooms.

▶

The view of the porch from across the pond shows the lattice of Unit Blocks that replaced the original screening on the lower level. Dow's change added visual weight to the structure while recalling the trellis wall at the entrance.

THE SCREENED PORCH

Underscoring the house's easy relationship with nature, Dow placed doors at almost every turn to provide access to the open air. One such portal, through a broad wood door just to the left of the dining room fireplace, leads to the retreat that put the family most in touch with the water ringing the home. This exceptionally wide door—it has been called "a passageway to nature"—opens onto the screened porch.

The porch is cantilevered over the pond, suspended like a tree house. Sheer copper mesh screens this outdoor room, with only a few delicate rails and posts to secure it. Otherwise the vista toward the Dow Gardens is unencumbered. Broad eaves on the hipped copper roof shield occupants from the weather. On a sunny day ripples from the pond reflect dancing patterns inside the porch.

The lower level was originally screened as well, but Dow later decided to encase it in Unit Blocks to support the cantilevered porch above. Repeating the lacy screen at the front of the house, the blocks are staggered to alternate solids and voids. This lightens the mass and adds visual interest while creating a platform for the upper porch.

Dow was bothered by muskrats whose construction work undermined the banks of the pond. "For a while," recounts his daughter Barbara Carras, "he even sat on the porch, B.B. gun in hand, until one day a muskrat sailed across the pond holding a big flower. Dad said that he must be taking it to his lady love—and he never bothered the muskrats again." It is pleasing to picture the architect in his elevated garden folly, doing battle to preserve his pond.

▶

Sitting on a carpet patterned like the house's Unit Blocks is a sofa as well as a selection of metal mesh chairs by Harry Bertoia, all from 1953: tall Bird chairs with footstools, low Diamond chairs, and dining chairs around a door turned into a table.

THE GUEST BEDROOM

The bedrooms on the second floor are carefully zoned into two areas: the family's rooms on the south side, off the living room, and the guest bedroom at the other end of the house, on the north side beyond the dining room, kitchen, and porch. This arrangement ensured privacy for both guests and family while giving the guest room its own verdant location slipped into the old Dow orchards.

A long hallway heightens the anticipation, its compressed ceiling signifying that a private space is ahead. Beneath a bank of windows, built-in wood cabinets provide surfaces on which to display part of the family's collections. An array of family photographs occupies the opposite wall.

The suite announces itself with a bright blue wall behind a built-in desk, a hint of an explosion of color to come. In the guest bedroom the sky is always blue, thanks to a breakaway ceiling exposing a peak that seems to open the room to the universe. Running around this mock skylight is a wood deck that holds decorative objects above and downlights below.

The hallway leading to the guest room was turned into a gallery for treasured family glassware, pottery, and photographs. A clean line of storage cabinets and windows points the way for guests along the hall.

When daughter Lloyd had more than one friend in to stay the night, the girls slept in the guest room's immense bed. The carpet continues the red orange hue begun in the dining area.

The guest bedroom's most notable feature is its dense blue sky of a ceiling. Downlights poised over the floor-level wood sill twinkle like stars. The blue desk chair is one of Dow's designs.

A broad picture window on the far wall is supplemented on the adjacent wall by a row of smaller operable windows resting on cabinets, both of which continue the line created in the hallway. Instead of adding another large window here, Dow installed the next best thing: a floor-to-ceiling mirror that visually expands the room's size and reflects light inside. It was a gift to guests—a little surprise left by the owner.

Another surprise is the size of the bed. To fill the room, the largest bedroom in the house, two double beds are pushed together and unified with a padded headboard of striped cloth. Placed directly in front of the picture window, the bed allowed for plenty of daydreaming. Long pulls operate a pair of square wooden reading lights attached to the ceiling's wood deck.

Cantilevered ledges above the corner desk and along the side of the cabinets offer yet more display space. In the room is a sensuous Georg Jensen pitcher, designed by Henning Koppel about 1956, which is part of the family's collection.

THE CHILDREN'S ROOMS

The second floor's entire southern wing was set aside for the Dow family's personal use. Designed seven years after the notorious kidnapping and murder of Charles and Anne Morrow Lindbergh's baby, it was also a secure place for the Dows' three young children. Lined up in a row, their bedrooms and their parents' bedroom all connect; the internal doorways do not lock, although the doors to the hall do. Today the rooms look different than they did when the children were growing up in the 1940s and 1950s because the Dows, like many parents, redecorated when Michael, Lloyd, and Barbara left home—changing carpet colors, among other things.

The family suite lies beside a long hallway that begins to the right of the entrance hall. It is raised two steps, emphasizing the wing's separation from the rest of the house. The hall first passes the powder room, called the coat room on the building plans, with a built-in cabinet and a baby grand piano marking its entrance. A little farther along is a door opening on stairs to the roof, giving Michael particularly easy access to this play area because his bedroom is the first in line.

Vada Dow recalled that her husband would phone her from his office to discuss whether the children's rooms should be small or large. Later in life, she said that she would have asked him to make them larger if she had known that the three would actually like to be in their own rooms so much. In the 1930s few people spent much time in bedrooms other than to sleep, but with the advent of record players and television, children—including the Dows'—began to drift away from some communal family activities.

The three bedrooms share similar features and details, some added over the years as the children's needs changed. For one, the rooms are irregularly shaped, roughly five sided if not equilateral pentagons in form. Picture windows offer views onto the terrace; narrow side windows were a response to security concerns after the Lindberghs' loss. Closets and drawers are built in.

In 1941, the year the Dows were finally able to move into their new home, Lloyd was four, Barbara was only a few months old, and Michael was six.

When they posed for their picture in Texas about 1943, the Dow children proved that bookcases can be multifunctional. They stacked themselves in alternating rows just like Alden Dow's Unit Blocks.

The bedroom hallway's ceiling is compressed to convey a sense of intimacy, yet a full-length run of windows opens it wide to the landscaped courtyard. A storage ledge rests on carpet as green as grass, a continuation of the living room floor covering.

In Michael Dow's bedroom, a mirror next to the broad picture window adds a touch of trompe l'oeil fun. Very narrow operable windows are behind the curtains at left and right. The wood band below the ceiling incorporates ornament directly into the walls.

▶

Handsome dresser drawers and closets of edge-grain fir were built into Michael's room. By using wood for the pulls and handles, Dow created a nearly seamless wall. Doors lead to the hall and the bathroom.

In Michael's bathroom, the intensity of the strawberry red, a color he liked, is heightened by its contrast with the white ceramic tile floor and the white fixtures. Elongated sconces light the mirror above the sink.

Each also has shelves on which to display treasures as well as a built-in desk added to encourage studying. Ledges under the windows carry the heating and cooling vents. Wood bands circle the rooms to tie together all the built-in elements. Mirrors fool the eye into perceiving the spaces as larger than they are. The bathrooms—Michael had his own, while the girls shared one in between their rooms—feature the richly colored tile that Dow liked to use, Mike's in strawberry red and Lloyd and Barbara's in a sylvan green.

When the family settled into the house in 1941, Barbara, the third child, was a baby. For a while she and her nurse occupied what was to be Michael's room. After he moved in, it grew to include typical childhood clutter representing his interests, among them model airplanes. After Michael and Lloyd simultaneously caught the measles, their mother sat between their rooms reading to them.

Lloyd's bedroom next door at one time had a purple and gold decor when she was permitted to have a say in its decorative scheme. She remembers putting together model airplanes and working on her stamp collection, messy hobbies that at least once spilled out into the hallway on long tables when cousins came over. For her freshman year in high school, she went off to the private Leelanau School on Lake Michigan, where Michael was enrolled as a junior.

The Dows wanted Barbara, as the youngest, to be next to their own suite. Her room, like the others, evolved over the years. Its end wall of built-in drawers and a door was a later addition, as was the desk. This door opened not into a closet but directly into her parents' room. Barbara, who finished high school in Midland, did not care for the original pink carpet in the room, so at one point she chose pink and purple striped curtains to ameliorate the effect.

As Lloyd reflected on the children's years in the Midland house, she noted: "My mother didn't tell us until years later that when Mike and I went away, she found it difficult to walk past our bedroom doors."

Looking into Lloyd's room, the open doors show the easy flow of space from one bedroom to another. Just beyond is a dressing area opposite the bathroom that the two girls shared.

▼

▲

Lloyd had an imaginary musical friend she named Moni Fago, who was immortalized by her father on the exterior wall outside her room.

▶

Tile recalling the green of the hall carpet distinguishes the girls' bathroom, accessed between their two bedrooms. A mirrored dressing area lines the passageway opposite the door.

The desk and the built-in drawers on the far wall were
added to Barbara's room as she grew older; the adjacent
translucent panel glows with behind-the-scenes lighting.
The "secret" door leads to the Dows' bedroom. Here
again a mirror visually expands the space and adds
a touch of good-natured confusion as to what is where.

THE MASTER BEDROOM

The Dows' master bedroom suite serves as the exclamation point at the end of the line of the family bedrooms. Nonetheless it generally continues the economical architectural features and decoration seen in the preceding children's rooms, with a few twists. Included in the suite is the airy bedroom as well as separate dressing areas for Vada and Alden Dow and a shared bathroom.

The bedroom itself is rectangular for the most part, the exception being that the corners nearest the pond are rotated forty-five degrees to achieve a floor-to-ceiling triangular bay window. Befitting the room's role as the Dows' own space, the peaked ceiling shows the complexity seen in major public areas of the Home and Studio. Up-lighting embedded in the substantial wood deck encircling the room adds a burst of brightness to the ceiling, highlighting its foil wallpaper covered in grass cloth; the wallpaper—a rare sight in a house by Dow—was added about 1950. After his death in 1983, Vada Dow removed one of the two beds originally in the room. Above the bed, a cloth "headboard" rises to meet a strip of windowlike wood-framed mirrors, more evidence of Dow's sense of play.

Behind the bed wall is the well-appointed dressing and bath area. As in the children's rooms, built-in closets and drawers simplify the lines of the dressing areas, eliminating the need for freestanding furniture. Vada's area features a long vanity under a mirror and windows, all kept low for sitting. Dow gave himself a corner window from which he could look down to his original drafting room.

In more closets lining one side of the bedroom Alden Dow kept his own clothes. It was a wardrobe as innovative and distinctive as his architecture. Bored by the drabness and uniformity of typical men's clothing, he flouted tradition by designing his own suits and vests. "He never had an ordinary vest on," remembered his sister Dorothy Dow Arbury. "Everything was just a little different." According to her, he thought, "'Why wear something if you don't like it? Design your own.'" His functional vests had long tacked-down lapels, a distinctive

side zipper, and slashes of pockets that were perfect for holding pencils, drawing tools, and notes; buttons were discarded because they got caught in his drafting materials. Dow favored bright colors for shirts under a sports jacket or for a tie (purple, for example). A spot of red might appear in his pocket linings or the cuffs of his suit trousers. Balanced, uplifting colors—that was the template for both his buildings and his own haberdashery.

The architect also let his sense of humor play out in the various forms of ingress and egress he allowed himself here. A Dutch door leads out onto the terrace, where a set of narrow stairs would let him escape to the water. A circular metal stairway spirals up from his office to a balcony outside the bedroom suite, allowing a quick getaway to or from the studio. And a floating wooden stairway took the railroad engineer up over the family's sitting room to monitor the progress of his trains as they traveled through this part of the house.

◄

In the Dows' bedroom, the most complex feature is the peaked ceiling, which terminates in a deep wood deck circumnavigating the room. Shelves are built into walls and the dressing areas behind the bed. The central opening leads to the family's sitting room, while the door at right opens onto the stairs Dow used to reach his train tracks over the sitting room.

▶

Covering the master bedroom's bay window are Mondrian-like drapes in the primary colors that Dow favored, similar to ones in the game room downstairs. Out of sight to the left is the door into Barbara's bedroom and at right a Dutch door to the terrace.

The trousers that Dow designed for himself were beltless and suspenderless. He favored tweeds and dark tones for his suits, which were typically hand-tailored by haberdashers in Grand Rapids and Saginaw. The hat on the built-in dresser in the dressing area testifies to another sartorial passion of his.

Dow was photographed in the 1950s wearing a vest of his own design. These custom items zipped up on the side and featured long, suitlike lapels. The architect did not like buttons that interfered with his work.

Vada Dow's dressing area features a built-in vanity designed at chair height as well as integral closets and dressers. Beyond is Dow's own dressing area, which also has a low basin. The couple's shared bathroom in between is tiled in a pheasant brown whose richness is a match for the colors used in the children's bathrooms.

The pondside terrace was never more than a few steps from the Dows' living quarters. At the far left is a white fountain that Dow designed to resemble petals; water gently cascades down an alternating series of spouts.

The terrace side of the Dows' bedroom suite was angled to provide an unobstructed view back toward the living room as well as down to the pond. The roof here projects forward to offer protection from sun and rain. In the foreground is one of Dow's naturalistic lanterns.

THE SITTING ROOM

Much of the family's private life together, other than their meals, took place in the sitting room adjacent to the Dows' bedroom suite. It was the gathering place closest to all four bedrooms, offered inviting warmth from a central hearth, and provided expansive views out to the courtyard and the old orchards beyond. The Christmas tree was here. And this is where the train buffs in the house came to ply their trade.

The sitting room started out to be Vada Dow's study but evolved into the family room. It is a whimsically shaped space inside and out, one of the most playful rooms in the residence. Where the living and dining area seems majestic, this is cozy and casual. The plan pivots around the fire-place, whose hearth of Unit Blocks points toward a glass-filled bay. This one-and-a-half-story wall of wood-framed windows, projecting toward the entrance arcade like the house's prow, was the best place in the house to watch the sunset. The other

A table for tea and games occupies the sitting room's prime space in front of the soaring glass prow. The space opens in several directions: to the courtyard, down the hall, and up through the wooden lattice to the train loft.

two walls are filled by bookcase-topped storage cabinets and a built-in desk.

The best surprise awaits above. Much of the ceiling dissolves into a lattice of woodwork—there but not there, intimate yet open. It rests at normal ceiling height but pulls one's gaze skyward, to apple-green walls reflecting the carpet. Here in the loft, Dow installed an oval track on plywood so that everyone could enjoy the thrill of seeing trains chug along their way, emerging from one tunnel and disappearing into another on their journey through the master bedroom and his office. As Dow might have asked, Who says that architecture has to be static?

Michael helped his father operate the trains when he got older. Barbara liked to play in the loft, which she called her "office," while her mother worked below at her desk. For Lloyd, who also played with dolls in the loft, the room came alive at Christmas. "The house was magical, with the Christmas tree sparkling with lights and silver tinsel in the sitting room." The feeling spilled over into other rooms, she recalled: "Candles in glass bowls were set along the wall above the front door, the dining room table was lighted with colored candles, and records of Christmas carols were heard throughout the upstairs."

The fireplace glows within and without, aided by shimmering gold wallpaper. Like other Dow fireplaces, it lacks any hint of a traditional mantel. An Eames lounge chair and ottoman by the bookcase wall underscore the room's role as a library.

▶

The lattice ceiling expands the view upward while making Dow's model trains visible as they move along the elevated track (one is visible at the upper left).

◄

A hanging bubble light by George Nelson glows at night like a full moon. An evergreen outside recalls the Christmas trees the family placed here in their sitting room.

▶

From the exterior the sitting room window resembles a partial octagon, a view reinforced by the broad side overhangs of the roof. Another of Dow's fanciful chimneys crowns the projecting space, this one made of tall interlocking stacks of blocks embracing a copper shaft. The door at the bottom right leads to the laundry room downstairs.

▶ Several years before designing his own home, Dow had used glass blocks, a staple of the International Style, for a two-story wall in the Pryor House (1936) in Grosse Pointe Park. In his own game room, he softened the effect by inserting just single rows of glass in between columns made of Unit Blocks.

▲ When the sectional sofa was red in the 1940s and 1950s, the Dows' daughter Barbara would throw slumber parties in this nook by the fireplace. Laminate-topped hexagonal tables made of plywood were easily moved or pushed together.

▲ Dow turned the game room wall into sculpture simply by leaving a series of voids to point the way toward his home theater. During parties—for his office staff, for example—votive candles would be placed inside the niches to festively light the space.

THE GAME ROOM

Nearly hidden in the house's entrance hall is a narrow, mysterious stairway that leads in a straight shot downstairs. Ahead is a true light screen: a wall of Unit Blocks interrupted just enough to allow stacks of light to filter in through glass blocks repeating the same geometric rhythm. This perforated wall announces the game room, one of two family spaces that fill most of the house's ground-floor level. It shares the generous L-shaped footprint of the living and dining area directly above it. And like it, space here also flows around corners, only slowly revealing the intimate nooks found within.

In the days before television, the family had to make its own entertainment—a task that Alden Dow was only too happy to embrace. He produced the most exuberantly cheerful room in the house as well as a good deal of the entertainment that took place in it. The quiet stairway, landing on a stepped curved platform of unfinished and thus more natural concrete, explodes into a burst of color, pattern, and expectations of fun. Balance comes from the playful juxtaposition of primary colors against the pure white Unit Blocks, of sinuous circles against hard edges. "Too much of any one color upsets the human equilibrium," Dow instructed.

In one area a horseshoe-shaped sectional sofa snuggles into a long rectangular space, its rounded back adding a welcoming counterpoint. The seating group focuses on a fireplace aligned with the one in the dining area upstairs. To the right, a mantel, if one can call it that, provides space in a lighted niche for displays of brass and copper objects to capture the fire's light. On the other side of the hearth, a door leads out onto the porch's lower level and then to the pond.

The sofa's curve mirrors the arc of the concrete platform, but an even more dominant circular form unfurls underneath. Abstract art of a kind that Dow may have seen when he first lived in New York in the 1920s fills the carpet with intersecting

forms of pure color. The disks recall the mobile marking the house's entrance hall on the level above, only lowered to let its pleasures be experienced underfoot. Circles float like balloons, coming to rest on squares and rectangles and bouncing into exclamation points. Originally the floor was covered in linoleum; in the 1970s Dow replaced the harder surface with carpeting replicating the original tones of yellow, green, red orange, blue, and dark purple on a field of off-white.

A blaze of two dozen bare ceiling lights—an overhead marquee whose colors can be easily changed—pulls the eye toward the room's far end, to the Dows' own little theater. Here the family shared the home movies that Dow loved to make and watched some commercial films he brought home. "Dad's movies were always popular, with Beethoven's Pastoral Symphony as the accompaniment," remembers Lloyd Mills, who also tried out Dow's shadow dances, called Somnophonics, with her friends. The audience could sit on the front-row, built-in green sofa or farther back on a balcony of chairs; a coffee table and side ledges provided places to put popcorn and soda.

Looking down on this scene is a fanciful montage of life-size figures in period dress—a reminder of one of the festive costume parties the Dows threw in their home in the 1960s. The occasion was the eightieth birthday of Eva Bennett, Vada Dow's mother. All eight of the Bennett children are depicted in the mural, with Vada in a yellow and blue gown on the left of the reigning Earl and Eva Bennett. Even after the party, the figures seemed too much fun to remove.

▲ No one could be surprised that the theatrical Dow would build a theater in his own home, a precursor of today's increasingly popular installations. The curtain reprises the geometric motifs seen in the master bedroom's window covering—a De Stijl pattern translated into textiles. It opened to reveal a retractable screen on which the family watched movies.

◄

The colorful carpet in the downstairs game room hopscotches toward the space's theater end, which is enlivened by a group of figures representing Vada Dow's family. The striped wall at left hides storage as well as mechanical units to heat and cool the house; air conditioning was added in the 1980s.

◄

A small projection room was built behind the theater's sitting area to show movies to family and friends. The projector was often fed with some of Dow's 16 mm films.

THE PLAYROOM

Of all the spaces in the Dow house, the play-room has changed the most. Only a few reminders hint at its earlier uses. An old black-and-white photograph on the counter (reproduced below) shows children at work and play here, documenting its early incarnation as a progressive nursery and elementary school. Three tiers of tracks filling the walls with Dow's trains and, above them, gatherings of mechanical toys in the compact window openings testify to its use much later as the architect's own playroom. Today, amid the trains and the toys, the space houses the Alden B. Dow Archives, where Dow's project records, correspondence, drawings, photographs, and films are stored.

At first the Dow children played in this unfinished "basement" built of double cement-block walls (for sound insulation) between a thick concrete ceiling and a wood floor. Like similar spaces in Dow's own clients' homes, it was left

In the 1940s the Dows' playroom welcomed Midland youngsters to the innovative Parents' and Children's School run by Vada Dow. Here they painted and learned by doing.

▼

What Alden Dow's toys, new when he purchased them, all had in common was that they moved. Whether racer or clown, duck or Howdy Doody, it was their mechanical nature that fascinated him. "We all enjoyed seeing him with wind-up toys," says his daughter Lloyd Mills. "He gave them to us as presents, or we gave them to him."

"to do." For a time the room was filled with the children's rocking horses and toys. Vada Dow also used it briefly in the 1940s for her Parents' and Children's School, attended by daughter Lloyd for kindergarten; the second grade was taught in the studio's workshop. Tables for ping pong and bumper pool and for airplane models eventually took over the space.

After his children were grown, Dow began to make the room his own. In the late 1960s and early 1970s, he brought in the trains he had long collected and had three levels of tracks laid for them in a point-to-point system. Then he added a wall where the game room's backstage area had been, separating it from the rest of the house so he could control the temperature and humidity; here he stored his 16 mm films and photographs. Dow created a third room at the rear as a workshop for train repairs and photo editing. He made the trains run through the walls of these three rooms and upstairs into the sitting room.

Receipts in Dow's files document some of his model train conquests. His goal was to purchase a replica of each key steam engine used in the United States. The collection, inventoried by wheel arrangement (such as 2–6–0 or 4–6–6–4, indicating lead, driving, and trailing wheels), is concentrated in O-gauge locomotives but includes a number of specialty cars, from a winged snowplow to Pullman passenger cars to a joyful circus train. A few by Lionel are toy trains, rather than scale models, including a streamlined 1936 Union Pacific passenger train with four coaches and an observation car. Dow also took an interest in efforts to preserve some of Michigan's old working steam engines.

In 1986 Vada Dow established the Alden B. Dow Archives to provide a resource on her husband's work. Two years later, what was originally an unfinished basement and then a playroom and a classroom became the repository for the life's work of the architect. In the center of the room, a large countertop was built over drawers in which his drawings are preserved. A state-of-the-art storage and cataloguing system, including environmental temperature and humidity controls, protects and manages a comprehensive collection of archival materials. In 2000 the American Institute for Conservation of Historic and Artistic Works and Heritage Preservation honored the Home and Studio for the care of these collections and the house itself.

◀ Although the Dow children's playroom has been adapted to accommodate the Alden B. Dow Archives, the architect's model trains remain against the far wall. Some of his mechanical toys fill the low window niches. The mural at left is a contemporary addition to the space.

▲

In a 1970 photograph, Dow is dressed in a train engineer's uniform given to him by his staff. "The picture of me in that railroad hat, goggles and red bandanna tickles me every time I go by it," he wrote to Jackson B. Hallett, one of his architects.

183

My father had a thought ... that
He said if you
or in other wo
gardening. La
peared behind planted areas. A p
bu
T
winding its way
to lead you on
it
He used this i
areas were always arranged so tha
areas. A po
nev
winding its w
a
to lead you on because that is th

My father had a thought … that has been a real inspiration for me. He said if you can see all of a thing from one position, it lacks appeal, or in other words, lasting expression. He used this idea in landscape gardening. Lawn areas were always arranged so that they disappeared behind planted areas. A pool of water was never a rectangle, but a ribbon path winding its way through planted and open areas. The effect of this is to lead you on because that is the only way to see it or understand it.

THE DOW GARDENS

■ In the 1970s the only thing separating Alden Dow's home from the Dow Gardens was a whimsical wooden footbridge crossing the pond outside his studio office. This is where, in his autumn years, Dow turned his sights. Here in this sylvan oasis he remembered as a boy running under the tree branches, canoeing and skating on its ponds, and enthusiastically embracing this unparalleled "back lot" transformed by Herbert Dow. Returning in the last decade of his life to work on the gardens allowed the architect to refine his father's accomplishments and secure what he thought was Herbert Dow's overlooked legacy as a horticulturalist. ■ Dow seldom failed to credit his father with giving him one of his chief architectural inspirations. "He said if you can see all of a thing from one position, it lacks appeal, or in other words, lasting expression." This was a lesson Herbert Dow himself learned as he shaped the gardens behind his home to tantalize with winding paths

ALL IN THE FAMILY

and to surprise by making lawns appear larger and anything but expected. ■ The Dow Gardens had opened to visitation in 1931, marking its transition from Herbert Dow's hobby and his family's private sphere to a public space. Elzie Cote and later his son Roy Cote continued to maintain the gardens, making few changes. By the start of the 1970s, the Herbert H. and Grace A. Dow Foundation, chaired by Willard Dow's son, Herbert H. Dow II, decided that modifications and improvements were needed to keep the garden vibrant and attract more than the three to four thousand visitors who then came each year. Alden Dow, his active work for his firm winding down, was eager to help. A plan was prepared in conjunction with a landscape consultant, and a horticulturalist, Douglas Chapman, was hired in 1974. ■ New features began to revitalize the Dow Gardens. A meandering stream was carved out along the eastern boundary in 1974. Pine stumps lining the old pathway were replaced with more pleasing rugged boulders. A rolling meadow dubbed the Bumps was sculpted in an area called the Pines. Not far away is a statue that Alden Dow had copied in 1926 from a sprite designed by Frank Lloyd Wright and Alfonso Ianelli for Midway Gardens (1915); it was one of his father's experiments with magnesite cement. A sixty-foot-square conservatory—a low glass pyramid with Dow's signature broad sheltering roof—opened in 1976 and a proper visitors center in 1979. New bridges also began to span the garden's hills and vales, adding distinctive architectural counterpoints to balance the natural beauty. In sensibility if not in outward appearance, the gardens maintained the oriental aspect that drew Herbert Dow to Japan in 1923 to learn more about the Japanese way of gardening. ■ Alden Dow frequently expressed irritation when people underplayed his father's role in creating the Dow Gardens or suggested that they had been designed by a family friend, Paul Tono, a young Japanese landscape architect whom the Dows met on their voyage following Tono's graduation from Cornell University. Two years later, in 1925, Herbert Dow invited Tono, who had gained renown for his work on Tokyo's parks, to come to Midland to help townspeople develop their own residential gardens, and Tono and the Dows kept in touch over a half century. "The Dow Gardens didn't pretend to be a finished idea," Alden Dow wrote a friend in 1969. Instead, he noted, they were "strictly an outlet for my father's creative interest in gardening and no outside experts ever laid a hand on them." The architect's work in the 1970s kept them all in the family. ■

Preceding page: Alden Dow's Home and Studio is linked to the Dow Gardens through history, family ties, and a fanciful wooden footbridge that he could see from his office. Outlined in red, it was just the sort of functional fun that the architect thoroughly enjoyed.

Alden and Dorothy Dow almost disappear beneath the towering Stump Cut wall, formed about 1918 of pines removed from the garden ponds. The trees' resin helped glue them tightly into artificial hills until the stumps were replaced with boulders in 1973.

Canoes and rowboats could be seen gliding through the quiet ponds in the 1920s. Here Alden Dow navigates from the back of a canoe decorated with Indian motifs.

The home of Willard Dow, Grace and Herbert Dow's elder son, backed up to the Dow Gardens and shared an imaginative rock-strewn landscape. His Tudoresque house would never be mistaken for one of his brother's projects, although Alden Dow designed alterations for it in 1934.

The Dows' visit to Japanese gardens in 1923 may have inspired this gently arched wooden truss bridge added to the Dow Gardens about 1925. It crossed the pond by the family swimming pool, leading to a path now called the Jungle Walk. Alden Dow photographed his nieces Ruth Hale and Dorothy Doan enjoying the playful crossing.

The openwork stick bridge in the maze was a good place for boys to hang out around 1918 but was taken down in the 1960s.

As a boy Alden Dow paddled a canoe beneath this picturesque arched span (he is visible by the arch's right side). It was built around 1904 using clinkers salvaged from The Dow Chemical Company. When Dow had to replace it in 1979, he retained the arch shape for his Sun Bridge.

For the first half century, the gardens' most modern-looking span was the concrete footbridge Alden Dow designed to connect his brother Willard's new home to the family gardens. It was built in 1927 while Alden was still a student at Columbia University, but it was removed around 1974, after the house was sold and the bridge then led onto private property.

To replace the original stick bridge in the maze, Dow designed a mazelike ribbon of concrete in 1975. Five decades earlier he had also turned to concrete, one of his favorite materials, for Willard Dow's bridge.

COMPOSED LANDSCAPE

"The Dow Gardens, as you see them today, are basically the same as my father designed them," said Alden Dow in 1978, as the revitalization of the Dow Gardens was under way. From Herbert Dow's eight acres of "pine stump lands" behind his home, he and his successors grew a world-renowned garden now encompassing 110 acres. Planted with 1,700 varieties of plants and trees, contrasting landscapes welcome spring with tulips and daffodils, magnolias and spectacular crab apples. Summer comes in with viburnum and lilacs, followed by rhododendrons and azaleas. Roses bloom from June through October, when the mature trees—maples, ash, dogwood, lindens, oaks, and birches—start to mix their color with the continuing array of perennials. In the winter, colorful witchhazel pokes through the snow.

Some two hundred thousand visitors each year start out in the Alden Dow–designed visitors center (1979) and meander down the Stream Walk and through the Boulder Pass, past the waterfall, and toward Dow's glass-sheathed greenhouse (1975). A Jungle Walk leads into the Homestead Area east of Herbert and Grace Dow's home. Beyond is the Color Garden, where walking on the grass is encouraged. Across the pond is the maze, one of the garden's oldest features, as well as the sculpted Bumps, Marshall Fredericks's *Leaping Gazelle* statue beside a reflecting pool dedicated to Herbert H. Dow II, and an overlook near Alden Dow's Home and Studio. The newest section, called the Exploration Garden, was carved from thirty acres bequeathed by Vada Dow upon her

Backed by some of the Dow Gardens' second-growth pines and venerable crab apples, banks of spring tulips zigzag across the lawn, which is contoured here to attract attention and compel a response. "Lawn areas were always arranged so that they disappeared behind planted areas," said Alden Dow in describing his father's naturalistic approach to landscape design.

This boulder-lined path replaced the old Stump Cut in 1973. It winds fluidly through the gardens, begging visitors to follow. As with the gardens' snaking water features, Dow pointed out, "The effect of this is to lead you on because that is the only way to see it or understand it."

In the late 1970s an old field in the gardens was transformed into sculpted lawns and appropriately dubbed the Bumps. On the same ground Herbert Dow had grown livestock crops at the turn of the century.

death on October 8, 1991; at its heart is an interactive Children's Garden designed to continue the process of learning about the natural world. A separate area, named Whiting Forest, was opened in 2004.

Linked by ponds and streams from the same source, the Dow Gardens and Alden Dow's Home and Studio form an exceptional union representing several generations of Dows. Along one side is the home where a young boy decided to become an architect, and at the opposite corner are key products of that career: Dow's visionary Midland Center for the Arts and the modern library dedicated to his mother, Grace Dow. Homes of other family members are nearby. It is a composed landscape of the highest order.

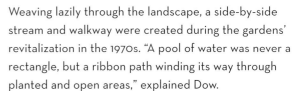

Weaving lazily through the landscape, a side-by-side stream and walkway were created during the gardens' revitalization in the 1970s. "A pool of water was never a rectangle, but a ribbon path winding its way through planted and open areas," explained Dow.

BUILDING BRIDGES

Dow's wonderful sense of architectural humor is most evident in a series of new bridges he added to the Dow Gardens in the 1970s. A half century earlier he had gotten his feet wet, architecturally speaking, by building two bridges, starting his career with a cubistic crossing for the sixth green of Midland's golf course in 1927; he called it "more sculpture than structure." That same year his Art Deco bridge trying out "the modern French style" linked Willard Dow's home to the family gardens.

As the garden spans that Herbert Dow had erected began to wear out or needs changed, new bridges were required. In 1974 he designed two of his most arresting bridges, both alluding to red wooden spans seen in Japanese gardens. His father, said Dow, "found Japanese gardens sympathetic to his ideas and thus anything Japanese became to the whole family an example of good composition." To replace a stepping-stone span in the northwestern part of the gardens, Dow produced a rigorously geometric design using steel but adding a shot of lacquer-bright red to balance the greens of the gardens. To bridge a pond near his new greenhouse, Dow created a two-part span that floats over the water in a stepped arch, its risers and delicate railings in the same red. A 1977 extension to the first bridge continued the same spare lines. All of these designs, as well as the red-trimmed wooden footbridge visible from Dow's office, recall the stickwork of several original bridges in the Dow Gardens. When it came time in 1979 to replace his father's original clinker bridge at the heart of the gardens, Dow retained the graceful

▶

The 1974 Lower Pond Bridge leading to the greenhouse in the Dow Gardens ranks among the architect's most memorable constructions. Like other spans he added in the 1970s, its sticklike form recalls some of the earlier bridges in the gardens, while its jolt of primary color seems to acknowledge Asian influences.

◄ Fresh snow highlights the color choice of Dow's 1977 Pond Bridge Extension. The railing cascades downward into squares, Dow's trademark. To lead to the new Exploration Garden, another red bridge was later built after the deaths of Alden and Vada Dow, continuing the Dow tradition of building with nature while having fun doing it.

arch shape but translated his own Sun Bridge into concrete, a comfortable material for him.

"Both my father and my grandmother loved to garden," Dow reminisced in 1976. "I suppose that's why I enjoy working with gardening and landscaping. Frank Lloyd Wright influenced me a great deal in my work with architecture, but he didn't understand landscaping at all." In his gardens as in his architecture, Dow made sure that whatever he set his hands to called out to be enjoyed and well used—even climbed. As Dow himself had asked, "Isn't fun a worthy goal, a kind of function?"

On August 20, 1983, Alden Dow died in his Midland home. His funeral was held in the Dow Gardens, the second of the two places he most revered and shaped, and he was buried in Midland Cemetery. A few days after Dow's death,

Judith O'Dell, executive director of the Alden B. Dow Creativity Center at Northwood Institute (now University), summed up his legacy:

Alden Dow has left much more than buildings which are works of art or writings printed on colorful sheets of paper. He has given us hope, encouraged us to open our own new worlds, and invited us to help our children discover their worlds, too.

Alden Dow has shared his life spirit. He will be with us as long as we seek solutions to unanswered questions—as long as we continue working together to improve the quality of life.

Dow's daughter Barbara Carras recalls a similar lesson: "He thought it very important that each of us contribute to this world in a positive way; the more you are given in this world," he believed, "the greater your responsibility."

▶ Sometimes Dow referred to his 1979 Sun Bridge as a fan, underscoring the Japanese aesthetic he brought to the Dow Gardens. Here he used water as a mirror to double the structure's impact. "Long lines like a vista," he said, "should end in a feature of some kind, like a brilliant bed of flowers, a bridge, a plain lawn area."

■ BEAUTY NEEDS FUNCTION; FUNCTION NEEDS BEAUTY. ■

FACTS

I believe that if all the profession ... standing of the re... of creativity migh... grow from feelings. Science, on the othe... edge that has been established as ... facts. he must let feelings express ... ap...eness of the facts, which ... wo... new facts established i... ca...nes generate new feelin... new feelings. Science is the mate...

I believe that if all the professions could come to a clearer understanding of the relationship between science and art, a great new era of creativity might follow. Without man there is no science, no art . . . just natural growth. Art is human, intuitive knowledge that springs from feelings. Science, on the other hand, is human, systematic knowledge that has been established as facts. For man to be creative with facts, he must let feelings express themselves. Feelings express the appropriateness of the facts, which in turn generates new facts. There would be no new facts established if feelings were not involved. Old facts can sometimes generate new feelings . . . but new facts always demand new feelings. Science is the material for creating. Art is the creator.

Alden Dow designed approximately six hundred structures, of which some three-fifths were built. More than one hundred of his designs were constructed in his hometown of Midland, Michigan. The architect's first built project, a modernistic concrete bridge connecting his brother Willard's home to the Dow Gardens, was erected when he was a university student in 1927, and his last came just over a half century later, in 1979—coincidentally, it was another concrete bridge for the family gardens. Two residential designs were built posthumously, with modifications, in 1988 and 1992. ■ Residences by far outnumbered Dow's designs for other building types, although about half remained unrealized dreams or prototypes. Commercial and education projects were next in number, followed by fewer civic and religious designs. In addition, Dow was responsible for planning and designing buildings in the new town of Lake Jackson, Texas, in the 1940s as well as for housing commissioned by The Dow Chemical Company in the nearby town of Freeport. Dow's day-to-day involvement with his firm, Dow Howell Gilmore Associates, continued through the late 1960s, after which his interests focused on two key projects in his hometown, the Midland Center for the Arts and the Dow Gardens. For the latter, he gently reinterpreted his father's gardens in the 1970s with a new master plan and striking bridges sprinkled throughout the landscape. During his long career, Dow also turned his hand to myriad other design ideas, from furniture to mechanical inventions to graphic designs. ■ The lists that follow survey Dow's architectural works, divided into built and unbuilt projects and organized by year of design (according to the date of the records); built commissions are additionally arranged by building type. Housing prototypes, to which Dow devoted considerable attention over the years, were sometimes theoretical and may not have been commissioned by a specific client for a specific location. ■ Remarkably, few of Dow's buildings have been demolished or altered beyond recognition—a tribute to the esteem in which he and his work have been held in Midland and beyond. Their longevity also testifies to the progressiveness of Dow's design vision. Fifty or seventy years later, many of his houses in particular continue to appear far more modern than residences being built today. ■ "I am convinced," wrote Dow in 1977, "that future great human expressions will result from one basic effort . . . that of a constant striving toward perfection." He put his faith in the future and in the potential of individual expression to compose a more perfect world. As pointed out in the 1989 report nominating his proudest achievement, his Home and Studio, as a National Historic Landmark: "Alden Dow was one of the very few 20th-century architects who could demonstrate with consummate skill his own theories concerning the principles of architecture." ■

THE BUILDINGS OF ALDEN B. DOW

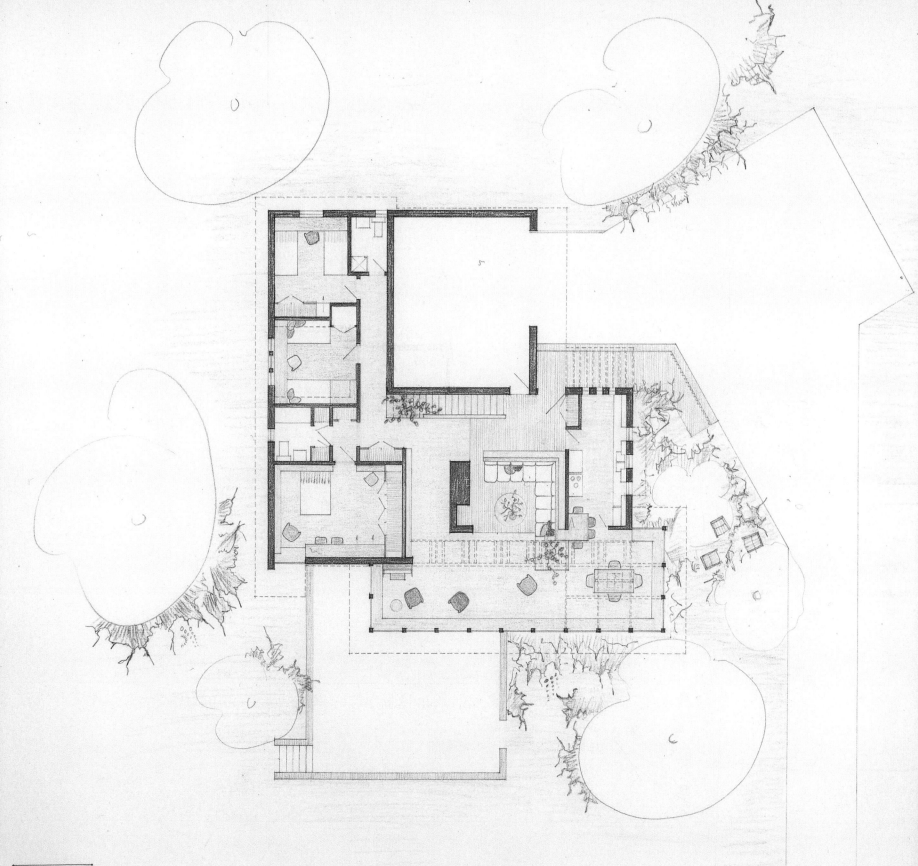

HOUSE for MR. & MRS. H. W. DOUMA
PETOSKEY, MICHIGAN
ALDEN B. DOW, INC. ARCHITECT   MIDLAND, MICHIGAN   APRIL 1, 1947
Revised April 8, 1947

HOUSES

Stein House

1931
Herbert H. Dow House
bathroom alteration[1]
Midland, Michigan

1932
Towsley House
Ann Arbor, Michigan

1933
Stein House
Midland, Michigan

Cavanagh House
Midland, Michigan

Lewis House[2]
Midland, Michigan

1934
Heath House
Midland, Michigan

Willard Dow House
addition and alterations[1]
Midland, Michigan

The Shanty for
Alden and Vada Dow[3]
Midland, Michigan

Hanson House
Midland, Michigan

Whitman House
Midland, Michigan

Ethyl-Dow Chemical
Company Houses (2)
Cape Fear,
North Carolina

1935
Anderson Arbury
Cottage alterations[1]
Midland, Michigan

Goodall House (with
Robert Goodall)
Midland, Michigan

Earl W. Bennett House
addition and alterations[1]
Midland, Michigan

Pardee House addition[1]
Midland, Michigan

Ball House
Midland, Michigan

Diehl House
Midland, Michigan

Leland I. Doan House
addition and alterations[1]
Midland, Michigan

Panter House
alterations[1]
Midland, Michigan

MacCallum House
Midland, Michigan

Stein House

Lewis House

Goodall House

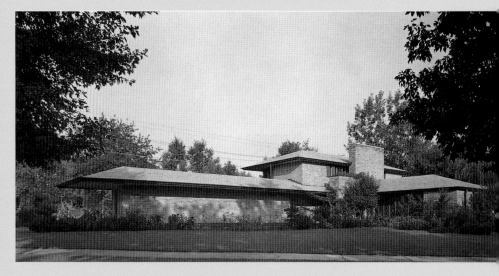

Diehl House

Diehl House

MacCallum House

MacCallum House

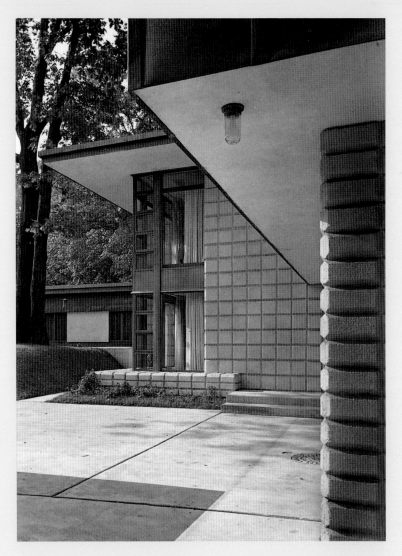

Pardee House

Mary Dow House

Mary Dow House

Pardee House

Greene House

Bachman House

Pryor House

Greene House

Pryor House

1936
Pardee House
Midland, Michigan

Mary Dow House[2]
Saginaw, Michigan

Earl W. Bennett
Cottage, Benmark Club
Roscommon, Michigan

Barstow House
alterations[1]
Midland, Michigan

Greene House
Midland, Michigan

Bachman House
East Lansing, Michigan

Koerting House
Elkhart, Indiana

Saunders House[3]
Bloomfield Hills,
Michigan

Pryor House
Grosse Pointe Park,
Michigan

1937

J. H. Sherk House
alterations[1]
Midland, Michigan

Brown House
Mount Pleasant,
Michigan

Herbert H. Dow House
alterations[1]
Midland, Michigan

Barstow Cottage
addition[1]
Ludington, Michigan

Rood House
Kalamazoo, Michigan

Barclay House[2]
Midland, Michigan

1938

Best House
(House for $3,000)[2]
Midland, Michigan

Wildes House[2]
Midland, Michigan

Hodgkiss House
Petoskey, Michigan

1939

Anderson Arbury
House
Midland, Michigan

Campbell House
Midland, Michigan

Fleming House
Elkhart, Indiana

The Dow Chemical
Company House 101
Midland, Michigan

Leland I. Doan Beach
House, Crystal Lake
Frankfort, Michigan

Morrison House
Midland, Michigan

Edick House
addition and alterations[1]
Midland, Michigan

Wells House
Grosse Pointe Farms,
Michigan

Alden B. Dow Home
Midland, Michigan

Rood House

Barclay House

Hodgkiss House

Anderson Arbury House

Anderson Arbury House

Anderson Arbury House

Leland I. Doan Beach House

Campbell House

Campbell House

1940

Grant House
Midland, Michigan

LeRoy Smith House
Algonac, Michigan

Rich House[2]
Midland, Michigan

Dreisbach House
Midland, Michigan

Robinson House
Grosse Pointe Park,
Michigan

1941

MacMartin House
Midland, Michigan

Grebe House
Midland, Michigan

Thomas Defoe House
Bay City, Michigan

Irish House
Midland, Michigan

Butenschoen House
Midland, Michigan

Reinke House
Midland, Michigan

Penhaligen House
Midland, Michigan

Boonstra House
Midland, Michigan

Bass House[2]
Midland, Michigan

Ballmer House
alterations[1]
Midland, Michigan

1943

Reed House
alterations[1]
Houston, Texas

1944

Charch House
West Chester,
Pennsylvania

1945

Ingersoll Housing
Prototypes (2)
Kalamazoo, Michigan

1946

Saxton House
Flint, Michigan

Small House 100
Midland, Michigan

Douma House
Petoskey, Michigan

Kirk House[3]
Midland, Michigan

1947

Whiting House
Midland, Michigan

Howard Arbury House
alterations[1]
Midland, Michigan

1948

Baptist Parsonage
Midland, Michigan

Anderson House
East Lansing, Michigan

Garfield House
addition[1]
Clare, Michigan

1949

Hoobler House
Ann Arbor, Michigan

George Duffy House
Port Huron, Michigan

Alden B. Dow Cottage
addition[1]
Higgins Lake, Michigan

Frisselle House
Midland, Michigan

1950

Ballmer House[2]
Midland, Michigan

Colpaert House
South Bend, Indiana

Myers House
Lapeer, Michigan

Sandwich Panel
House no. 1
Midland, Michigan

Comey House
St. Clair Shores,
Michigan

Yates House
Midland, Michigan

Robert Bennett House
Midland, Michigan

1951

Josephine Ashmun
House
Midland, Michigan

Bergstein House
Midland, Michigan

1952

Colburn House
Midland, Michigan

Goldberger House
Saginaw, Michigan

Sandwich Panel
House no. 2
Midland, Michigan

Sandwich Panel
House no. 3
Midland, Michigan

Herbert H. Dow II
House
Midland, Michigan

LeRoy Smith House

Irish House

Robert Bennett House

Josephine Ashmun House

Ballmer House

Herbert H. Dow II House

Leland I. Doan House

Leland I. Doan House

Lynn Townsend House

Dow Test House (Carras House)

Dow Test House (Carras House)

Michael Dow House

1953
Herbert Doan House
addition and
alterations[1]
Midland, Michigan

1954
J. L. Sherk House
Midland, Michigan

Birmingham House
Adrian, Michigan

George Olson House
Midland, Michigan

Herbert Doan Cottage[2]
Higgins Lake, Michigan

Harlow House
Midland, Michigan

James Duffy House
St. Clair Shores,
Michigan

1955
Dick House
Grand Rapids,
Michigan

Herbert Doan House[2]
Midland, Michigan

Herbert H. Dow II
Cottage, Crystal Lake
Frankfort, Michigan

1956
Heber Ashmun House
alterations[1]
Midland, Michigan

Rowland House
Midland, Michigan

Leland I. Doan House
Midland, Michigan

1957
Oppermann House
Saginaw, Michigan

Keeler House
East Grand Rapids,
Michigan

Marshall House
Midland, Michigan

Cannon House
Muskegon, Michigan

Gabel House
Midland, Michigan

Pierson House
Saginaw, Michigan

1958
Howell House
Midland, Michigan

Schuette House
Midland, Michigan

Reed House
Houston, Texas

House for
Blackhurst Realty
Midland, Michigan

1959
Freligh House
Adrian, Michigan

Washburn House
Okemos, Michigan

Emry-Kraus Houses
Mount Pleasant,
Michigan

Branch House[4]
Midland, Michigan

Davis House
Mount Pleasant,
Michigan

1960
Jameson House
East Tawas, Michigan

Oberlin House
Canton, Ohio

Collinson House
Midland, Michigan

1961
Riecker House
Midland, Michigan

Dow Test House
(Carras House)
Midland, Michigan

1962
Morris House
Ann Arbor, Michigan

1963
Duke University
President's House
Durham,
North Carolina

Lynn Townsend House
Bloomfield Hills,
Michigan

1966
Michael Dow House
Okemos, Michigan

1968
Gillaspy House
Harrison, Michigan

1971
Carras Cottage
Benmark Club
Roscommon, Michigan

1973
James Duffy Cottage
St. Clair, Michigan

1988
Donald Smith House[5]
Midland, Michigan

1992
Mills Summer Home[6]
Higgins Lake, Michigan

Donald Smith House

W Frame House (adapted for Mills Summer Home)

RELIGIOUS BUILDINGS

St. John's Lutheran Church

1937
Presbyterian Church
Manse addition[1]
Midland, Michigan

1940
Reorganized Church
of Jesus Christ
of Latter-day Saints
Midland, Michigan

1947
First Methodist Church
Midland, Michigan

1948
Indian River
Catholic Church
Indian River, Michigan

1949
St. John's
Episcopal Church
Midland, Michigan

Fountain Street
Baptist Church Chapel
Grand Rapids,
Michigan

1952
St. John's
Episcopal Church
Parsonage and
Apartment
Midland, Michigan

1953
St. John's
Lutheran Church
Midland, Michigan

Ashman Street
Church of God[2]
Midland, Michigan

1954
Messiah
Lutheran Church
Bay City, Michigan

1955
Bay City Jewish Center
Bay City, Michigan

Grand Haven
Methodist Church
Grand Haven, Michigan

1957
Midland Jewish Center
alterations[1]
Midland, Michigan

Ward Memorial
Presbyterian Church[3]
Livonia, Michigan

Kalamazoo
Christian Church
Kalamazoo, Michigan

1958
Eastminster
Presbyterian Church
East Lansing, Michigan

Christ Episcopal Church
Adrian, Michigan

Holy Family
Episcopal Church
Midland, Michigan

1960
First Presbyterian
Church
Dearborn, Michigan

First Presbyterian
Church addition[1]
Alma, Michigan

Salvation Army Citadel
Midland, Michigan

Roscommon
Congregational Church
Roscommon, Michigan

1961
Seventh-day
Adventist Church
Midland, Michigan

Temple Beth El
Spring Valley, New York

Church of the
Nazarene addition[1]
Nease Memorial
Midland, Michigan

1962
Hellenic Orthodox
Community Church
of St. George
Bloomfield Township,
Michigan

1964
Lutheran Church,
Missouri Synod
Michigan District
Headquarters
Ann Arbor, Michigan

St. John's Lutheran Church

Indian River Catholic Church

Roscommon Congregational Church

First Methodist Church

Church of the Nazarene/Nease Memorial

Temple Beth El

EDUCATION BUILDINGS

1937
Merrill School addition[1]
Merrill, Michigan

1938
Parents' and
Children's School[7]
Midland, Michigan

Barrett School
District no. 7
Midland, Michigan

1949
Northeast Intermediate
High School
Midland, Michigan

1950
Alma College
Jerry Tyler Commons
Alma, Michigan

University of Michigan
Women's
Swimming Pool
Margaret Bell Building
Ann Arbor, Michigan

1951
Northeast
Elementary School
Midland, Michigan

1953
Midland High School
Midland, Michigan

1954
Nelson Street School
Midland, Michigan

1957
Delta College
Master Plan
Bay City, Michigan

1958
University of Michigan
Botanical Gardens
Ann Arbor, Michigan

Hillsdale College
Dining Hall
Hillsdale, Michigan

Hillsdale College
Olds Women's
Dormitory
Hillsdale, Michigan

Interlochen Arts
Academy
Girls' Dormitory
Interlochen, Michigan

Midland High School
Stadium
Midland, Michigan

1959
Hillsdale College
Knorr Memorial
Student Center
Hillsdale, Michigan

Hillsdale College
Parking
Hillsdale, Michigan

Hillsdale College
Master Plan
Hillsdale, Michigan

University of Michigan
Botanical Gardens
Superintendent's
Residence
Ann Arbor, Michigan

Regina Catholic
Girls High School
Midland, Michigan

1960
Interlochen Arts
Academy
Master Development
Plan
Interlochen, Michigan

University of Michigan
Institute for
Social Research
Ann Arbor, Michigan

Mapleton Elementary
School addition[1]
Midland, Michigan

Chestnut Hill
Elementary School
addition[1]
Midland, Michigan

1961
Wayne State University
Physical Education and
Recreation Building
Detroit, Michigan

Interlochen
Arts Academy
Classroom Building no. 1
Interlochen, Michigan

Meridian High School
Sanford, Michigan

North Intermediate
School
Midland, Michigan

Delta College
Addition
Bay City, Michigan

Interlochen
Arts Academy
Kresge Auditorium
Interlochen, Michigan

Interlochen Arts
Academy
Gymnasium
Interlochen, Michigan

1962
Northwood Institute
Site Plan
Midland, Michigan

Northwood Institute
Classroom Building
Midland, Michigan

Northwood Institute
Dining Hall
Midland, Michigan

Northwood Institute
Men's and Women's
Dormitories
Midland, Michigan

Interlochen Arts
Academy
Science Building
Interlochen, Michigan

Interlochen
Arts Academy
Maddy Administration
Building addition[1]
Interlochen, Michigan

1963
Delta College
Technical
Education Wing
Bay City, Michigan

Northwood Institute
Faculty Housing
Midland, Michigan

Interlochen
Arts Academy
Language Arts Building
Interlochen, Michigan

Northwood Institute
Gatehouse
Midland, Michigan

Hillsdale College
Strosacker
Science Center
Hillsdale, Michigan

Muskegon County
Community College
Muskegon, Michigan

Wayne State University
University Center
Detroit, Michigan

Northeast Intermediate High School

Classroom Building no. 1, Interlochen Arts Academy

Hillsdale College
Maintenance Building
Hillsdale, Michigan

Saginaw Valley
State College
Master Plan
Saginaw County,
Michigan

Interlochen Arts
Academy Store
Interlochen, Michigan

1964
Northwood Institute
Men's and Women's
Dormitories addition
(1964)
Midland, Michigan

Hillsdale College
Nursery
Hillsdale, Michigan

Northern Michigan
University
Learning Resource
Center
Marquette, Michigan

Northwood Institute
Men's and Women's
Dormitories addition
(1965)
Midland, Michigan

Wayne State University
Handball and Squash
Court addition
Detroit, Michigan

University of Michigan
Administration Building
Ann Arbor, Michigan

Delta College
Administration Wing
addition
Bay City, Michigan

Northwood Institute
Student Activities
Building
Midland, Michigan

Northwood Institute
Tennis House addition
Midland, Michigan

1965
Interlochen
Arts Academy
Boys' Dormitory
Interlochen, Michigan

Herbert Henry Dow
High School
Midland, Michigan

University of Michigan
Continuing Education
Center
Ann Arbor, Michigan

1966
Greenhills School
Ann Arbor, Michigan

Northwood Institute
Texas Campus
Cedar Hill, Texas

Mid-Michigan
Community College
Instructional Facility
Harrison, Michigan

Saginaw Valley
State College
Instructional
Facility no. 1
Saginaw County,
Michigan

Northwood Institute
Student Union
Midland, Michigan

1967
Kalamazoo Valley
Community College
Kalamazoo, Michigan

Interlochen
Arts Academy
Grand Traverse
Performing Arts Center
Interlochen, Michigan

Northwood Institute
Strosacker Library
Midland, Michigan

1968
Woodcrest
Elementary School
Midland, Michigan

Northwood Institute
NADA Center
Midland, Michigan

1972
Northwood Institute
Griswold Communi-
cations Center
Midland, Michigan

Northwood Institute
AOT Hall of Fame
Midland, Michigan

Griswold Communications Center, Northwood Institute

Kalamazoo Valley Community College

COMMERCIAL BUILDINGS

1934
Alden B. Dow Studio
Midland, Michigan

1935
Frolic Theater
alterations[1]
Midland, Michigan

1936
The Dow Chemical
Company
Clock Room
Midland, Michigan

1937
The Dow Chemical
Company
East Clock Room
addition
Midland, Michigan

The Dow Chemical
Company
Building 47 addition[1,3]
Midland, Michigan

1938
The Dow Chemical
Company
Golden Gate
International
Exposition Exhibit
San Francisco, California

1939
Brown Lumber
Company[1]
Midland, Michigan

The Dow Chemical
Company
Building 47, second-
floor addition[1,3]
Midland, Michigan

1940
The Dow Chemical
Company
Biochemical Research
Laboratories and
Greenhouse[4]
Midland, Michigan

The Dow Chemical
Company
RCA Building Office
additions and
alterations[1]
New York, New York

The Dow Chemical
Company
Seal Beach Office
Long Beach, California

The Dow Chemical
Company
Great Western Division
Pittsburg, California

1943
Barnes Manufacturing
Company alterations[1]
Mansfield, Ohio

Dow Corning
Corporation
Service Building and
Laboratory
Midland, Michigan

1944
The Dow Chemical
Company
Sales Office
St. Louis, Missouri

1946
The Dow Chemical
Company
Office Building and
Laboratory
Ann Arbor, Michigan

The Dow Chemical
Company
Plastic Sales Office
and Warehouse
Midland, Michigan

LaPelle's Flower Store[3]
Midland, Michigan

Rich Publishing House
alterations[1]
Midland, Michigan

Moutsatson Store
alterations[1]
Midland, Michigan

Midland National Bank
alterations[1]
Midland, Michigan

The Dow Chemical
Company
Administration Building
Sarnia, Ontario, Canada

1947
Dow Corning
Corporation
Empire State Building
Office[1]
New York, New York

Patrick Block
alterations[1]
Midland, Michigan

Midland Federal
Savings and Loan
Midland, Michigan

Heisman Company
Store alterations[1]
Midland, Michigan

Lape Building[2]
Midland, Michigan

Chemical State
Savings Bank
alterations and
additions[1]
Midland, Michigan

The Dow Chemical Company, Golden Gate International Exposition Exhibit

The Dow Chemical Company, Building 47 addition

The Dow Chemical Company, Building 47 addition

1951
The Dow Chemical
Company
Medical Building
Midland, Michigan

Chemical State
Savings Bank
Midland, Michigan

1953
The Dow Chemical
Company
Biochemical Laboratory
Midland, Michigan

1954
Smith's Flower Shop
Midland, Michigan

New Midland
National Bank
Midland, Michigan

1955
The Dow Chemical
Company
Polymer Research
Laboratory
Midland, Michigan

The Dow Chemical
Company
Nuclear Research
Laboratory
Midland, Michigan

Consumers Power
Company
Midland, Michigan

The Dow Chemical
Company
Agricultural Chemical
Research Laboratory
Midland, Michigan

The Dow Chemical
Company
2020 Chemical Building
Midland, Michigan

1956
Consumers Power
Company
Bay City, Michigan

The Dow Chemical
Company
Abbott Road Center
Master Plan
Midland, Michigan

The Dow Chemical
Company
2010 Central Service
Building
Midland, Michigan

The Dow Chemical
Company
2030 Abbott Road
Center
Midland, Michigan

1960
Dow Corning
Corporation
Building 114 addition[1]
Midland, Michigan

Leonard
Service Station
Ann Arbor, Michigan

Bay Refining Gas
Station and Car Wash[2]
Midland, Michigan

1961
Conductron
Corporation Offices
Ann Arbor, Michigan

Midland National Bank
Circle Branch
Midland, Michigan
The Dow Chemical
Company
Bio Products
Department
Midland, Michigan

1962
People's National Bank
and Trust Company
Bay City, Michigan

1963
New First National
Bank and Trust
Company
Circle Branch
Midland, Michigan

Osburn and
Goodnight Office[3]
Midland, Michigan

The Dow Chemical
Company
2040 Plastics Building
Midland, Michigan

Phoenix Sprinkler
and Heating
Midland, Michigan

University Microfilms
Ann Arbor, Michigan

1964
Gillespie Building
Midland, Michigan

1965
Church and Guisewite
Advertising
Midland, Michigan

1966
Holiday Inn
Traverse City, Michigan

1967
Laboratory for
Macromolecular Science
Midland, Michigan

1968
The Dow Chemical
Company
Abbott Road Center
Covered Walkway
Midland, Michigan

Cassiday Theater
Restaurant and Bar
alterations[1,3]
Midland, Michigan

1970
General Aviation
Lansing, Michigan

1974
Carras Law Office
Midland, Michigan

The Dow Chemical Company, 2020 Chemical Building

Laboratory for Macromolecular Science

CIVIC STRUCTURES

1927
Bridge on Sixth Green[3]
Midland Country Club
Midland, Michigan

1930
Midland Country Club[2]
Midland, Michigan

1938
Midland (Central Park)
Band Shell
Midland, Michigan

Central Park
Bathhouse and Pool[3]
Midland, Michigan

Midland Hospital[2]
Midland, Michigan

Midland Homecoming
and Dow Field Day
Information Booth
Midland, Michigan

1949
Phoenix Civic Center[2]
Phoenix, Arizona

1950
Bay County
War Memorial
Bay County, Michigan

Midland Public Library
Midland, Michigan

1953
Midland Community
Center
Midland, Michigan

1954
Midland Skating Rink
Midland, Michigan

1955
Fire Station no. 1
Midland, Michigan

Ann Arbor
Public Library
Ann Arbor, Michigan

Midland County
Courthouse Jail and
Office addition[1]
Midland, Michigan

1956
McMorran Memorial
Auditorium
Port Huron, Michigan

Bridge on Sixth Green, Midland Country Club

King's Daughters Home
Midland, Michigan

1957
McMorran Sports Arena
Port Huron, Michigan

1958
Dunbar Community
Center
Ann Arbor, Michigan

Cottage Grove
Boat House
Higgins Lake, Michigan

1960
Young Women's
Christian Association[2]
Saginaw, Michigan

Ann Arbor City Hall
Ann Arbor, Michigan

1961
Winterberry
Girl Scout Camp
Midland County,
Michigan

Tri-City Airport[2]
Freeland, Michigan

Paul Bunyan
Boy Scout Camp
Oscoda, Michigan

Kalamazoo
Nature Center
Kalamazoo, Michigan

1965
Cleveland Manor
Midland, Michigan

1966
Chippewa Nature Center
Midland, Michigan

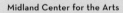

Midland Center for the Arts

Phoenix Civic Center

McMorran Memorial Auditorium

Midland Public Library

Midland Center
for the Arts
Midland, Michigan

Higgins Lake Boat Club
Higgins Lake, Michigan

1967
Seven Ponds Nature
Center addition[1]
Dryden, Michigan

1973
Farmers Market
Midland, Michigan

DOW
GARDENS

1927
Willard Dow House
Bridge[3]
Midland, Michigan

1974
Dow Gardens
Master Plan
Midland, Michigan

Lower Pond Bridge
Midland, Michigan

Upper Pond Bridge
Midland, Michigan

1975
Concrete Maze Bridge
Midland, Michigan

Greenhouse
Midland, Michigan

1976
Visitors Center
Midland, Michigan

1977
Pond Bridge Extension
Midland, Michigan

1979
Sun Bridge
Midland, Michigan

Pond Bridge Extension

Lower Pond Bridge

TEXAS COMMISSIONS

1940

The Dow Chemical
Company
Houses
Freeport, Texas

The Dow Chemical
Company
Apartment Building
Freeport, Texas

The Dow Chemical
Company
Hotel
Freeport, Texas

The Dow Chemical
Company
Plant no. 2
Office Building
Freeport, Texas

Lake Jackson and
Freeport Defense Maps
Brazoria County, Texas

Freeport
Primary School
Freeport, Texas

Hospital[3]
Freeport, Texas

1941

Beutel House additions
and alterations[1]
Freeport, Texas

The Dow Chemical
Company
Magnesium Corporation
Clock Room, Cafeteria,
and First Aid Building
Velasco, Texas

Lake Jackson Planta-
tion Townsite Maps
Lake Jackson, Texas

Greene House
addition[1]
Freeport, Texas

House no. 34 alteration
Freeport, Texas

1942

U.S. Defense Housing
Project
Lake Jackson, Texas

Dow Chemical Housing
Building 50
Freeport, Texas

Dow Chemical Housing
Building 51
Freeport, Texas

Tract Houses Area B
Lake Jackson, Texas

Tract Houses Area C
Lake Jackson, Texas

The Dow Chemical
Company
Laboratory Building
Freeport, Texas

Grocery Store,
Drug Store,
and Service Station
Lake Jackson, Texas

Barber and Beauty Shop
Lake Jackson, Texas

Recreation Building
Lake Jackson, Texas

Barbecue Pit
Lake Jackson, Texas

Comfort Station
Lake Jackson, Texas

Fire House
Lake Jackson, Texas

Telephone Building
Lake Jackson, Texas

Elementary School
Lake Jackson, Texas

Lake Jackson
Area Maps
Lake Jackson, Texas

Oyster Creek
Pump Station
Lake Jackson, Texas

Bridge Over
Fresh Water Flume
Lake Jackson, Texas

1943

The Dow Chemical
Company
Fire Protection
Building
Freeport, Texas

The Dow Chemical
Company
Display Booth, Houston
Fat Stock Show
Houston, Texas

Office Building
Lake Jackson, Texas

The Dow Chemical
Company
Guard and Clock Room
Freeport, Texas

A. P. Beutel Office
Freeport, Texas

Freeport Primary
School addition
Freeport, Texas

Rodeo Arena
Lake Jackson, Texas

Trash Receptacle
Shopping Center
Lake Jackson, Texas

"No Parking" Sign
Lake Jackson, Texas

1944

Dry Goods Store
Building
Lake Jackson, Texas

Theater
Lake Jackson, Texas

Variety Store Building
Lake Jackson, Texas

Sweeny Grade School
Sweeny, Texas

1945

First Methodist Church
Lake Jackson, Texas

Elementary and Junior
High School
Lake Jackson, Texas

Primary and
Elementary Schools
Clute, Texas

Primary, Elementary,
and Junior High
Schools
Velasco, Texas

1946

Lake Jackson Clinic
Lake Jackson, Texas

Lake Jackson State
Bank
Lake Jackson, Texas

The Dow Chemical
Company
Clock Room 1A
Freeport, Texas

Freeport High School
Gymnasium Building
Freeport, Texas

Sweeny Independent
School District
Campus Layout
Sweeny, Texas

1947

Brazosport
Independent
School System
Shop Buildings
Freeport, Texas

Elementary School
Building no. 6
Freeport, Texas

NOTES, pages 204–22

1 Additions and alterations by
Dow to non-Dow buildings

2 Buildings with major
alterations since construction

3 Demolished structures

4 A 1940 laboratory converted
by Dow to a residence in 1959

5 Posthumous adaptation of the
Washburn House (1959)

6 Posthumous adaptation of the
W Frame House (1955)

7 Converted to a residence in
1943

Projects are listed in
chronological order by the
design date except when the
exact date is unknown.

The Dow Chemical Company Houses, Freeport

Tract House, Lake Jackson

Alden B. Dow House, Freeport

Elementary School, Lake Jackson

Theater, Lake Jackson

Comfort Station, Lake Jackson

UNBUILT PROJECTS

1932
Goal for Humanity
House
No location

Putnam House
Midland, Michigan

House for Mr. X
No location available

Vinewood Boulevard
House
Ann Arbor, Michigan

St. Andrews Boulevard
House
Midland, Michigan

Day Forest Golf Club
No location available

Yocum House
No location available

1933
House 1933
No location available

Heatley House
Midland, Michigan

1934
U.S. 10 and State Road
Intersection Building
Midland, Michigan

Oviatt's Bakery Garage
Midland, Michigan

1935
Morrison House
Midland, Michigan

Mitts House
Saginaw, Michigan

Dubois House
Flint, Michigan

Jonescue House
Dearborn, Michigan

House with Copper
Roof
No location available

Low-Cost Housing
Midland, Michigan

Gordon Oil Company
Atha Supply Company
No location available

Johnston Cottage
Lansing, Michigan

1936
Eman and Mauris
Houses
Grand Rapids, Michigan

Emerson Park
Concert Stage
Midland, Michigan

MacGregor House
Flint, Michigan

Wycoff House
Mount Pleasant,
Michigan

Towsley Cabin,
Benmark Club
Roscommon, Michigan

Colignon House
Muskegon, Michigan

Apartment Building
Mount Pleasant,
Michigan

1937
Low-Cost House
Midland, Michigan

1940 Ethocel House
No location

Sundstrom House
Saginaw, Michigan

Flint Theater
Flint, Michigan

Hotel
Ann Arbor, Michigan

Midland Band Shell
Midland, Michigan

The Dow Chemical
Company
Organic Laboratory
Midland, Michigan

1938
Gatley House
Pontiac, Michigan

Keller Houses
No location available

Cummings House
Ypsilanti, Michigan

Carlson Houses
No location available

House with a Future
No location

Judson House
Midland, Michigan

Soslosky Store
Midland, Michigan

Henry Defoe House
Bay City, Michigan

1939
Ingleside Housing
Project
Detroit, Michigan

Erickson House
No location available

Low-Cost House no. 10
Midland, Michigan

Brown House
Detroit, Michigan

Roush House
No location available

Dowell, Inc.
Prefab Demountable
Field Office
No location available

ca. 1940
The Dow Chemical
Company House
No location available

The Dow Chemical
Company Office
No location available

1940
Dowell, Inc.
Exhibition Building
Tulsa, Oklahoma

Low-Cost Housing
No location

Carr House
Mount Pleasant,
Michigan

Houses for Narrow
Lots
No location

Towsley Nursery School
Ann Arbor, Michigan

Brown Clinic
Mount Pleasant,
Michigan

Carr Apartments
Mount Pleasant,
Michigan

Loose House
Midland, Michigan

Fred Olsen House
Alton, Illinois

1941
Short House
Midland, Michigan

Homasote Panel House
No location

Low-Cost Housing
No location

MacMartin Store
Winter Park, Florida

Starbuck House
No location available

School Tax Collector's
Office and Bus Garage
Freeport, Texas

Freeport High School
Freeport, Texas

Colored School addition[1]
Freeport and Jones
Creek, Texas

Reed House
Houston, Texas

House
Lake Jackson, Texas

1942
Camp Chemical
Freeport, Texas

Salvation Army Chapel
Midland, Michigan

Masonry House
Lake Jackson, Texas

Sewage Treatment Plant
Lake Jackson, Texas

1943
Dow Corning Corpor-
ation Guard Tower
Midland, Michigan

The Dow Chemical
Company
Homestead Housing
Development
Midland, Michigan

Low-Cost Housing
No location

Lutheran Church
Freeport, Texas

Dow Corning
Corporation
Power House
Midland, Michigan

Houses no. 1 through 8
No location

Dow Corning Corpor-
ation Boiler House
Midland, Michigan

Goal for Humanity House

House for Mr. X

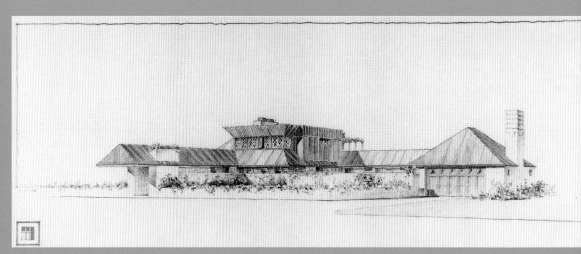

Heatley House

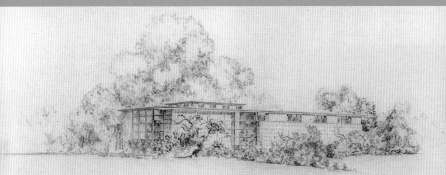

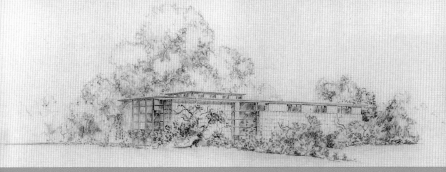

Mitts House

Oviatt's Bakery Garage

Keller House

Towsley Nursery School

Ingleside Housing Project

Circle House

A House for the Southwest

1943 House no. 3

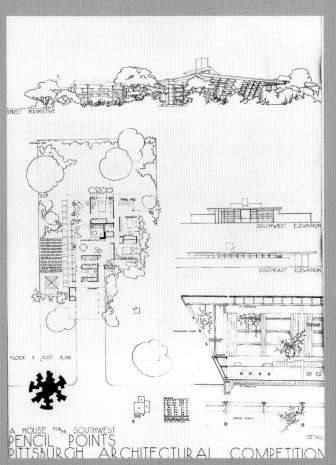

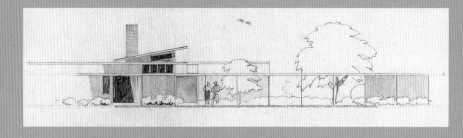

Mode Motors

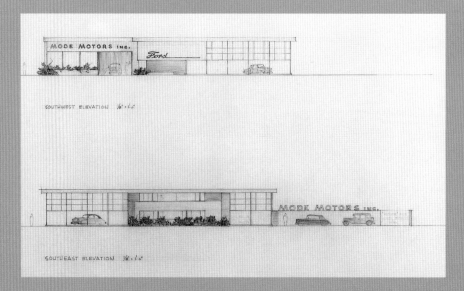

Circle House
No location

Bay Front Estates
Sarasota, Florida

Hospital
Texas

House Type 201
No location

1944
Donnell House
Findlay, Ohio

Lutheran Church
Midland, Michigan

Community Building
Sweeny, Texas

Kreger House
Grosse Ile, Michigan

36th Division War
Memorial Competition
Temple, Texas

U.S. Plywood House
No location

1945
Memorial Chapel
Midland, Michigan

Burdick House
Midland, Michigan

A House for
the Southwest
No location

Baptist Church
Sweeny, Texas

American Legion
Clubhouse and
Bowling Alley
Grayling, Michigan

Knepp's Store
alterations[1]
Midland, Michigan

The Dow Chemical
Company
Composite Laboratory
Midland, Michigan

Draper House
Houston, Texas

Maher House
Midland, Michigan

Alpha Omicron Pi
Sorority House
East Lansing, Michigan

Okoonian House
No location

Hanchett House
Big Rapids, Michigan

Michigan Solar House
No location

School Play Courts
Sweeny, Texas

Manufacturing Plant
Building
No location available

Addington House
No location available

The Dow Chemical
Company
Building 47 addition[1]
Midland, Michigan

1946
School
No location available

Governor's House
Lansing, Michigan

Peloubet House
Midland, Michigan

Hayworth House
East Lansing, Michigan

MacMartin Store
Harbor Springs,
Michigan

Freeport High School
Site Plans
Freeport, Texas

Dowell Corporation
Laboratory and
Engineering Building
Tulsa, Oklahoma

Tri-City Airport
Freeland, Michigan

Detroit Edison
Display Kitchen
Detroit, Michigan

Crystal Lake Boathouse
Crystal Lake, Michigan

First Presbyterian
Church
Lake Jackson, Texas

Apartment Building
Midland, Michigan

Gardner House
No location available

Midland Hospital
Nurses Home
Midland, Michigan

Fred Olsen House
Guilford, Connecticut

Dow Homesite Project
Contra Costa County,
California

Church of Jesus Christ
of Latter-day Saints
Grand Rapids, Michigan

House 1946
No location available

Zass House
Long Island, New York

The Dow Chemical
Company
Auditorium Building
Freeport, Texas

1947
The Dow Chemical
Company
Engineering Building
Freeport, Texas

Bradley Block Stairway
Midland, Michigan

River Drive
Midland, Michigan

Church of the Nazarene
alterations[1]
Midland, Michigan

Burgess Music Store
Midland, Michigan

Elementary School
Building no. 5
Freeport, Texas

Rogner's Beauty Shop
Midland, Michigan

Towns House additions
and alterations[1]
No location available

Love House
No location available

1948
Mode Motors
Midland, Michigan

Wilson Funeral Home
additions and
alterations[1]
Midland, Michigan

Saginaw Methodist
Church
Saginaw, Michigan

House for Standolind
Gas and Oil Company
No location available

Willard Bennett House
Ludington, Michigan

1949
Sarnia Riding Club
Sarnia, Ontario, Canada

Wright Store alterations[1]
Midland, Michigan

1940s
Emerson Park
Midland, Michigan

Howe House
Midland, Michigan

Gas Station/Store/House
No location available

1950
Harrington Cottage
Indian River, Michigan

Bulmer House
Midland, Michigan

Elks Club
Midland, Michigan

Ward House
Big Rapids, Michigan

1951
Children's Home
Midland, Michigan

Alliance Clay Products
Company
Alliance, Ohio

Housing Project
on M-20
Midland, Mchigan

Arcade Building
alterations[1]
Midland, Michigan

1952
Thomas Defoe
Lakeside House
No location available

LeFevre House
Midland, Michigan

1953
MacDonald House
Ann Arbor, Michigan

Housing Project
on M-10
Midland, Michigan

Experimental House
with Folded-Plate Roof
No location available

Airport Site
Elementary School
Midland, Michigan

1954
Upjohn House theater
addition[1]
Kalamazoo, Michigan

Dau House
Harbor Springs,
Michigan

Evans House
No location available

The Dow Chemical
Company Laboratories
Midland, Michigan

1955
Munson House no. 1
(W Frame House)[2]
Midland, Michigan

A Proposed X for Z, Inc.
No location

Chrysler Carousel
Display
Miami, Florida

Chieftain Hotel-Motel
Mount Pleasant,
Michigan

Braden House
Grosse Isle, Michigan

Indian River Shrine
Stations of the Cross
Indian River, Michigan

New Holland Hotel
East Tawas, Michigan

Homestyle Center
Foundation House
Grand Rapids, Michigan

Vosburgh House
addition[1]
Midland, Michigan

U.S. Department of
State Seafront Housing
Manila, The Philippines

1956
Kilian Office Building
Frankfort, Michigan

Munson House no. 2
Midland, Michigan

Webster House
Midland, Michigan

Midland Hospital
Intern Housing
Midland, Michigan

1957
Shopping Center
Midland, Michigan

Surath House
Midland, Michigan

Post Office
Houghton Lake, Michigan

1958
A Motel Idea
Midland, Michigan

Cottage Grove
Control Tower
Higgins Lake, Michigan

Grebe House
Midland, Michigan

Interlochen Arts
Academy Opera House
Interlochen, Michigan

1959
Midland County
Infirmary
Midland, Michigan

Hrobron House
Columbus, Ohio

Collinson House
(W Frame House)
Midland, Michigan

1960
Chick House
Bloomfield Hills, Michigan

Webb House
(W Frame House)[2]
Traverse City, Michigan

Emma McMorran
Murphy Park
Port Huron, Michigan

Port Huron Hotel
Port Huron, Michigan

Mid-State Broadcasting
No location available

Crown Petroleum
Service Station
Bay City, Michigan

Post Street Workshop
addition
Midland, Michigan

Kalamazoo Clinic
Kalamazoo, Michigan

Hunter House
Midland, Michigan

1961
Midland Professional
Building
Midland, Michigan

Delta College
Sign and Gate
Bay City, Michigan

Laird House
Ann Arbor, Michigan

Delta College
Somnophonic Garden
Bay City, Michigan

Wayne State University
Theater
Detroit, Michigan

1962
University of Michigan
Alumni Living
Ann Arbor, Michigan

Hillsdale College
Administration Building
alterations
Hillsdale, Michigan

1963
Bildor Idea House
Midland, Michigan

Hillsdale College
Classroom Building
Hillsdale, Michigan

Beth Israel
Community Center
Ann Arbor, Michigan

First Methodist Church
Lansing, Michigan

Anderson House
East Lansing, Michigan

Midland Hospital
Medical Building
Midland, Michigan

Northwood Institute
Sundial
Midland, Michigan

Donald Bennett House
Midland, Michigan

Birmingham-Bloomfield
Bank
Birmingham, Michigan

1964
University of Michigan
Theater
Ann Arbor, Michigan

Delta College
Union, Dormitories, and
Television Building
Bay City, Michigan

Tri-City Airport
Car Rental Center
Freeland, Michigan

Northwood Institute
Amphitheater
Control Center
Midland, Michigan

Interlochen
Arts Academy
Girls' Dormitory
Interlochen, Michigan

Tri-City Airport Motel
Freeland, Michigan

1965
Interlochen
Arts Academy
Boys' Dormitory
Interlochen, Michigan

Markley House
Bloomfield Hills, Michigan

Bloomfield Country
Day School
Birmingham, Michigan

1966
Oppermann Cottage
Higgins Lake, Michigan

1967
First Church
of the Nazarene
Southfield, Michigan

1968
Retreat for Mr. and
Mrs. Herbert H. Dow II
Frankfort, Michigan

1969
Northwood Institute
Classroom Building
Midland, Michigan

1970
Hillsdale College
Chapel
Hillsdale, Michigan

1971
Northwood Institute
Creative Discussion
School
Midland, Michigan

1973
Carras House
Midland, Michigan

Farmers Market Murals
Midland, Michigan

No dates
Weckler House
No location available

Townsend Dude Ranch
restaurant
Lansing, Michigan

NOTES, pages 224–28

1 Additions and alterations by
Dow to non-Dow buildings

2 Later modified for the Mills
Summer Home (1992)

Projects are listed in
chronological order by the
design date except when the
exact date is unknown.

PATENTS AND INVENTIONS

1940 Ethocel House with Structural Facing Units

1938
Unit Blocks. A building system of sixteen precast rhomboid and triangular concrete blocks designed to be laid in overlapping courses to produce a strong bond and a continuous line of joints. Each block (12 or 6 inches) is a unit of measure. (With Robert Goodall) Patent granted.

1939
Structural Facing Units. One-foot square blocks of Ethocel® and Styron used for walls and roofs. Available in transparent, translucent, and opaque versions, the panels included a flange for nailing to a wood frame. Insulating air space was left between the panels.

1939
Railway Crossing Signal. Only the patent application is available (no drawings), and there is no documentation that a patent was granted.

1941
Playing Cards. The face of the cards is conventional, but the back is ornamental and displays the order of a poker hand. Patent granted.

1941
Boat Steering Mechanism. A self-propelling steering apparatus for small and moderate-size watercraft. It allows a boat to be turned on a relatively short radius. Patent granted.

1946
Display Folders. A matchbook-type display folder. Its outer cover has a transparent pocket in which to slip printed or pictorial advertising information. Patent granted.

1949
Plastic Windows. Windows with a flexible plastic pane of simple and economical construction free from weights, cords, and movable sashes. Windows can be opened and closed by manipulating the flexible panes. Patent granted.

1949
Sandwich Construction Panels. A lightweight, prefabricated, economical construction system using sandwiches of Styrofoam® panels between plywood sheets.

1965
Dispensing Container. An adhesive applicator that provides improved distribuation of adhesives on the face of surfaces to be joined. Patent granted.

1971
Insulated Building Structure. A furlike insulation material to be used on building exteriors or interior partitions for thermal and sound protection. Patents granted in Belgium (1972), Great Britain (1972), Italy (1973), Switzerland (1974), and Canada (1975).

1973
Self-Choreographing Musical or Luminescent Appliance (Moodical). A cagelike machine with keys, bars, switches, panels, and rods activated by an operator's movements to provide a synthesis of music and light, all reflecting the person's moods. Patent granted.

HONORS

1931
Society of Beaux-Arts Architects, Second Medal, Architecture

1937
Paris International Exposition, Diplome de Grand Prix, Best Residential Design, Whitman House and Alden B. Dow Studio, Midland

1944
36th Division War Memorial Competition, Temple, Texas, First Place (unbuilt)

1947
House and Garden Architectural Award, Honorable Mention, Irish House, Midland

1956
American Institute of Architects, Honor Award, First Methodist Church, Midland

1957
American Institute of Architects, Election to Fellowship

Southern Christian Leadership Conference, Certificate of Appreciation

1958
Miami Window Corporation, Fenestration Award, St. John's Lutheran Church, Midland

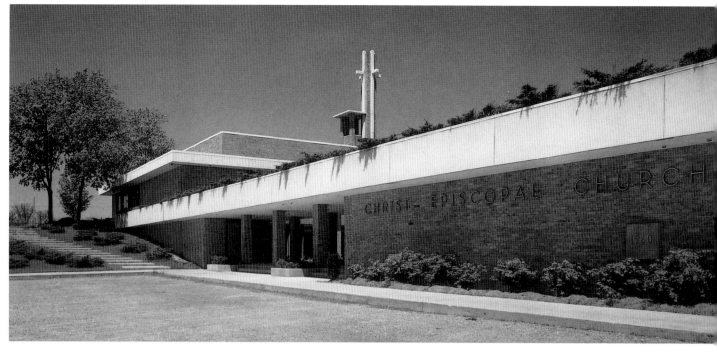

Christ Episcopal Church

1960
Michigan Society of Architects, Gold Medal

Hillsdale College, Honorary Degree, Doctor of Fine Arts

1961
Columbia Architectural Alumni Association, President's Award (second recipient)

1962
Northwood Institute, Outstanding Service

Saginaw Valley Chapter, AIA, First Honor Award, Christ Episcopal Church, Adrian; Honor Award, Keeler House, East Grand Rapids

1963
Saginaw Valley Chapter, AIA, Honor Award, Northwood Institute Campus, Midland

Lake Jackson, Texas, Founders Monument (with Dr. A. P. Beutel) on twentieth anniversary

University of Michigan, Honorary Degree, Doctor of Architecture

1964
Michigan Society of Architects, Certificate of Appreciation, President (1949–50)

Saginaw Valley Chapter, AIA, Certificate of Merit, Ann Arbor City Hall

Albion College, Honorary Degree, Doctor of Fine Arts

1965
Flint (Michigan) Institute of Arts, Retrospective Exhibition

Saginaw Valley Chapter, AIA, Certificate of Merit, Carras House, Midland

1966
The Dow Chemical Company Board of Directors, Resolution Commending Service on Retirement (1941–65)

Michigan Society of Architects, Award of Merit, Carras House, Midland; Honorable Mention, Riecker House, Midland

Kalamazoo Valley Community College, "Opportunity for All" Medal

Michigan State University, Honorary Degree, Doctor of Laws

1967
Saginaw Valley Chapter, AIA, First Honor Award, Roscommon Congregational Church; Certificates of Merit, First Presbyterian Church, Dearborn, and Institute for Social Research, University of Michigan, Ann Arbor

1969
Saginaw Valley College, Dedication Medal

Northwood University, Honorary Degree, Doctor of Humanities

Saginaw Valley Chapter, AIA, Certificates of Merit, Greenhills School, Ann Arbor; Muskegon County Community College

Saginaw Valley College, Honorary Degree, Doctor of Humane Letters

1970
Michigan Association of Nurserymen, Landscape Award

1971
Midland Board of Realtors, Community Leader of the Year

1971–72
Midland Center for the Arts, Bronze Plaque

1974
Keep Michigan Beautiful, Outstanding Service Award

Federated Garden Clubs of Michigan, Michigan Award of Merit

1975
Midland Center for the Arts, Retrospective Exhibition, A Way of Life

Mid-Michigan Community College, Harrison, Alden B. Dow Week (June 1, 1975); The Alden B. Dow Way of Life Center

Interlochen Arts Academy, Medal of Honor

1978
Northwood University, Alden B. Dow Creativity Center

National Music Camp, Interlochen Arts Academy, Fifty Years of Service to Gifted Youth

1980
Boy Scouts of America, Recognition Dinner and Award

1981
Michigan Fraternal Order of Police, Certificate of Appreciation

American Association of Nurserymen, National Landscape Award, Dow Gardens

1982
Frank Lloyd Wright Foundation, Frank Lloyd Wright Creativity Award (first recipient)

1983
Michigan Senate, Resolution, Architect Laureate (first recipient)

1989
U.S. Department of the Interior, National Historic Landmark, Alden B. Dow Home and Studio

PROFESSIONAL AND HONORARY MEMBERSHIPS

1933
Frank Lloyd Wright Fellowship, Taliesin, Spring Green, Wisconsin

1946
Michigan Capitol Building Commission, Governor's Appointment

1949
Michigan Engineering Society

1949–50
Michigan Society of Architects, President

1957
Michigan Society of Architects, Sustaining Member

Michigan Library Association, Honorary Member

1958
Church Architecture Guild of America

1960–61
Michigan Cultural Commission, Governor's Appointment

1961
American Society for Church Architecture, Honorary Membership

1962
Bricklayers, Masons, and Plasterers International Union, Honorary Membership

1963
Delta Kappa Phi, Northwood University, Honorary Membership

Michigan State Council for the Arts, Governor's Appointment

1965
Guild for Religious Architecture

1966
Michigan Council for the Arts, Environmental Arts Committee

1972
Michigan Society of Planning Officials

1979
Bertram A. Barber Society, Hillsdale College, Distinguished Member

Muskegon County Community College

ALDEN B. DOW ARCHIVES

The Alden B. Dow Archives opened in 1988 to collect, preserve, and interpret the architect's papers, drawings, and related collections. These materials are divided into roughly two categories—professional and personal papers—and include approximately 560 project files, 22,000 drawings, 1,425 publications, 330 16 mm films, as well as sketchbooks, photographs and slides, model trains, and mechanical toys. Dow's professional library of books on the shelves in his office is considered part of the archival collection. Overlaps occur, especially in the case of sketches and sketchbooks, patents, lectures and speeches, photographs, motion pictures, videos, and the library.

Professional Papers. Included in this collection are the administrative files of the architecture firm, project files, drawing files, financial records (restricted), sketches and sketchbooks, speeches and writings, patents, oral histories, photographs and transparencies, motion picture films and videos, publications by and about Dow, audiotapes, the architect's library, and awards and ephemera. Many of the motion picture films and some of the still photographs were taken by Dow himself to record family life, document buildings, and explore aesthetic issues.

Personal Papers. This collection encompasses personal correspondence and topical files, financial records (restricted), objects (toys, cameras, musical instruments, and the collections in the Home and Studio), and clothing.

The Alden B. Dow Archives is located on the lower level of the Dow residence in three ground-floor rooms, including the former playroom, backstage, and workshop. Researchers with an interest in Alden Dow's work and philosophy are welcome to visit the archives, which is open to the public by appointment.

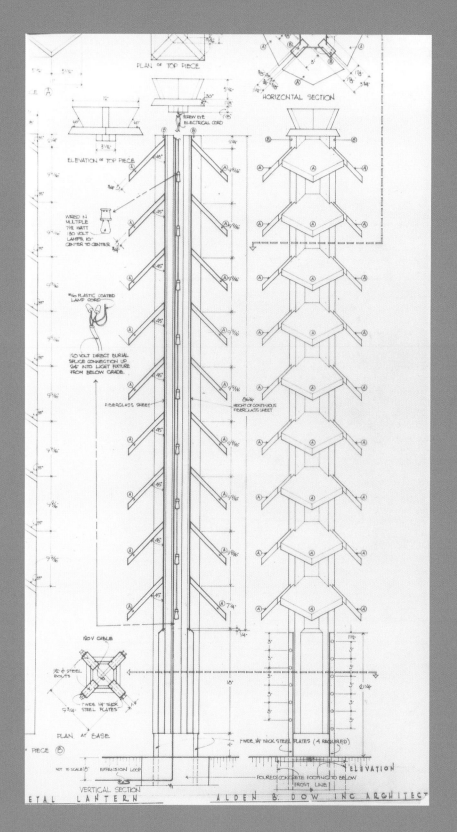

Dow designed a variety of lanterns to please the eye as much as to light the site. The version in this archival drawing evokes the stalk of a long-stemmed flower.

SOURCES

The writings by and about Alden Dow are extensive. The architect gave many lectures to civic and professional groups, wrote for publication as well as for his own satisfaction, and maintained an active correspondence with clients and associates. His work was likewise recorded frequently in national, state, and local publications from architectural journals to daily newspapers over a half century. The majority of this material is preserved by the Alden B. Dow Archives, along with his project records, correspondence, architectural drawings, sketches, films, and photographs of his work (see a more detailed description of the archives on page 232); additional family correspondence and photographs of the Herbert H. Dow family are located at the Post Street Archives, the repository of Herbert Dow's papers and an archive of The Dow Chemical Company. Research for this book was drawn primarily from these two sources, both located in Midland, Michigan, just steps from one another.

With *The Architecture of Alden B. Dow*, published by Wayne State University Press in 1983 (the year of Dow's death), Sidney K. Robinson produced the first critical study of Dow's work. This monograph on the architect, aided by Robinson's personal relationship with Alden Dow, served as an important reference point for preparation of this new volume. Robinson's earlier publication, *Life Imitates Architecture: Taliesin and Alden Dow's Studio* (Ann Arbor: Architectural Research Laboratory, University of Michigan, 1980), offers incisive comparisons of how Dow and Frank Lloyd Wright approached the challenges of designing their own homes and studios. Between 1989 and 1991, the Alden B. Dow Archives conducted oral histories with many family members, professional associates, and friends of Dow's, all of which contain invaluable insights and details from the people who knew him best; several interviews with Dow's sisters were conducted by the Post Street Archives. More recently, Alden Dow's children also offered additional remembrances of life at 315 Post Street for this book. Tawny

Ryan Nelb's book *The Pines: 100 Years of the Herbert H. and Grace A. Dow Homestead, Orchards, and Gardens* (Midland, Michigan: Herbert H. and Grace A. Dow Foundation, 1999) proved helpful for its careful telling of the story of the Dow family home and the "back lot" that grew into the Dow Gardens. Architectural and historical information on Dow's work was also found in the forms nominating the Home and Studio and other Dow buildings to the National Register of Historic Places, including one on the Home and Studio prepared by Carolyn Pitts and multiple-property nominations researched by Robert G. Waite, Elizabeth C. Panhorst, and Samantha Harrison Stand. Alden Dow's own book, *Reflections* (Midland, Michigan: Northwood Institute, 1970), summarized his architectural philosophy and served as a guide for how a new book such as this might approach the architect's work and life.

A number of important magazine articles featuring Dow's architecture also provided useful contemporary commentary on his designs. Among them are "Alden B. Dow, Architect," *Architectural Forum*, September 1936; "Alden B. Dow: Midland, Michigan," *Progressive Architecture*, February 1955; *Architecture and Design*, vol. VII, no. 7, June 1943 (an issue devoted to Dow's work); Douglas, Helen, "Alden Dow and His Houses" (a study drafted for *Time*, May 28, 1947; unpub.); Hamlin, Talbot F., "The Architect and House 8: Alden B. Dow of Michigan," *Pencil Points*, May 1942; "Profile in Design 1: Houses by Alden Dow of Midland, Michigan," *House and Home*, February 1961; Silver, Cathy, "Historic Architecture: The Legacy of Alden Dow," *Architectural Digest*, July 1985; Snyder, Tim, "Alden Dow's Studio and Residence," *Fine Homebuilding*, August-September 1982.

These basic sources, used throughout this book, were supplemented by specific materials and publications in various chapters, as follows. All archival materials, including oral histories (some restricted), are found in the Alden B. Dow Archives except where otherwise noted.

Photographic Essay
Page 2: Dow, Alden B., "A Way of Life Cycle" (brochure), 1976; Dow, Alden B., speech to Friendly Garden Club, Traverse City, Michigan, October 13, 1970. Page 5: *Architecture and Design*, vol. VII, no. 7, June 1943. Pages 6–7: *Architecture and Design*, vol. VII, no. 7, June 1943. Page 9: Dow, Alden B. Page 10: *Architecture and Design*, vol. VII, no. 7, June 1943. Pages 12–13: "Patterns in Thought: An Interview with Alden Dow, FAIA," *Monthly Bulletin*, Michigan Society of Architects, November 1962.

MIDWESTERN MODERN
Dow, Alden B., "A Way of Life Cycle" (brochure), 1976.

Alden B. Dow
Dow, Alden B., typescript (draft of speech in Midland, Michigan), ca. 1936. *The Continental Magazine*, May–June 1963. Hamlin, Talbot F. "Alden B. Dow of Michigan," *Pencil Points*, May 1942. "Profile in Design 1: Houses by Alden Dow of Midland, Michigan," *House and Home*, February 1961.

Tomorrow's City Today
Florey, Virginia, *Midland: The Way We Were*, edited by Leona Seamster, Images of America (Chicago: Arcadia Publishing, 2001). "Midland County's New Court House," *Midland Sun*, November 1926. "New Midland County Courthouse" (rotogravure supplement), *Detroit Free Press*, October 18, 1925. "Snapshots," *Modern Homes in Michigan*, June 1943. Works Progress Administration, *Michigan: A Guide to the Wolverine State* (New York: Oxford University Press, 1941). Yates, Dorothy Langdon, *Salt of the Earth: A History of Midland County Michigan* (Midland, Mich.: Midland County Historical Society, 1987).

The Works
Brandt, E. N., *Growth Company: Dow Chemical's First Century* (Lansing: Michigan State University Press, 1997). Brandt, E. N., and Barbara Schettig Brennan, *The Papers of Herbert H. Dow: A Guide for the Scholarly*, Post Street Archives (Midland, Mich.: Northwood Institute Press, 1990). Dow, Herbert H., "Why I Came to Midland," *Midland Republican*, October 16, 1930.

Nelb, Tawny Ryan, *The Pines*. "Our Founder," *Dow Diamond*, February 1938. Towsley, Margaret Dow, interview by E. N. Brandt, December 4, 1989 (Post Street Archives). Whitehead, Don, *The Dow Story: The History of The Dow Chemical Company* (New York: McGraw-Hill, 1968). Yates, *Salt of the Earth*.

A "Tight Ship"
Arbury, Dorthy Dow, interview by E. N. Brandt, January 18, 1989 (Post Street Archives). Arbury, Dorothy Dow, interview by Judith O'Dell, August 21, 1989. Dow, Alden B., "Memories of My Mother," August 15 and 16, 1974 (unpub.). Hatton, Harrison, notes on conversations with Alden B. Dow, June 22, 1949, and April 19, 1950. See also Murray Campbell and Harrison Hatton, *Herbert Dow: Pioneer in Creative Chemistry* (New York: Appleton, Century, Crofts, 1951). Nelb, *The Pines*. Schmidt, Bea, "H. H. Dow, Founder and Father," typescript, n.d.

Sanctuary
Dow, Alden B., letter to Derwin H. Bass, June 2, 1969. Dow, Alden B., notes on Dow Gardens, 1978. Hatton, notes on conversations with Alden B. Dow, June 22, 1949, and April 19, 1950. Nelb, *The Pines*. Whitehead, *The Dow Story*.

Born to Build
Arbury, Dorthy Dow, interview by E. N. Brandt, January 18, 1989 (Post Street Archives). Arbury, Dorothy Dow, interview by Judith O'Dell, August 21, 1989. Barstow, Ormond, taped memories of Alden B. Dow, May 31, 1975. Dow, Alden B., letter to James Marston Fitch, August 29, 1974. Dow, Alden B., "My Famous Fling at Fisticuffs," typescript, n.d. Dow, Vada Bennett, interview by Judith O'Dell, August 1989. "First Passenger Train Wreck in Midland Takes Two Lives," *Midland Republican*, August 11, 1923. Mi-Hi Annuals, Midland High School, 1921, 1922. Nelb, *The Pines*. Schmidt, Bea, "H. H. Dow, Founder and Father," typescript, n.d. Towsley, Margaret Dow, interview by E. N. Brandt, December 4, 1989 (Post Street Archives). Towsley, Margaret Dow and Harry, interview by Judith O'Dell, August 24, 1989. Whitehead, *The Dow Story*.

Setting Sail
Dow, Alden B., "An Architect's View of Creativity," address to Symposia on Creativity, Michigan State University, 1958; reprinted in *Journal of the American Institute of Architects*, February 1959, and *Creativity: and Its Cultivation*, edited by Harold H. Anderson (New York: Harper and Brothers, 1959). Dow, Alden B., letter to James Marston Fitch, August 29, 1974. Dow, Alden B., letters to Herbert H. and Grace A. Dow, 1923–26 (Post Street Archives). Dow, Alden B., "Toward Perfection," typescript, June 1977. Dow, Alden B., typescript, March 1, 1938. Dow, Herbert H., letter to Alden B. Dow, December 1, 1924. Nelb, *The Pines*.

Schooled in the Jazz Age
Arbury, Dorothy Dow, interview by E. N. Brandt, January 18, 1989 (Post Street Archives). Arbury, Dorothy Dow, interview by Andy Rapp, *Day by Day* (television program), June 2, 1975. Dow, Alden B., letters to Herbert H. and Grace A. Dow, 1926, 1927, and 1929. Homberger, Eric, *The Historical Atlas of New York City: A Visual Celebration of Nearly 400 Years of New York City's History* (New York: Holt, 1994). Koolhaas, Rem, *Delirious New York: A Retroactive Manifesto for Manhattan* (New York: Oxford University Press, 1978). LeBlanc, Sydney, *20th Century American Architecture: A Traveler's Guide to 200 Key Buildings*, 1993, 2d ed., rev. (New York: Whitney Library of Design, 1996). Morris, Lloyd, *Incredible New York: High Life and Low Life from 1850 to 1950*, 1951 (Reprint, Syracuse, N.Y.: Syracuse University Press, 1996). Naylor, David, *American Picture Palaces: The Architecture of Fantasy*, 1981 (Reprint, New York: Prentice Hall Press, 1991). Polshek, James Stewart, letter to Alden B. Dow, December 2, 1977. Roberts, Michael, "Alden Dow Talks About Art, Order and Midland," *Midland Daily News*, December 6, 1978.

Vada
Barstow, Ormond, taped memories of Alden B. Dow, May 31, 1975. Alden B. Dow, letters to Herbert H. and Grace A. Dow, 1929 (Post Street Archives and Alden B. Dow Archives). Dow, Vada Bennett, interview by Judith O'Dell, August and October 1989. Oppermann, Peters "Pat," interview by Judith O'Dell, August 22, 1989.

Avant Garde
Dow, Alden B., letter to Grace A. Dow, November 5, 1929. Dow, Alden B., letter to James Marston Fitch, August 29, 1974. Dow, Herbert H., letter to Alden B. Dow, November 12, 1927 (Post Street Archives). "Midland Country Club," *Architectural Record*, June 1932. Robinson, Sidney K., *The Architecture of Alden B. Dow.* "Unique Clubhouse Brings Congratulations to Midland," *Midland Republican* (special edition), April 30, 1931.

Fellowship
"Alden Dow Gets Wisconsin Job," *Midland Republican*, May 4, 1933. Dow, Alden B., letter to Dorothy Costopoulos, November 6, 1970. Dow, Alden B., letters to Grace A. Dow, 1929, 1930, and 1933. Dow, Alden B., letters to Edgar Tafel, August 3, 1935, and June 10, 1974. Dow, Alden B., letters to Frank Lloyd Wright, March 11, 1933; March 31, 1933; and April 10, 1933. Dow, Vada Bennett, interview by Judith O'Dell, August and October 1989. Guggenheimer, Tobias S., *A Taliesin Legacy: The Architecture of Frank Lloyd Wright's Apprentices* (New York: Van Nostrand Reinhold, 1995). Robinson, Sidney K., *Life Imitates Architecture.* Tafel, Edgar, letter to Alden B. Dow, July 30, 1935. Wright, Frank Lloyd, letter to Alden B. Dow, ca. April 12, 1930. "Wright Lauds Midland Modernistic Homes," *Midland Republican*, May 1, 1937.

Not Your Father's House
Dow, Alden B., letter to James Marston Fitch, August 29, 1974. Dow, Alden B., letters to Earl Stein, June 30, 1933, and September 19, 1933. Robinson, *Life Imitates Architecture.* Rossiter, Maggie, "Dow's Credo: Never Copy Anything," *Saginaw News*, August 27, 1978. Towsley, Margaret Dow, interview by E. N. Brandt, December 4, 1989 (Post Street Archives). Towsley, Margaret Dow and Harry, interview by Judith O'Dell, August 24, 1989.

Geometric Poetry
Architectural Forum, December 1936 and April 1937. Dow, Alden B., letter to Martha M. Whiting, November 6, 1969. Hamlin, Talbot F., "Alden B. Dow of Michigan," *Pencil Points*, May 1942. Helmling, Greg, "Landmark Status Sought for Alden Dow Home," *Midland*

Daily News, April 1989. "House in Michigan," *Architectural Record*, October 1941. Martineau, Janet I., "Architect Receives National Recognition," *Saginaw News*, June 14, 1990. National Register of Historic Places Multiple Property Documentation Form: Residential Architecture of Alden B. Dow in Midland, Michigan, 1933–1938.

Invention for Its Own Sake
Robinson, *The Architecture of Alden B. Dow.* Robinson, *Life Imitates Architecture.* Snyder, Tim, "Alden Dow's Studio and Residence," *Fine Homebuilding*, August– September 1982.

Pillar to Post Street
Dow, Vada Bennett, interview by Judith O'Dell, August and October 1989.

COMPOSED ORDER
Dow, Alden B., speech to Friendly Garden Club, Traverse City, Mich., October 13, 1970.

Architectural Bouquets
Dow, Alden B., "An Essay on Quality," *Midland Daily News*, October 21, 1977. Dow, Alden B., letter to Daniel Wildenstein, November 8, 1946. Dow, Alden B., speech to Friendly Garden Club, Traverse City, Mich., October 13, 1970. Robinson, Sidney K., *Life Imitates Architecture.*

"Composer of Composers"
Bryce, Ken, interview by Judith O'Dell, November 4, 1992. Dow, Alden B., "Introduction" (selected quotations from his writings and conversations), typescript, n.d. Gilmore, William, interview by Judith O'Dell, November 25, 1992. Howell, James, interview by Judith O'Dell, ca. 1992. Knopf, Dick, interview by Judith O'Dell, April 11, 1991. Lee, Jack, interview by Judith O'Dell, October 30, 1992. "Patterns in Thought: An Interview with Alden Dow, FAIA," *Monthly Bulletin*, Michigan Society of Architects, November 1962. Robinson, *Life Imitates Architecture.* Snyder, Tim, "Alden Dow's Studio and Residence," *Fine Homebuilding*, August– September 1982. Warner, Francis E., interview by Judith O'Dell, November 1, 1992.

A Way of Life
Dow, Alden B., *Way of Life: Alden B. Dow, FAIA, Architect* (exhibition catalogue excerpted from *Reflections*) (Midland: Northwood Institute, 1973). Dow, Alden B., "A Way of Life Cycle" (brochure), 1976. Dow, Alden B., letter to Harold Anderson, March 19, 1959. Dow, Alden B., "Toward Perfection," typescript, June 1977. Dow, Alden B., typescript, March 1, 1938. Hamlin, Talbot F., "Alden B. Dow of Michigan," *Pencil Points*, May 1942. Howell, James, interview by Judith O'Dell, ca. 1992. Neutra, Richard, in "Modern Houses Across the U.S.A.," *Time*, August 15, 1949. Roberts, Michael, "Light Plays Upon Alden Dow," *Midland Daily News*, August 25, 1983.

The Tao of Dow
"Alden B. Dow: Midland, Michigan," *Progressive Architecture*, February 1955. Allison, Margaret, "Washington Students Meet Architect Alden Dow," *Bay City Times*, February 2, 1964. *Architecture and Design*, vol. VII, no. 7, June 1943. Dow, Alden B., "An Essay on Quality," *Midland Daily News*, October 21, 1977. Dow, Alden B., "Appreciating Architecture," typescript, May–July 1976. Dow, Alden B., in "Michigan Style Mixes Past, Present, Future," *Detroit Free Press*, March 19, 1981. Dow, Alden B., letter to Hillis Arnold, June 29, 1945. Dow, Alden B., letter to Daniel Wildenstein, November 8, 1946. Dow, Alden B., speech to American Association of University Women, Midland Country Club, March 4, 1935. Dow, Alden B., speech to American Institute of Architects, Great Lakes District Seminars, October 4, 1947. Dow, Alden B., speech to Chicago AIA, January 7, 1959. Dow, Alden B., speech to Friendly Garden Club, Traverse City, Mich., October 13, 1970. Dow, Alden B., speech to Monday Club, May 13, 1935. "Profile in Design: Houses by Alden Dow of Midland, Michigan," *House and Home*, February 1961. Robinson, *The Architecture of Alden B. Dow.* Rossiter, Maggie, "Dow's Credo: Never Copy Anything," *Saginaw News*, August 27, 1978.

Designs for Living
"Alden B. Dow Homes Are a Lived-in Legacy," *Midland Daily News*, February 19, 1988.

Dow, Alden B., "Plastics in Houses of the Future," *Construction*, November 1944. Dow, Alden B., "Typically Midland," *Midland Republican*, April 30, 1931. National Register of Historic Places Multiple Property Documentation Form: Residential Architecture of Alden B. Dow in Midland, Michigan, 1933–1938. National Register of Historic Places Multiple Property Documentation Form: Residential Architecture of Alden B. Dow in Midland, Michigan, Since 1939. Raulet, Joan, letter to Alden B. Dow, November 11, 1972. Rich, Philip T., "Our Real Frontiers," WJR (radio station), Detroit, March 30, 1940. Roberts, Michael, "Alden Dow," *Midland Daily News*, August 22, 1983.

Dream Houses
"Alden Dow Employs Sloping Window Walls and Ceilings to Lend Space and Interest to a Compact House," *Architectural Forum*, February 1946. Dow, Alden B., interview on low-cost housing, ca. 1945 (unpub.). Dow, Alden B., letter to Bruce Biosset, December 1, 1945. Dow, Alden B., "Planning the Contemporary House," *Architectural Record*, November 1947. Gilmore, William, interview by Judith O'Dell, November 25, 1992. "The House for the Growing Income—The Home with a Future," *Bulletin*, Michigan Society of Architects, November 22, 1938. "House in Midland, Mich., Alden B. Dow, Architect," *Architectural Forum*, April 1939. "Low Cost Houses," *Architectural Record*, July 1946. "Sandwich Homes Wearing Well," *Journal of Homebuilding*, January 1961. "Small House Gives Maximum Space in Minimum Area," *Architectural Forum*, December 1947. Welsh, James P., "Your Home Tomorrow: Great Alden B. Dow Forecasts Brilliant Colors in Postwar Residences," *Ohio Motorist*, August 1945.

Boomtowns
"Camp Chemical: The City Built from Scratch," *Dow Diamond*, September 1942. Dow, Alden B., essay on Lake Jackson, 1944 (unpub.). Dow, Alden B., "Home and Housing," n.d. (unpub.). Dow, Vada Bennett, interview by Judith O'Dell, August and October 1989. "Dream Town by the Gulf," *Houston Chronicle Magazine*, February 19, 1950.

"A Feud, a Murder, a Model City: Dow Carves Functional Community Out of Lost Plantation," *Dow Diamond*, March 1942. "Freeport, Texas," *Architectural Record*, April 1942. "Hotel," *Architectural Record*, May 1942. Mintz, Yvonne, "Lake Jackson Throws Party for City Founder, *The Facts*, April 11, 1999. "A One-Story Hotel for a Texas Town," *Architectural Record*, January 1944. Ratcliff, J. D., "Boom Comes to Town," *Collier's*, December 28, 1940. Robinson, *The Architecture of Alden B. Dow.* Warren, Susan, "Lake Jackson, Texas, Has Strange Ways that Baffle Many, *Wall Street Journal*, December 15, 1999. Welles, George D., Jr., "It's True—What They Say About Lake Jackson," *Dow Diamond*, May 1944. Whitehead, *The Dow Story.*

Striving to Inspire
"Alden Dow Urges Churches Do More Creative Thinking," *Saginaw News*, February 20, 1958. Dow, Alden B., "Life Is Growth" (on First Methodist Church, Midland, Michigan), ca. 1950. Martin, Martin E., "The Architecture of Growth: The Five Dow-Designed Churches of Midland, Michigan," *The Christian Century*, March 27, 1957. *Time*, September 19, 1955.

Rethinking the Schoolhouse
Dow, Alden B., "A New Campus Concept," in *Crusade for Continuing Independence* (Hillsdale, Mich.: Hillsdale College, ca. 1968). Keith, James, "Kresge, Dow, Mott and Stone Foundations Giving for a Greater Interlochen," *Lawyers Title News*, December 1966. National Register of Historic Places Registration Form: Parents' and Children's Schoolhouse, 1995. "Nature and Aesthetics Interwoven in Alden Dow's Design at Northwood," *Midland Daily News*, October 26, 1962. "Northeast Intermediate School," *Better Building and Equipment*, April 1952. Woods, John A., "Fleeing 'The Fortress,'" *Ann Arbor News*, July 13, 1997.

Tending to Business
"Color Is Catching On," *Chemical Week*, July 28, 1956. Dow, Alden B., "An Architect's View of Creativity," *AIA Journal*, February 1959. Dow, Alden B.,"Color—A New Element in Chemical Plant Design," *Chemical Industries*, January 1945. "National Bank Ready to Open Tomorrow,"

Midland Daily News, August 8, 1947. "New St. Louis Blues," *Dow Diamond*, June 1945. "Scientific Color Job Done on Newly Leased Office on Olive Street," *St. Louis Post-Dispatch*, May 13, 1945.

Civic Pride
Brashear, Jay, "Art Building Termed Inspirational Center," *Phoenix Gazette*, ca. 1949. Douglas, Helen, "Alden Dow and His Houses" (drafted for *Time*, May 28, 1947; unpub.). Dow, Alden B., "Careful Planning Makes Each a Cheerful Room," *Hospitals*, June 1945. Dow, Alden B., in *Bay City Times*, March 29, 1963. Dow, Alden B., in *Saginaw News*, March 31, 1963. Dow, Alden B., letter to Dorothy Costopoulos, November 6, 1970. Dow, Alden B., answers to behavioral research questionnaire, San Francisco State College, 1970. "Five Buildings by Alden B. Dow," *Architectural Record*, September 1967. Dow, Alden B., "Typically Midland," *Midland Republican*, April 30, 1931. "Integration of Components," *Progressive Architecture*, October 1963. Kamphoefner, Henry L., "The Acoustics of Music Shells," *Pencil Points*, September 1945. Morrill, Claire, and Alden B. Dow, "Color in Balance," *Hospitals*, June 1945. "New Addition to Court House to Mark Another Milestone," *Midland Daily News*, January 15, 1958. "Outdoor Music and Drama Require a Scientific Design: Band Shells," *Architectural Record*, April 1941. "Spectator Accommodations for Organized Sports: Bath Houses," *Architectural Record*, April 1941. Thinnes, Tom, "Climate-Controlled Nature Center," *Muskegon Chronicle*, November 5, 1964.

A New Language
"Building the Home of Tomorrow," *Dow Diamond*, ca. 1940. "Construction Units Appear," *Modern Plastics*, February 1940. Dow, Alden B., "Discussion of the Model" (Circle House), typescript, ca. 1944. Dow, Alden B., letter to Eugene Masselink, September 5, 1946. Dow, Alden B., letter to Vernon D. Swaback, June 26, 1968. Dow, Alden B., "Michigan," *Your Solar House* (New York: Simon and Schuster, 1947). Dow, Alden. B., "Plastics in Houses of the Future," *Construction*, November 1944. Dow,

Alden B., speech to Women of Kiwanis Club, May 7, 1936. Dow, Alden B., "System for Unit Wall or Roofing Covering," typescript, July 30 and August 23, 1937. Gilmore, William, interview by Judith O'Dell, November 25, 1992. Lee, Jack, interview by Judith O'Dell, October 30, 1992. "Outdoor Museum for Houses," *Architectual Forum*, September 1956. "Plastic Houses," *Newsweek*, December 1939. Warner, Francis E., interview by Judith O'Dell, November 1, 1992. "When Building Starts Again," *Motor News*, August 1945.

Our Town
Douglas, Helen, "Alden Dow and His Houses" (drafted for *Time*, May 28, 1947; unpub.). Dow, Alden B., notes for a lecture, May 25, 1971. Dow, Alden B., speech to Midland Art Association, November 12, 1965. Dow, Vada Bennett, interview by Judith O'Dell, August and October 1989. Morrill, Claire, "In 10 Years, You May Not Know Midland," *Midland Daily News*, June 29, 1944.

Reflections
"Alden B. Dow: Cinematography," Alden B. Dow Archives, n.d. Alexander, Judith Dow Towsley, interview by Judith O'Dell, April 11, 1991. Arbury, Dorothy Dow, interview by Judith O'Dell, August 21, 1989. Brandt, E. N., interview by Robert Maddex, October 24, 2003. Doan, H. D. "Ted," interview by Judith O'Dell, November 3, 1989. Douglas, Helen, "Alden Dow and His Houses" (drafted for *Time*, May 28, 1947; unpub.). Dow, Alden B., letter to E. N. Brandt, June 20, 1978. Herbert Henry Dow (nephew), interview by Judith O'Dell, November 1, 1989. Dow, Vada Bennett, interview by Judith O'Dell, August and October 1989. Herring, Betty, "Dow's Moodical Concocts Fantasies in Sight, Sound," *Midland Daily News*, October 7, 1971. Mills, Mary Lloyd Dow, interview by Judith O'Dell, June 22, 1991. Plummer, Elaine, and Jean Stark, "A Picture Painted in Sound," *Etude*, September 1956.

THE STUDIO
Dow, Alden B., "Appreciating Architecture," typescript, July 21, 1976.

General sources for information on the Alden B. Dow Home and Studio presented in the parts of this book entitled The Studio and The Home include the following: Douglas, Helen, "Alden Dow and His Houses" (drafted for *Time*, May 28, 1947; unpub.). Interviews by the author with Michael Lloyd Dow, Mary Lloyd Dow Mills, and Barbara Alden Dow Carras, 2005 and 2006. Mills, Mary Lloyd Dow, interview by Judith O'Dell, June 22, 1991. National Register of Historic Places Registration Form: Alden B. Dow House and Studio, 1989. Robinson, Sidney K., *The Architecture of Alden B. Dow* (Detroit: Wayne State University Press, 1983). Robinson, Sidney K., *Life Imitates Architecture: Taliesin and Alden Dow's Studio* (Ann Arbor: Architectural Research Laboratory, University of Michigan, 1980). Snyder, Tim, "Alden Dow's Studio and Residence," *Fine Homebuilding*, August–September 1982. Tour narrative, Alden B. Dow Home and Studio, 2004 (unpub.). Quinn Evans, Architects, "Alden and Vada Dow Home and Studio Sustainability Study," 2003 (unpub.). Additional sources follow.

Earth, Air, Fire, and Water
"Alden B. Dow, Architect," *Architectural Forum*, September 1936. *The 50 Most Significant Structures in Michigan* (Detroit: Michigan Society of Architects, 1980). Foxe, David M., "The Saunders Residence: Vignettes of a Deceased Architecture," *Pinup 6*, spring 2001. Guggenheimer, Tobias S., *A Taliesin Legacy: The Architecture of Frank Lloyd Wright's Apprentices* (New York: Van Nostrand Reinhold, 1995). Hamlin, Talbot F., "Alden B. Dow of Michigan," *Pencil Points*, May 1942. Silver, Cathy, "Historic Architecture: The Legacy of Alden Dow," *Architectural Digest*, July 1985.

The Site
Dow, Alden B., "Creative Design for Inspired Living," speech to Detroit Annual National Joint Conference on Church Architecture and Church Building, February 18–20, 1958. Silver, Cathy, "Historic Architecture: The Legacy of Alden Dow," *Architectural Digest*, July 1985.

The Entrance
Hamlin, Talbot F., "Alden B. Dow of Michigan," *Pencil Points*, May 1942.

Alden Dow's Office
Allison, Margaret, "Washington Students Meet Architect Alden Dow," *Bay City Times*, February 2, 1964. "Garden Lights Should Do More Than Light," *House Beautiful*, June 1962. Gilmore, William, interview by Judith O'Dell, November 25, 1992. Reeves, Barbara E., "Personal Home, Studio Were Dow's Masterpiece," *Midland Daily News*, October 16, 1992.

THE HOME
Dow, Alden B., "Typically Midland," *Midland Republican*, April 30, 1931.

A Machine for Living
Dow, Alden B., "Typically Midland," *Midland Republican*, April 30, 1931. Dow, Vada Bennett, interview by Judith O'Dell, August and October 1989. Stanton, Barbara, "The Dow Who Hated Chemicals, But . . . He's Changed the Face of His World," *Detroit Free Press*, July 23, 1967.

The Entrance
Architecture and Design, vol. VII, no. 7, June 1943. Dow, Alden B., letter to James Marston Fitch, August 29, 1974.

The Entrance Hall
Allison, Harvey "Cle," interview by Carol Coppage and Craig McDonald, August 3, 1993.

The Living Room
Dow, Alden B., letter to Hillis Arnold, June 29, 1948. Dow, Vada Bennett, interview by Judith O'Dell, August and October 1989.

The Dining Room
"Bronzes by Fredericks," *Midland Daily News*, December 15, 1977.

The Kitchen
Thomas, Fern, interview by Judith O'Dell, August 19, 1989.

The Guest Bedroom
"A Look at Silversmith Georg Jensen," *Midland Daily News*, May 12, 2000.

The Master Bedroom
Arbury, Dorothy Dow, interview by Judith O'Dell, August 21, 1989. Thomas, Fern, interview by Judith O'Dell, August 19, 1989.

The Playroom
Dow, Alden B., letter to Mr. and Mrs. Jackson B. Hallett, January 23, 1976.

THE DOW GARDENS
Dow, Alden B., "Creative Design for Inspired Living," speech to Detroit Annual National Joint Conference on Church Architecture and Church Building, February 18–20, 1958.

A general source for this part was Tawny Ryan Nelb, *The Pines: 100 Years of the Herbert H. and Grace A. Dow Homestead, Orchards, and Gardens* (Midland, Michigan: Herbert H. and Grace A. Dow Foundation, 1999).

All in the Family
Dow, Alden B., letter to Derwin H. Bass, June 2, 1969.

Composed Landscape
Chapman, Douglas, interview by the author, December 20, 2005. Dow, Alden B., "Creative Design for Inspired Living," speech to Detroit Annual National Joint Conference on Church Architecture and Church Building, February 18–20, 1958. Dow, Alden B., typescript, 1978.

Building Bridges
Dow, Alden B., "Appreciating Architecture," typescript, May 3, 1976. Dow, Alden B., letter to Herbert H. Dow, ca. 1927 (Post Street Archives). Dow, Alden B., letter to James Marston Fitch, August 29, 1974. Dow, Alden B., letter to Henry Whiting, September 11, 1974. "Let's Talk Landscaping with Alden Dow," *Benzol*, July 1976. O'Dell, Judith, letter to *Midland Daily News*, August 25, 1983. "Patterns in Thought: An Interview with Alden Dow, FAIA," *Monthly Bulletin*, Michigan Society of Architects, November 1962.

FACTS
Dow, Alden B., "I Believe," typescript, January 4, 1974, and "Five Buildings by Alden B. Dow," *Architectural Record*, September 1967.

ILLUSTRATIONS

Illustration Credits

Alden B. Dow Archives: case binding, 11, 19, 30 bottom, 34 top, 35 top, 37 bottom left, 39, 40 top and bottom, 43 top and center, 53 center, 55 bottom, 58 top, 59 bottom, 72 bottom, 79 top and bottom, 85 top and bottom, 92 bottom, 94 left and right, 106 right, 107 center, 124–25, 125, 131 top, 133, 134–35, 137 left top and right top, 143 inset, 162 bottom, 180, 183 inset, 184 top, 184 bottom, 185, 188 bottom, 188–89, 190 bottom, 191 top, 200 top, 201, 212 center right, 213 left, 215 bottom left and bottom right, 217 bottom left, 218 bottom left, 229. See also specific photographers.

R. Wayne Anderson, Alden B. Dow Archives: 86–87 bottom

Ralph Appleman, Alden B. Dow Archives: 65 top

Elmer L. Astleford, Alden B. Dow Archives: 51 top and bottom left, 55 top, 57 bottom, 61 top, 64, 70 both, 71 top right, 77 top, 86 top, 93, 107 bottom, 204 bottom, 205 left bottom, right top, right center, and right bottom; 206 top left, top right, bottom left, and bottom right; 207 top, center left, center right, bottom left, and bottom right; 208 left, center, and bottom; 209 top left, top right, center left, center right, bottom left, and bottom right; 210 left and right, 215 top right, 216, 218 top, 223 row 2 left and right, row 3, and row 4 left and right

Beinlich Photo, Alden B. Dow Archives: 221 left top

Beutel Photo, Alden B. Dow Archives: 51 bottom right, 204 top left

Doug Chapman, courtesy Dow Gardens: 195 bottom

R. Chickering, Alden B. Dow Archives: 52 right, 53 top right, 205 left top

Cooper-Hewitt National Design Museum, 38

Marcia Dilling, Alden B. Dow Archives: 120, 151 all

Display Illustrations

Endpapers: Pond photographs by Alden B. Dow, ca. 1968

Pages

1: Alden B. Dow, 1930s

2–3: Living room of the Josephine Ashmun House, Midland, Michigan

4–5: Perforated-block trellis wall near the entrance to the Alden B. Dow Home

6: Lower Pond Bridge in the Dow Gardens

7: Stepping stones outside the Alden B. Dow Studio

8–9: Sketches by Alden B. Dow of oganic architectural inspirations, including orchids and a grape leaf, 1933

10: *Little Beach Blossom* (1953), a film by Alden B. Dow

11: Alden B. Dow with a movie camera, 1940s

12–13: Trains in the Alden B. Dow collection: a scale model of a Denver and Rio Grande Western Challenger steam engine (4-6-6-4), ca. 1937, and a toy Lionel Lines Union Pacific passenger train, 1930s

14–15: Sketch of tumbling blocks by Alden B. Dow, ca. 1960s

18–19: Alden B. Dow, ca. 1914, 1930s, and 1970s

60–61: University of Michigan Administration Building, Ann Arbor; Pryor House, Grosse Point Park, Michigan; Alden B. Dow, ca. 1960s

68–69: James Duffy House, St. Clair, Michigan

98–99: Alden B. Dow Studio conference room; second drafting room; Alden B. Dow in conference room, 1937

130–31: Alden B. and Vada Dow in the residence's game room, 1940s; the house from the pond; the mobile in the entrance hall

184–85: Dorothy Dow Arbury, Loretta Macomber Poffenberger, Margaret Dow Towsley, and Lee Doan Jr., 1920s; Alden B. Dow walking with his dog, ca. 1940s; Alden B. Dow, ca. 1982

200–201: Riecker House, Midland, Michigan; Seafront Housing, Manila; Alden B. Dow, ca. 1940s

240: Alden B. Dow Studio conference room reflected in the pond

(continued)

Alden B. Dow, Alden B. Dow Archives: endpapers, 8–9, 10, 14–15, 44–45, 46 center, 47, 50 both, 56 top left and right, 57 top left, 58 bottom, 58–59 center, 59 top, 64–65, 66, 68–69, 73, 74 top and bottom, 78–79, 83, 90, 91 top and bottom, 95, 110, 138 top, 139 bottom, 187, 190 bottom right, 191 bottom, 203, 212 bottom, 220 top, 225 all, 226 all, 232

Alden B. Dow, Post Street Archives: 31 bottom, 37 top, 41 all

Dow Diamond, Alden B. Dow Archives: 78, 85 center and bottom

Ferriby Photo Service, Alden B. Dow Archives: 75 bottom left and right

Frank Lloyd Wright Preservation Trust: 36

Gerald Gard, Alden B. Dow Archives: 215 top left and center left, 221 left bottom

Earl R. Gilbert, Alden B. Dow Archives: 226 top

Gittings Studio, Alden B. Dow Archives: 61 bottom

Glenn Photography, Alden B. Dow Archives: 23, 167

Pedro E. Guerrero: 46 left

Haley Illustration, Alden B. Dow Archives: 42

K. G. Harding, Alden B. Dow Archives: 219 bottom

C. M. Hayes, Alden B. Dow Archives: 18 left, 33 center left and bottom

Hedrich Blessing, Alden B. Dow Archives: 57 top right, 82–83, 98 top, 104, 105 top, 106 left, 107 top, 131 bottom, 135 bottom, 136 top and bottom right, 137 left bottom, 200 bottom, 211 top left, top right, and bottom left; 212 center left and center middle, 215 center right, 217 top and bottom right, 220 bottom, 231

Balthazar Korab: 6 both, 7 both, 48 top, 60, 72 right, 87 top, 92 top, 100–101, 114 top, 119, 121, 123, 126, 127, 141, 144–45, 153, 158 bottom, 159, 161 right, 169, 173 top, 174, 175, 176 top, 177, 178, 194, 195 top, 198, 211 bottom right, 212 top left and top right, 213 right, 219 top, 221 left center, 230

Richard Lee, Detroit Free Press: 136 bottom left

Martha Mardirosian, Alden B. Dow Archives: 84

Lynn Marvin, Alden B. Dow Archives: 108–9

(continued)

Midland County Historical Society: 22

Glen Calvin Moon, Alden B. Dow Archives: 2–3, 4–5, 12–13, 21, 28, 29 all, 49 both, 54 both, 63, 72 top left, 80 both, 81 both, 88, 103, 112–13, 113, 114 bottom, 115, 116–17 all, 118, 122, 124 top and bottom, 128 both, 129, 140, 142–43, 146–47, 148–49, 150–51, 152, 154–55, 156, 157, 158 top, 160, 161 left, 162–63, 164 both, 165, 166 all, 168, 170 center and bottom, 171 both, 172, 173 bottom, 176 bottom, 179 both, 181, 182–83, 192–93, 196–97, 199, 214, 221 right top and right bottom, 240

MWM Color Litho, Aurora, Missouri: 89

Elwood M. Payne/Paralta Studios, Alden B. Dow Archives: 76, 77 center both, 223 top

Post Street Archives: 24 all, 25, 27 both, 30 top, 31 top, 32, 33 top and center right, 34 bottom, 35 bottom, 37 top and bottom right, 41 all, 43 bottom, 99, 188 top, 190 bottom left

Quinn Evans, Architects, adapted by Robert L. Wiser: 111, 138 bottom, 139 top

Shelburne Studios, Alden B. Dow Archives: 170 top

Smith Photo, Alden B. Dow Archives: 26

Preston Sweet, Alden B. Dow Archives: 1, 130, 162 top

R. W. Tebbs, Alden B. Dow Archives: 48 bottom

William Vandivert, Alden B. Dow Archives: 18 right, 98 bottom, 105 bottom

Robert L. Wiser, adapted from plans by Quinn Evans, Architects: 111, 138 bottom, 139 top

Wright Photo, Alden B. Dow Archives: 52 left, 53 top left, 71 bottom left, 137 right bottom, 204 top right, 218 bottom right

INDEX

Dedicated to the memory of Alden B. Dow, whose vision of a humane architecture is one that continues to resonate.

Published by the
Alden B. Dow Home and Studio
315 Post Street
Midland, Michigan 48640
989–839–2744
www.abdow.org

Craig R. McDonald, Director
Daria Potts, Director,
    Alden B. Dow Archives

Produced by
Archetype Press, Inc.
Diane Maddex,
    Project Director
Robert L. Wiser, Designer
Robert L. Maddex,
    Research Assistant

Distributed by
W. W. Norton & Company, Inc.
500 Fifth Avenue
New York, NY 10110
www.wwnorton.com
W. W. Norton & Company Ltd.
Castle House
75/76 Wells Street
London W1T 3QT

**Library of Congress
Cataloging-in-Publication Data**
Maddex, Diane.
Alden B. Dow: midwestern
modern / Diane Maddex.
p.   cm.
Includes bibliographical
references and index.
ISBN 978-0-393-73248-1
(alk. paper)
1. Dow, Alden B., 1904–83.
2. Architects—United States—
Biography. I. Title.
NA737.D67M33 2007
720.92—dc22
                    2007007766

Printed in Singapore

10 9 8 7 6 5 4 3 2 1

Ethocel® (ethylcellulose
ether), Styrofoam® insulation,
and Styron® (polystyrene)
are trademarks of The Dow
Chemical Company.

A Note on the Typography
This book was typeset in
Neutraface, a font designed
by Christian Schwartz for
House Industries in 2002
based on the hand lettering
of the midcentury architect
Richard Neutra, a contemporary of Alden B. Dow's.

Acknowledgments
This book would not have
been possible without the
encouragement and support
of Craig McDonald, director
of the Alden B. Dow Home and
Studio, who patiently guided it
through the long process of
development. The burden of
furnishing information and
images in the Alden B. Dow
Archives fell chiefly to Daria
Potts, its director, who unfail-
ingly offered her assistance
whenever asked and provided
meticulously organized illustrations and answers to questions too numerous to count.
Much appreciation also goes
to others at the Home and
Studio who participated in this
work, among them Margaret
Allen and Barbara McGregor
in the archives as well as
Regina Curtis, Rebecca
Gillette, Jo Ellen Griese,
Clyde Hoover, Dick Schell,
Roger Schmidt, and Mary Lou
Timmons in the Home and
Studio. Special thanks go to
Beth Todd for her cheerful
help in copying material.
    I am grateful as well to the
children of Alden B. Dow—
Michael Lloyd Dow, Mary

Lloyd Dow Mills, and Barbara
Alden Dow Carras—for sharing
with me recollections of their
parents and early life spent in
their unique environment;
they and their own children,
including Diane Dow Hullet,
Bonnie Kendall Mills, and
Stephen Peter Carras, provided guidance by reviewing
the book at various stages
when it was a work in progress. Several owners of Alden
Dow houses, including Nancy
and R. William Barker, Ray
and Sharon Leenhouts, and
Donald Smith, graciously
opened the doors to their
lovingly cared-for homes.
    At the Post Street Archives,
Tawny Ryan Nelb, chief
archivist, and Kathy Thomas,
reference librarian, shared
their collection of resources on
the Herbert H. Dow family,
both written and photographic.
E. N. Brandt, the former
historian of The Dow Chemical Company, was generous
in providing his insights
on the company and the
Dow family. Kathy Chapman
at the Dow Gardens also
assisted with illustrations on
the gardens.

    In addition, I wish to
recognize the writers and
researchers on Alden Dow
who have laid the groundwork
for this book, notably
Sidney K. Robinson and Tawny
Ryan Nelb, and including
people such as Judith O'Dell,
Robert G. Waite, and Samantha Harrison Stand, who
have sought out the story of
Dow's work and ideals to help
perpetuate his legacy.
    Deep thanks also go to the
photographer Balthazar Korab,
a good friend whose enthusiasm for Alden Dow's work
and the year-round beauty of
the Dow Gardens first inspired
me to undertake this book.
Robert Maddex kindly assisted
with research in Midland, and
Robert Wiser has once more
provided a design to match
its subject.

                    — Diane Maddex